AROUND THE
BEND I GO

AROUND THE
BEND I GO

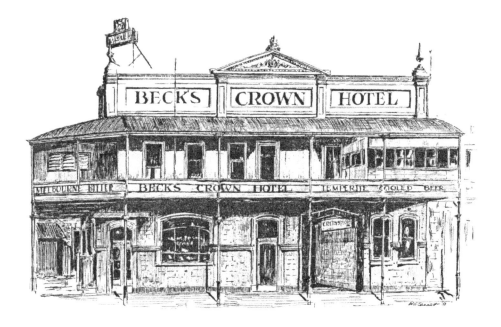

The true story of a boy surviving childhood
in a Bendigo city hotel in the 1950s and 1960s

MAX C.S. BECK

Published by Max C. S. Beck
mcsbeck@bigpond.com

First published 2022

 A catalogue record for this
book is available from the
National Library of Australia

ISBN 978 0 6456577 0 8 (pbk)
ISBN 978 0 6456577 1 5 (ebk)

Edited by Sheryl Allen
Front cover illustration, *Beck's Crown Hotel*,
ink drawing by W. G. Shapcott, 1958
Designed and typeset by Helen Christie, Blue Wren Books
Printed by Ingram Spark

In memory of Reg Beck, a capable businessman and manager, an excellent host and an all-round good bloke, who was, to use one of his favourite phrases, "as straight as a gun barrel" and could be relied on always.

ABOUT THE AUTHOR

After graduating with two law degrees and practising for many years as a barrister and solicitor, Max became a Magistrate and Coroner. As a child, raised in the Crown Hotel, he had little supervision, functioning at times on the fringe of the law as a promising juvenile delinquent. Fortunately, he was never caught by the cops. His book is a collection of tales embracing a narrative romp of his life as a young boy growing up in central Bendigo. They are all true and will grab your attention, entertain, inform and make you laugh or cringe.

Writing skills have always formed an important part of Max's life in the law. This is his second book. His first was *A Different Earth*, a true story of a pioneering widow who walked over land, with six children, from South Australia to the Victorian diggings in the 1850s, published by Cornwall Editions with an introduction by Professor Philip Payton, Flinders University, Adelaide, Australia.

You can contact Max at mcsbeck@bigpond.com

ACKNOWLEDGEMENT

I am greatly indebted to my wife Prue who tolerates my self-imposed isolation when I research and write. Her supporting word processing and computer skills have been invaluable along with her proofreading, critical appraisals, artistic design input, encouragement, patience and wise counselling.

I am indebted also and convey my sincere thanks to Madge Nicholas, Heather McLeod, Robert Iser and Tony Conolan for helping to rebuild and corroborate my memory with the names of students who were at Gravel Hill State School.

PREFACE

This book is a collection of tales embracing a narrative romp of my life as a young boy growing up in The Crown Hotel and Bendigo city. They are all true. I hope they will grab your attention, entertain, inform and make you laugh or cringe and cry. The book is also a part record of the historical times of the 50s and 60s, including school days, the teenage revolution encompassed by the Rock 'n' Roll era and the golden age of pop music. It is also the story of the last days of the old Crown Hotel.

Max Beck

CONTENTS

LIST OF ILLUSTRATIONS

Chapter 1

EMERGENCE

It is said that Bendigo was named after former sailor and bullock driver James Mouat, a shepherd on the Ravenswood Run, who was known around the district to be an accomplished bareknuckle boxer. He had a style similar to the then famous British prize fighting champion, William Abednego Thompson who was nicknamed 'Bendy' due to his constant bobbing, weaving and incredible contortions around the ring sometimes even including somersaults. His speed and agility together with his personality and sense of humour endeared him to spectators and drew crowds of 10 to 15,000 people. The cry "Let's see Abednego!" soon evolved to "Let's see Bendy go!" and then to the name "Bendigo" which stuck throughout his career.

Bendigo lived from 1811 to 1880 and during his time boxed under The London Prize Ring Rules for bareknuckle boxing. He had been at his peak just before gold was discovered at Bendigo. After his last fight on 5 June 1850 he stepped down as undefeated champion with two prize belts and four silver cups to his name. He was perhaps the last of the 'Great Prize Fighters' and considered by some to be the champion of champions. He had a massive fan base, including Sir Arthur Conan Doyle who wrote a verse to the fighter titled *Bendigo's Sermon*. After retiring he took up an unofficial role as Boxing Coach at Oxford University teaching rich young gentleman the noble art of pugilism. On his death his funeral procession was a mile long and thousands lined the streets including many famous people of the period. *The Times* newspaper published his obituary, which was normally reserved for very illustrious people. Years later in Sneiton, Nottingham, they named a pub 'Bendigo's' after its famous resident.

There is little doubt that local bareknuckle boxer and shepherd, James Mouat would have been flattered to be called Bendigo, and to know that the creek which flowed through his Ravenswood Run was called Bendigo's creek. The point of this narrative, in part, is that when I was born my father was seriously keen to name me 'Bendigo'. He was then a hotel keeper between hotels and thought, so I am told, that the name Bendigo Beck would be of substantial promotional value in the event that sometime in the future his son became a publican. Thankfully, my mother was totally against the idea arguing that in the environment of country Victoria I would most likely be given the nickname of 'Diggo' for short! Ultimately my father gave me the nickname of 'Mickey' or 'Mick'. He never gave me a satisfactory answer why, but the name is still used by my earliest and closest friends.

I was born in the middle of the biggest event of the 20th century—World War II. The years leading up to my birthday on 25 October 1944 were perhaps the darkest and most challenging in the history of Australia and arguably not the best time to start a family. A hell of a lot of dreadful stuff was going on. What were my parents thinking? Truth be known, they probably weren't. Anyway they had established a precedent already with the birth of my sister Zelda just 16 months before me.

There were already 23,000 Australian prisoners of war incarcerated at Changi prison in Singapore and more elsewhere. Japanese air raids had hit Darwin and surrounding areas about 60 times. Newcastle and Sydney had been torpedoed by Japanese submarines and bombed from the air. The Japs also sunk scores of ships around the Australian coastline. Out of our total population of around seven million, 1.7 million were in the armed services or war industries resulting in manpower shortages especially in food production and farming where we had 120 million sheep to look after. More than 6,780 Australians had been rounded up and interned as potentially dangerous aliens and, where possible, put to work to support the war effort. Their efforts were supplemented by a further 18,000 Italian prisoners of war who were shanghaied wherever possible into the workforce.

Schools and private households were counselled to dig slit trenches as a precaution against air raids. Communal shelters in parks and other open spaces were excavated, boarded with timber and covered with sandbags or soil. Many homes in Bendigo had their own self-dug 'air raid shelters' and special blackout blinds on their windows, black paper pasted on the glass or window panes painted black. Daylight saving was introduced together with blackout rules that dimmed city lights and car lights at night. Citizens took their turn on enemy aircraft watch at the top of the lookout tower in Rosalind Park and the police placed air raid sirens on the poppet heads of the Central Nell Gwynne and the North Deborah mines as a civil defence measure. With its Commonwealth Ordnance Factory devoted to the war effort, Bendigo was a possible enemy target.

Everyone had to use coupons in a government ration book for the purchase of tea, sugar, clothing and petrol, for which the basic ration was reduced to 800 miles (1,287 kilometres) per year for ordinary citizens. New tyres were not available to private motorists but it was possible to get your old ones retreaded. Such restrictions caused many people to revert back to the horse and cart days. With the almost total absence of coffee, roots of chicory plants were baked, roasted and ground into a coffee essence substitute. Tea was rationed at the rate of half a pound (227 grams) per adult for five weeks. Tea leaves in the pot were reused again and again with just a smidgen of new leaves added on top each time. Waistcoats, double-breasted coats and cuffs on trousers were banned to save material. Housewives were counselled to make new clothes from old for their family so that factories could concentrate on producing essentials for the armed forces. Belts could be no wider than a regulation five centimetres. Dry-cleaning was regulated, hotel hours shortened and the production of beer and other alcohol reduced. Tobacco was in short supply and the manufacture of non-essential items such as bath heaters, toys, many cosmetics and lounge suites was halted. Even confectionery was rationed. Around 6,000 varieties on the market pre war were reduced to about 70. Typewriters were controlled and the export of pigeons prohibited. Deliveries by shopkeepers were banned causing women to take along prams and pushers to carry purchases home when shopping.

Government censorship of news excluded the reporting of anything that might damage morale. There was industrial as well as military conscription and everyone carried an identity card. The government decided what work you did and whether a person changed jobs or was sacked. Wages, prices and profits were generally frozen for the duration. In March 1944, 2,000 women were 'called up' by the Manpower Board because there were not enough workers for the fruit and vegetable canning factories in Bendigo and elsewhere. Not until May 1946 were all manpower controls lifted enabling workers to again choose where they worked. Minister for rationing J. J. Dedman became known as "the man who killed Santa Claus" when he tried to ban the use of Santa Claus emblems in advertising. By 1944 you needed ration coupons to buy any meat at all. Rationing also extended to butter, and beer with restrictions on many items lasting long after the war. A black market in rationed goods flourished. Sugar rationing ended in 1947, meat and clothing in 1948, butter, tea and petrol in 1950.

But while life in Bendigo was annoying, everyone was on easy street compared to the poor wretches in England and Europe. Meanwhile, the Japanese got close to Australia—more than 200,000 of them reached Papua New Guinea and they carried out 97 air attacks on Australia before the war was over. After I had remained safely snuggled up inside my mum for some five months the largest battle in history between aircraft carriers took place in the Philippine Sea from 19 to 20 June 1944. American airmen nicknamed it "The Great American Turkey Shoot" due to the huge losses inflicted on the Japanese. They lost three aircraft carriers, more than 433 carrier aircraft plus around 200 land-based aircraft and more than 3,000 men. The USA lost only 134 aircraft, recovering some 50 or more pilots from the sea.

Back in Australia as I completed my first six months since conception, the largest prisoner of war outbreak ever recorded occurred at Cowra in New South Wales. On 5 August 1944 at least 1,104 Japanese prisoners armed with baseball bats and gardening tools, attempted to escape with some 334 going over the wire. During the escape and ensuing manhunt four Australian soldiers died and another four were injured, 231 Japanese prisoners were

1. Emergency Ration Cards, Commonwealth of Australia World War II.
Source: Australian War Memorial.

killed and 108 wounded. Over the 10 days that it took to round up and re-imprison the escapees, panic was rife in the local community and for a considerable time thereafter. No civilians were harmed, but 25 escaped prisoners committed suicide by hanging, drowning, ritual disembowelment or throwing themselves under a train.

Five days before I was born General Douglas MacArthur returned to the Philippines to keep his promise. Then on the day I was born, 25 October 1944, the largest naval battle in modern history, in terms of the number of personnel involved, took place between Japan and the USA in the Philippines at Leyte Gulf. It involved nine large aircraft carriers, 27 small carriers, 21 battleships, 175 destroyers, 42 cruisers and 1,829 aircraft. This was no small show. On the morning of 24 October a 250 kilogram bomb was dropped on the USS *Princeton* aircraft carrier causing it to sink and my mother to go into labour. To get even the US Navy threw at least 10 bombs and fired 19 torpedoes at the enormous Japanese battleship *Musahi* causing her to go down. The next day, on my birthday, the Japanese produced for the first time their most fearsome weapon of the Pacific War—the kamikaze suicide plane. (More than 5,000 similar attacks would follow.) One hit and severely damaged the USA carrier *Suwannee* and another destroyed the escort carrier task unit *Saint Lo*. As this was going on the USA aircraft carrier *Gambier Boy* and the destroyer USA *Johnston* was sunk by Japanese naval gunfire. In all the USA lost six ships plus a submarine during the battle, but the Japanese lost 28 ships. Allied forces suffered around 2,800 casualties and the Japanese 12,500. After my birthday the weakened naval fleet of Japan declined.

Back in the maternity ward at Bendigo's hospital, my mum had won her battle. But, in a worldly context, it was not a happy birthday. On top of the war, eastern Australia was going through one of its most serious droughts in history with dust storms in the Mallee being the worst for 20 years and the Murray River running at its lowest level in memory. By the end of the following year more than 10 million sheep had died. From my parents' perspective my arrival could have been regarded as a spectacular example of poor judgement. In fact it turned out that being born in Australia was like winning the lottery. I may not have arrived in the Age of Aquarius but I had arrived in the Age of Antibiotics. By the end of the year penicillin was, for the first time, in common use in the war theatre. Meanwhile in Moscow, Churchill and Stalin were arguing the toss about how they were going to divide up Europe after Hitler, who at the time was firing 300 V2 rockets a day at London, had been given the mother of all hidings by the allies. My arrival into the context of this brave new world was a muddled circumstance indeed.

Chapter 2

CONTEXT

I t's hard to imagine an entire year full of more inhumanity, horror, tragedy, death, evil and bitterness than the year I was born. Obviously I knew nothing about this at the time. The historical context of my arrival later meant more to me than just a moment of contemplation as I began to develop an understanding and love of history and an appreciation of how fortunate my life has been since then. My understanding of the history of World War II brought with it a component of guilt connected with the fact that I had, in part, a German ancestry.

The Germans had invaded Hungary in March 1944 and by May full-scale deportation of Hungary's Jews to Auschwitz had begun. By 16 June, 109 trains with Jews on board had arrived. Russian war correspondent Vasily Grossman describing an extermination camp for Jews at Treblinka near Warsaw in Poland wrote in March/ April 1944:

> *There was a chamber with moving knives, it was in a basement ... The bodies were cut into pieces and then burned. There were mountains of ashes, 20 to 25 metres high. In one place Jews had been chased into a pond full of acid. Their screams were so terrible that local peasants abandoned their homes.*

He then found that in Berezovska,

> *... 58,000 Odessa Jews were burned alive ... Some of them were burnt to death in railway carriages. Others were taken to a clearing where Germans poured petrol over them and set them on fire.*

Grossman described an SS man called Zepf who specialised in killing children:

> *This beast, who possessed a massive physical strength, would suddenly seize a child out of the crowd, and either hit the child's head against the ground waving the child like a cudgel, or tear the child into two halves.*

He described how victims, stripped of all clothing were driven through open doors into gas chambers as SS men unleashed trained Alsatian dogs which threw themselves on the crowd and tore the naked bodies with their teeth. One Commandant by the name of Kurt Franz had specially trained his dog called Barry "to jump at the doomed people and tear their private parts."

After gassing,

> *... the corpses were examined by SS men. If someone was discovered to be still alive, was moaning or moved, this person was shot with a pistol. Then the crews armed with dentist tongs would set to work wrenching platinum and gold teeth out of the dead people's mouths. The teeth were then sorted according to their value, packed into boxes and sent to Germany.*

Eventually Australia, per capita, would take in more holocaust survivors than any other country except Israel.

On 20 July 1944, a namesake of mine Ludwig Beck, a former Chief of Staff of the German Army High Command, together with other conspirators attempted to assassinate Adolf Hitler, Fuhrer of Nazi Germany, at his Wolf's Lair field headquarters in East Prussia with a briefcase bomb placed under a table. Had the plot known as operation 'Valkyrie' succeeded it was proposed to appoint Beck as President or Regent of a new provisional German government. Three people were killed, but not Hitler. He ordered the Gestapo to arrest more than 7,000 people and executed 4,980—many of whom were in the German military. Beck offered to commit suicide and shot himself but failed in that attempt as well accomplishing only a severe self-wounding. He had to be finished off by a German sergeant who administered a *coup de grace* with a pistol shot in the back of his neck.

In the end it was the communists that succeeded in finishing off Hitler. The world had never before seen a fighting force like Stalin's army. By the end of 1944 it was well over one million strong and contained the greatest concentration of fire power ever amassed. On 21 April 1945, when I was only four days shy of six months of age, the Russians fired 1.8 million shells in a single day in their assault on Berlin. They could hardly lose the battle, out-numbering the Germans in men (five to one), tanks (five to one), guns (15 to one) and planes (three to one). Still, another 500,000 people died before it was over. Hitler suicided on 30 of April and Germany officially surrendered on 8 May 1945. The Soviets took nearly 3.5 million prisoners back to Russia and nearly half of them died in captivity. Some 50,000 were kept for 11 years in concentration work camps until they were released in 1956 when I was 12 years old.

In Japan, where the war continued, pitiless fire raids were carried out on every major city. On Tokyo alone more than three million incendiary bombs were dropped. One US saturation raid in March 1945 destroyed the city with an unbelievable thoroughness. Vast firestorms consumed wooden buildings with whirlwinds of flames that writhed and lashed the shattered population. Thousands suffocated, thousands baked to death in timber buildings that turned into ovens, and thousands drowned in the crush as they fled to the river. On that night alone 250,000 buildings were destroyed and almost 100,000 people obliterated.

The ultimate incentive for the closure of the war came in the form of atomic bombs. I was just short of 10 months of age and still very much a little boy when, in August 1945, the first atomic bomb codenamed 'Little Boy' dropped and flattened 42 square miles of Hiroshima city. It killed 80,000 people outright and seriously injured 37,000. Another 10,000 were declared missing having apparently 'evaporated' or vaporised by the intense heat leaving only their shadows on the ground. People suffocated as all available oxygen fed the massive fireball. With no indication of surrender, a further A bomb was then dropped on Nagasaki, killing 35,000, severely injuring 6,000 and leaving 5,000 'missing'. By the end of 1945, a further 80,000 people had died from 'radiation sickness'. Then on 14 August 1945, at least another 800 US bombers poured bombs over every military target on Japan's main island. Next day the Japanese Emperor publicly capitulated. It was the end of all things to the Japanese. Hundreds of them from common civilian workers to generals killed themselves. In Launceston, Tasmania, the effigy of the Emperor Hirohito on his white horse was burned in a bonfire and in Martin Place Sydney they burned an effigy of a Japanese soldier as girls danced, snatched hats from servicemen and traded kisses for autographs. In Bendigo, the pubs were full, as were the customers.

For me it was just the beginning. Like anyone else who did not actually experience World War II first hand I can't imagine the scale of human tragedy it encompassed. It did however define the Australia that I was to live in and it was the catalyst that sparked a quantum leap of growth and change like a starburst in every direction. The year 1945 changed the world. The nuclear age would result in a new world order. The hard-fought victory of 1945 brought with it a period of unequalled peace, prosperity and relative stability. At the end of the war Australia's population was estimated to be 7.4 million. In the two decades following and beyond Australia was to enjoy an easy prosperity. This was to be my purple patch.

While the war was being fought, the people in Bendigo remained largely oblivious to its horror. They were removed from it and censorship prevented them from finding out the really adverse details that might negatively influence public morale. On a daily basis life went on much as it did before the war. Business, politics and pleasure mostly went on as usual. Compared with the reality, ignorance was bliss for most. Apart from the annoying effects of rationing and other government regulations the closest they came to the war was when trains arrived at the railway station loaded with American soldiers sent to Bendigo on 'R and R' furlough, some of whom had not had their boots off for months. After being assembled and lined up outside the station they would, at the call of a number, file off either to the left or the right to be billeted with a volunteer family. Locals willingly welcomed the 'Yanks' and showed sincere appreciation for their efforts fighting the Japanese to keep them out of Australia.

As American forces had built up in the Pacific, the number of US soldiers in Australia on furlough grew until, by mid 1944, it was estimated that at any given time there were up to 250,000 GIs in the country and, by the end of the war, 860,000. The Australian government made US dollars legal tender in the country and the free spending habits of Yanks gained favour from taxi drivers, waiters, publicans and goodtime girls. While Aussie men envied the Yanks with their higher military pay, smart uniforms and endless supply of cigarettes, chocolates and nylons to entice the girls, they stood up and honoured them at theatres and concerts whenever the 'Star Spangled Banner' was played. With the winning of the war in 1945, American soldiers reached the peak of their popularity and influence. Jitterbug dancing they introduced reached a high point with jitterbug jamborees and, when they left, they took with them 10,000 Aussie brides back to the USA.

Puckapunyal army camp near Seymour was a popular furlough station for American soldiers during the war. At the time my father, Reg Beck, was licensee and proprietor of The Canadian Hotel in Seymour. He had not been eligible for war service after the accident he had in the 1930s driving his Buick which ran off the road, hit a tree and caused permanent injury to his left lung. A considerable portion of his lung containing a pocket of air was closed off and rendered useless. I never knew it to bother him much except on one occasion in a 1950s flight in a low pressurised DC3 with ANA to Tasmania when the air pocket in his lung expanded, reducing the operational capacity of his other lung causing him considerable pain and shortness of breath. He claimed that the medical diagnosis for his condition was a "permanent, spontaneous, natural, numeroid thorax" and often gave that description as an anecdote, when relevant, to his many stories.

With a name like 'The Canadian' my father's hotel was popular with the American troops who, when granted leave, would march into town and 'dismiss' in front of the hotel and invade the bar. Often the thirsty soldiers were up to 10 men deep at the counter.

Men at the front of the bar would refuse to leave their position of advantage causing the back markers to hand their money forward to the front men to make purchases for them. Many had no understanding of the Aussie currency or exchange rate and would simply hand up a wad of notes and say, "Take what you need pal," or throw a handful of coins on the counter, some of which would finish on the floor. The front positions were so well held that many men, instead of going to the toilet would piss in situ on the bar wall. To deal with this my father laid sawdust on the floor of the public side of the bar.

When he lost a diamond out of a gold signet ring that had been given to him by my mother, he set up a water sluicing trough, one Sunday, in the backyard of the hotel and shovelled all the sawdust through it. He recovered the missing diamond and such a very substantial and worthwhile amount of coinage that he repeated the procedure every Sunday thereafter. The Canadian Hotel proved to be a very profitable business and it was the funds derived from that establishment that enabled my father to later purchase The Crown Hotel in Bendigo.

Chapter 3

FAMILY

I lived as a toddler at 109 Queen Street Bendigo, now the location of The Golden Twin Cinemas. Our house was a substantial red brick Federation style building, formerly owned by a doctor, that backed on to King Street with a frontage to Queen Street, and apart from the usual bedrooms included a separate lounge/dining room, billiard room, cellar, large veranda with sleepout plus a garage and workshop outbuildings. A wood-fired stove in the kitchen and large fireplaces in the lounge and billiard room kept the place warm in winter. At house parties my father conducted race meetings with yabbies on the billiard table. Having sold the Canadian Hotel in Seymour he was now between pubs and looking to buy another in Bendigo.

My mum had no refrigerator and made do with an ice chest for our meat, butter and milk. Once a week the iceman would come with a gleaming translucent block held by a hook on a sugar bag over his shoulder to replenish the chest. Refrigerators were in short supply and expensive after the war.

Another weekly visitor was the rabbit catcher who drove past yelling out "rabbio rabbio" selling pairs of rabbits for a few shillings. They were skinned on the spot if requested by mum when she ran out to buy a pair. She was a good rabbit cook, pot roasting them over a slow fire for at least two hours with beef dripping and a few rashers of bacon added. Farmed meat was rationed for the first four years of my life from 1944 to 1948, but fortunately it did not extend to rabbits which were in plague proportions.

My grandmother said I ate snails raw, straight out of the garden. I have no independent recollection of that and doubt that anyone witnessed it. My father claimed, that around the periphery of my mouth and dribbling off my chin, he had seen evidence of shells and slime allegedly derived from said snails. Maybe I was hungry. My grandmother said I wasn't because try as she might she was unable to force feed me with her concoction of mashed banana. I vividly recall gagging on the stuff and thereafter felt repelled from eating them until well past middle age. I still retain a preference for protein over fruit and vegetables.

My grandmother's name was Sarah Johanna Janetta Von de Merwe, born in South Africa to Dutch Africana parents on 28 May 1869 and was 75 years old when I arrived. My sister, Zelda, and I called her 'Nana'. Her accent was pronounced and her skin old and leathery but still, paradoxically, so soft. When she wasn't carrying me around on her hip she made home-made mint sauce or crocheted lace doilies with bead fringes to cover milk jugs and other like containers to keep the flies out. She had served as a military nurse in the action against the British during the Boer War in South Africa at the end of the 19th century during which she was captured and imprisoned in a British concentration camp. She had no time for the British but took a fancy to a journalist, Charles Walker from Cressey in Tasmania, who had gone to South

Africa to cover the war. Charlie, who had been born in 1852, was 17 years older than Sarah and had a deceased wife with six children from his first marriage, but none of that stopped her from falling in love and marrying him at Bloemfontein on 25 May 1903. When Charlie's mother died he returned to Tasmania to finalise her estate as executor, leaving Sarah and their first child, Anne, in South Africa. After a lengthy period of time Sarah became tired of waiting and decided that she would chase after Charlie to Australia. When she arrived on the wharf in Tasmania with child in arms, he was standing there with his bags packed ready to board ship to return to South Africa. Luckily, she spotted him.

The couple decided to stay and settle in Launceston where my mother, Madge, was born. Eventually the family settled in Seymour, Victoria, where Charles got a job in the local newspaper until his eyesight failed due to cataracts and he became blind. Sarah then became the sole breadwinner for the family and, to support them, ran a guesthouse. Charles died in 1930. After meeting in Seymour when my father was running The Canadian Hotel, my parents married in 1939 and when they came to reside at 109 Queen Street Sarah took up residence with them and later went with them to The Crown Hotel.

My grandfather, Alec Beck, had been a 'gun' blacksmith whose skills extended to wheelrighting, buggy and jinker construction and equine dental work. In 1905, at the age of 31, he entered a mounted display of various intricate styles of horseshoes he had made in the Royal Melbourne Show and won first prize. His wife, my grandmother Mabel Elizabeth (née Dunstan), died in 1947 when I was aged three after they had been married 46 years. He then took up residence with us at the Queen Street house. By the time World War I had started, the couple had three children (Roy, my father Reg, and Mabel, aged twelve, eleven and nine) and he was aged 40. He never drove a car for his entire life and was always happiest when reminiscing about his old blacksmithing and horse and harness days. When the first east-west crossing took place in a car in 1912 he was aged 38 years. They were machines he did not fancy and he rightly blamed them for the demise of the horse and buggy era.

From the very beginning it was a love/hate relationship between my grandfather and me. He started the ball rolling when he noticed that I was fascinated with sparrows coming into the garden and tried to catch them. As a three-year-old I had no chance but he counselled me that I could easily do so if I could put salt on their tails. Accordingly, he equipped me with a loaded salt shaker and let me loose in the garden with his words of encouragement while he sat back and laughed for days on end at my futile endeavours. Eventually my mother confiscated the salt shaker. Due to infantile amnesia many of us remember nothing about being a toddler but I certainly remember this. I have little doubt that my memory was reinforced by my grandfather retelling the story many times, in my embarrassed presence, to others. Many years later I had the last laugh when I discovered, that while we lived at the house in Queen Street, he had built a wooden wheelbarrow in the workshop and only found out when the job was done that it was too big to go out through the narrow doorway. That was a story I could tell.

When living at the house in Queen Street my father was working as a barman for the licensee of the City Club Hotel, Sarah Fordyce, who became my Godmother at my christening. It was an easy walk from our house in Queen Street to the shopping centre and I have early memories of often accompanying my mother and sister Zelda is as a toddler to the City Club Hotel and other licensed premises such as The Queens Hotel at the corner of Queen and Mitchell streets where the licensee was Minnie O'Shea and The Arcade Hotel that fronted what is now Hargreaves Mall. I loved walking through the old livery stables, accessed from Queen Street, at the rear of The Arcade Hotel and looking at the horses and carriages. Unlike many women of the time my mother was comfortable in the environment of hotels after serving the previous seven years helping my father in managing the residential and dining facilities of The Imperial Hotel at Castlemaine and The Canadian Hotel at Seymour. The setting and surroundings of a hotel ladies lounge was a place where she felt comfortable and could relax with a drink and a smoke, and women were welcome to go there with their babies in prams or toddlers in pushers.

2. 109 Queen Street Bendigo, our 1948 home.
Now the site of the Golden Twin Cinemas.

3. Arcade Hotel Stables. The livery stables that led from Queen Street
through to the Arcade Hotel in Hargreaves Street.
Source: Travis McScratchey, 'Lost Bendigo and District', 1952
lostbendigodistrict.weebly.com.

Chapter 4

THE CROWN HOTEL

I n 1949 when Australia's rabbit plague was reaching its peak, my father purchased The Crown Hotel at 238 Hargreaves Street Bendigo. I was only four years old when he took possession of the freehold and business on 2 May that year. While Australia then had a population of a little over eight million, Bendigo and district had less than 40,000 residents. He apparently was not concerned about the fact that between 1945 and 1948 there had been frequent shortages of beer and that, with 72 hotels Bendigo had a pub for less than every 600 people including men, women and children, or that 12 of those hotels were within 250 to 400 metres from The Crown—as the crow flies. [See Appendix 1 for their names and locations.]

The original Crown Hotel had been built in the 1860s and was probably a timber structure. Around 1911 the present front section was constructed, then including a magnificent front veranda with cast iron lacework. During the 1930s the rear portion of the hotel was added with additional upstairs guest accommodation and large dining room and kitchen downstairs. At the same time the veranda was 'modernised' by replacing the cast iron lacework with painted metal panels. In the late 1950s it was removed altogether and replaced with the present cantilever on the order of the Bendigo City Council motivated by their concern over the risk of parking cars running into posts that supported verandas throughout the city.

A small foyer at the front of the hotel led to the heavy double main entrance doors framing bevelled glass panels engraved with elaborate crowns and fitted with large solid brass handles and push plates. On entering you saw the grand wooden staircase with right angled turns around the walls of the stair hall leading to three levels. The balustrade or system of railing and banister that kept people from falling over the edge was made from a hard reddish-brown mahogany-like timber with turned posts supporting the scalloped banisters running between large shaped corner posts crowned with spherical wooden tops at each landing. At the bottom of the stairway the banister curved slightly to the right into a much larger post topped with a bigger wooden sphere. Upon reaching the upper floor the balustrade continued to the left before turning again at 90 degrees to the left to follow a short passageway to complete at its end a one and a half circle around the stair hall. The width of the stair allowed three people to pass with room to spare and natural light filtering through a large stained-glass window halfway up the stair flight completed the impression that The Crown was a quality hotel. From my point of view, the staircase was one of the hotel's most redeeming features as I quickly learned how to slide down the banisters and bailout just before each 90 degree turn to avoid the large corner posts. The last slide was the best with the banister bearing to the right enabling me to just shoot off the end.

The hotel office at the far side of the entrance hall featured Victorian style clear and opaque ornamental lead glass windows, displaying the word "Office" in gold leaf, that could be slid up when open for business. Next to the office was the guests' telephone booth made from the same hard reddish-brown mahogany-like timber as the staircase. To remove any doubt the structure was clearly labelled "Telephone" with a shiny brass plate. It was then thought that people were entitled to privacy when making a phone call. Similar clear and opaque ornamental lead glass windows provided some natural light in the top of the booth.

A partitioned washroom near the entrance door of the dining room, where guests could freshen up before a meal, continued the Victorian theme with the same style of ornamental lead glass windows and reddish-brown mahogany wood work. In the stair hall there were three large leather club chairs for the comfort of guests, a substantial and fabulous painting by Dora Meeson featuring a gold miner entering through the door of his cottage to show his wife a large gold nugget in his hand, a mirrored hall-stand for coats and several brass jardinieres on pedestals to display plants.

Somehow you didn't notice the sound of ticking clocks around the hotel. There was one in the stair hall, two in the bar and one in the ladies lounge. They were all old-style mechanical station clocks with pendulums and huge round dials that had to be wound regularly. This task fell to my grandfather who told me that it was important to wind them up in the middle of the day when the temperature was stable and to count each turn of the key to make sure they were not overwound. At the end of a gold chain in his vest he kept a pocket watch to keep track of the time which he set daily by the post office clock, readily visible from the backyard of The Crown. This was a practice that most people had followed all their lives before radio was invented. For those who couldn't see the post office clock it struck in loud clear notes every hour and quarter hour during the day which reminded me constantly, as a child, of the time.

Residential accommodation included four double bedrooms, three twin bedrooms plus single rooms that provided for a total of 29 guests. There were no ensuites and all guests had to share the three bathrooms, two separate showers and three toilets. This was a time when motels didn't exist. It was not until 1956 that the first one opened at Oakleigh in Melbourne and it took some years after that before they started to arrive in Bendigo. Hotels were still the go-to place for accommodation and The Crown was one of the best accommodation hotels in Bendigo.

During the time my father ran the hotel, dignified guests included ten Supreme and County Court judges, nine Knights of the Realm, which included a Deputy Prime Minister and two State Premiers, three Police Superintendents, two Police Inspectors, Major General George Rankin and Dame Flora McLeod, Chieftainess of the Scottish Clan McLeod. [See Appendix 2 and 3 for further details.]

All VIPs were given special treatment which was incorporated in the significant bill they received at the end of their stay. Most stayed in Room 3 which had a doorway leading onto the balcony that overlooked the town hall gardens. They were given exclusive access to a lockable lounge/dining room upstairs and a separate parlour room downstairs with a wood fire. Those who preferred to be served in the main dining room were provided with a special reserved table and waitress dedicated to their needs. Like all guests, some were a delight to attend to and others were demanding arrogant tyrants. My mother looked after the finer details of their accommodation including any special meal requirements, laundry needs and so forth.

If a judge elected to use the dining room my mother instructed the waitresses that the correct protocol was to wait at the dining room door so that they could open it and welcome His Honour to dine. One morning, when waitresses were fully occupied, my mother told me to sit at the bottom of the staircase in one of the club leather chairs and "watch out for the bloody old judge and let me know when he is coming." At the time I was probably in Grade 1 at Gravel Hill State School where repetition learning was the order of the day. Having taken her instructions literally, as soon as I saw the judge coming down the stairs I yelled out "Mum! The bloody old judge is coming down the stairs!"

When she craned her neck around the office window, there he was to bid her good morning but expressing some disquiet at the way he had been announced by me, stating that I must have picked up the expression "bloody old judge" from some other person who had described him similarly. She explained that it was difficult to protect me from all the influences of some less desirable hotel patrons and apologised to him profusely. That was one job I was never given again.

Successfully running a hotel like The Crown was a substantial undertaking. Employed staff included two waitresses for the dining room, a cook and two kitchen maids, one full-time and one part-time barmen, a general 'useful' man and two housemaids. A total of ten in all plus my mother and father providing extra hands-on backup in the kitchen and the bar in addition to their managerial duties. At very busy times such as Christmas, Easter, Bendigo Cup day, Bendigo Agricultural Show and Grand Final day, additional part-time bar, waiting and kitchen staff were employed.

Most of the hotel guests were ordinary people either on holidays or commuting through Bendigo to another destination. A number were a separate cohort of 'commercial travellers'. They were men who acted as agents for various manufacturers anxious to sell their wares in Bendigo and dealt in diverse products from jewellery to floor tiles and soap powder, often bringing small samples with them to show their clients. There was a special room allocated to their needs in The Crown called The Commercial Room where they could set out trestle tables to display their goods. As regular returning guests, many became familiar friendly faces whose names, unfortunately, have now vanished into the fog of my past. One I particularly recall was a Mr Cameron who was a tall thin bloke with curly hair and an orange complexion. He was notorious for drinking a bottle of whisky a day during his stay and had an unending repertoire of jokes and wisecracks. His nickname was 'Carroty Cameron' as he always brought with him his own carrot juicing machine together with a supply of carrots to reduce to juice. He conned my mother into allowing him to have access to the kitchen during afternoon quiet periods to juice his carrots which then formed the mixer base for his whisky which seemed to be a substantial part of his diet and probably the reason for his orange complexion. He was terribly thin and I wonder how long he ultimately lasted.

The Crown also attracted its fair share of entertainment and show people. Perhaps it was because of my father's early background as a violinist and his love of variety and entertaining. He had been professionally taught, and during the era of silent movies was employed as lead violinist in the orchestra pit of a Melbourne theatre producing music to accompany the silent thunder of horse hooves in mostly western movies. Not long after the first talking movie *The Jazz Singer* arrived here around 1928, he lost his job due to soundtrack movies rendering his position redundant. Maybe it was just the popular venue of the Town Hall for entertainers and its proximity across the road from The Crown that made it a convenient place for them to stay. In any event all entertainers and show people were made especially welcome as guests.

Once a year during the fifties the Royal Victorian Institute for the Blind brought their concert show *Variety on Parade* to Bendigo as part of its state wide tour. As well as providing much needed money and publicity for the institute, touring played an important and challenging role in the lives of the singers and musicians most of whom were blind. For years the institute had made the best of music in its educational program for blind students. Several institute members had Bachelor of Music degrees. Many had been trained to play various instruments or were trained in singing and others had learned how to tune pianos. Concerts were held at the Town Hall and played to packed houses for two or three nights on each visit. I often went to every performance each year. The variety show had its own orchestra, choir, singers, solo instrumentalists, comedians, magicians, jugglers, ventriloquist and impersonators. My father was in awe of a solo violinist and I particularly remember a brilliant saxophonist. Many of these performers stayed at the crown where particular attention was paid to their care.

The proximity of the Town Hall was probably also responsible for drawing others to stay at The Crown, such as Hector Crawford conductor of the Melbourne Symphony Orchestra, Glenda Raymond operatic soprano and Gladys Moncrieff concert singer. One regular visitor during Agricultural Showtime and the Bendigo Easter Fair was Tom Wittingslow, who at the time was probably the leading showman of merry-go-rounds and all things that whizzed around or went bump in the night. He and my father seemed to enjoy each other's company and became good friends. Country and western folk singers, The Legarde Twins and actor

Frank Thring also stayed and I recall my father having to extend one of the single beds to accommodate a man who was billed as "The Giant of The World" in one of the sideshows.

Off street car parking for up to 15 cars in the large backyard of The Crown was one of its attractions. There was no other hotel in the central business district of Bendigo that could provide such a facility. Many guests also arrived by train and then taxi to the hotel. Two or three taxis turned up with guests every night after the last train arrived around 9 p.m. Most bookings were done by phone with requests for accommodation also received in the twice daily mail deliveries to Bendigo's central business district and from the uniformed boys riding red post office bicycles delivering telegrams originating from transcribed chattering Morse code. If available, the boys were instructed to send the reply "Accommodation confirmed." On most nights during the working week accommodation was close to fully occupied. Sunday was the quietest.

Weary travellers could spread bedbugs from the luggage they brought with them. There had never been a sign of bedbugs at The Crown until my father received an alarming report that they were in some of the bedrooms. An adult bedbug is about the size of an apple seed, reddish-brown, flat and happy living in tight spaces such as the joint of a bedframe, the back of a bedside table or even the head of a screw where it patiently waits until the next victim arrives. On sensing the carbon dioxide from human breath or the heat of a body, they venture forth for a drink of blood, during which their body can double in size. They then creep back to their hidey holes and pack in tight with anywhere from five to a dozen others. Their bites can cause mild irritation to severe allergic reaction, depending on the individual victim. Commonly, painful, swollen red splotches are the result.

In the 1950s and 1960s they developed a hearty resistance to conventional pesticides. My father was aware of this and resolved to kill them by whatever means possible. Having been around before the invention of DDT he was aware that back in 'the old days' various methods of extermination had been used including flammable liquid such as turpentine, petrol and kerosene painted into the homing crevices of bed frames, and even spreading gunpowder in the cracks and then setting it alight. He chose to make a noxious paste with arsenic which he had witnessed his father use in the past with great efficacy. It was then legally possible to acquire the substance from the chemist if you filled out the appropriate forms, gave legitimate reasons and signed for it. In any event, by fair means or foul, he acquired it, made a paste and painted it into every bedframe and furniture crack he could locate on the premises. The end result was bedbug genocide. I vividly recall walking into one of the bedrooms while he was applying the stuff and receiving an unexpected and amazingly vociferous lecture about the dangers of arsenic and the necessity of using it on bloodsucking bed buggers. Subsequently, there were no reports of any customers suffering from arsenic poisoning.

4. Young Zel and Max (aka Mickey), about 1948/49.

CROWN HOTEL
BENDIGO
(REG. W. S. BECK, Proprietor)

Tariff:

PER DAY	**£2-0-0**
DINNER, BED AND BREAKFAST	**£1-15-0**
BED AND BREAKFAST	**£1-10-0**
PER WEEK	**£12-12-0**

5. Crown Hotel tariff card, circa 1950s.

Chapter 5

ENTERTAINMENT
AND DINING

The entrance doorway to the dining room was elegant and stylish. A large dark wood surround housed double doors of bevelled glass framed in the same wood with huge brass handles on each door. The words "Dining" and "Room" were painted separately on each door in gold leaf, and a modest amount of glass frosting on only the upper and lower parts of the doors provided a hint of privacy to the occupants.

On entry you realised at once that this was a significant dining room. Ahead was a large portrait of Queen Elizabeth II displayed above the mantle of a big faux fireplace. To the left were three very grand and double hung leadlight windows framed in red velvet pelmets edged in gold braid. Curtains of the same red velvet flowed down to be tied back with gold tassels. The high ceiling was not just ornate but in heavy relief made up of large squares of decorative plaster hiding the supporting beams. The four walls, furnished with wood panelling to shoulder height, displayed three magnificent Victorian sideboards with bevelled glass mirrors.

A total of sixty diners could be seated at eleven round tables of four each and two rectangular tables of eight each, all on straight-backed dining chairs with padded leather upholstered seats. The commencement of each dining sitting, breakfast at 8 a.m., lunch at 12:30 p.m. and dinner at 6 p.m. was heralded by a waitress striking a large polished brass gong engraved with dragon symbols. The deep-toned resonation echoed throughout the entire hotel and was impossible to ignore.

All tables were 'silver service' with a full complement of cutlery for each diner, cruet sets containing pepper, salt, mustard and vinegar, a glass crock for bread, a jug of water and glasses and white linen tablecloths. The linen napkins folded in the shape of a crown would have been the pride of any origami master. A typed formal menu was presented in a silver-framed stand and two waitresses in black dresses with white cuffs, collars and white aprons provided service.

In the far-left corner from where you entered the dining room my father Reg had built a small stage for the provision of entertainment on special occasions such as Christmas dinner, New Year, Easter Saturday and Cup Day. The platform was equipped with a piano and music stands for instrumental performers but there was no amplification. Performers had to rely on their acoustic ability.

The usual variety concert consisted of diverse acts including my father as master of ceremonies and violin player, Arthur Norman on the piano and Mac McQueen on the squeezebox who, in addition to singing, stood upside down on his hands and drank a glass of beer. Another star attraction was Teddy Motram, known as "one-man band". He wore a big bass drum on his back, a kettle drum on his front, cymbals on his knees, a mouth organ on a frame under his chin and held a concertina in his hands. Somehow he was able to play them all at the same time.

George English sung 'Old Man River' and 'The Bluebird of Happiness' beautifully, although in normal conversation he had such a severe stutter that he could sometimes barely put two words together. George, who worked at the ordnance factory, was a regular customer at The Crown and a gentleman who always had a lovely smile, a twinkle in his eye and a warm greeting for me. He rode a small pedal assisted motorbike to and from work and parked it in the backyard of The Crown when he called in for a drink. After observing George stop and start it for several months, the temptation became too much for me and I purloined it myself for a test run around the yard. George caught me red-handed but just smiled and counselled me, for safety sake, not to do it again.

One day George turned up at the hotel after work and explained to my father that he was in serious trouble. It was winter time and he said that he had been travelling home from the hotel in the semi-darkness after 6 o'clock closing the previous evening, when a man ran out and he had hit him with his motorbike. George said that because he had a few drinks he kept driving, but that he was really worried about the consequences of his actions and the extent of any injuries he might have caused the man. Reg said that it was unlikely that George had done any serious injury with his small bike to the man and it would be best if he just shut up and said nothing to anyone about it. At this point George became quite distressed and, after a terrible bout of prolonged stuttering, eventually blurted out to my father that he had found "this" in the spokes of the back wheel of his bike as he pulled out a tobacco tin from his pocket.

"What the hell is it, George?" said my father.

George lifted the lid and there, in the tobacco tin, was a human finger lying in bloodstained cotton wool.

"Christ!" said Reg. "Give me a look."

Then, as he peered more closely at the item in the tin, suddenly the finger stood up vertically. The finger was George's that had come up through a hole in the bottom of the tin! History doesn't record exactly what my father's subsequent remarks were, but the joke was on him and so was the shout with free drinks around the gathered throng.

At the dining room variety shows my sister Zelda reluctantly performed with some tap-dancing routines while I volunteered with my own acts, which included singing, at Christmas, 'Rudolph the Red-Nosed Reindeer' wearing a red nose and antlers. At other times I did an imitation of Chad Morgan with plastic false teeth singing 'I'm the Sheik of Scrubby Creek' and acting the part of an idiotic, illiterate bushwhacker, a role which seemed to come naturally to me.

My father was a highly skilled violinist and a great raconteur. One of his favourite numbers was 'Home Sweet Home' which he introduced with a long sentimental introduction that had most people on the verge of crying before he started his performance. By the time he finished playing they had tears rolling down their cheeks. He brilliantly performed classical numbers such as 'Méditation De Thaïs', 'The Nuns Chorus', 'Souvenir' and compositions of Fritz Kreisler's.

Above all else he was a showman and after a few drinks was liable to claim he could play the 'Minute Waltz' in 52 seconds!

His signature performance was undoubtedly playing the bagpipes on his violin. He began by rolling up his pants to reveal long underwear and garters with tartan rosettes on his calves. Removing his coat, he turned it inside out and tied it behind his back with the sleeves so that the inside lining made a makeshift kilt in front. He then produced a feather duster, which he hung with a hook from the front as a facsimile sporran. He grabbed his Akubra hat, which just happened to be handy, punched it inside out and put it on his head upside down, stuck with a large goose feather. Undoing all the strings from his bow he held them in one hand while he ran the wooden part of the bow under his violin with the other hand and then passed the bow hairs, still held in hand, over the top of the violin strings. The sound that came from his instrument as he moved the bow hairs across all the violin strings together at once was remarkably like the drone of the bagpipes. So equipped, he would then march off the stage and 'waddle' in and around the tables of the dining room playing the bagpipes with renditions of such popular numbers as 'Scotland the Brave' and others. The act was always a huge hit.

If it came to it, Reg was also capable of singing a song. His favourite number was 'Pat McGinty's Goat' about Paddy, an Irishman of note, who came into a fortune and bought himself a goat. Said Paddy, "Of goats milk I mean to have my fill!" But when he got his Nanny home, he found it was a Bill! [See Appendix 4 for full text.]

Another of Reg's performance tricks was 'The One-Armed Fiddler'. He would walk on stage wearing a coat jacket with the right sleeve hanging free. In his left arm he would hold his violin and bow. His right arm was hidden from the audience in his pants. As he fumbled in his endeavours to turn pages on the music stand with his left arm that still held the violin and bow, two fingers appeared from the fly of his pants to hold the bow and violin by the neck thus freeing his left arm to turn the pages.

For novelty variety he also played the lagerphone, an Aussie percussion instrument he made by loosely tacking more than 100 beer bottle tops to an old worn-out broomstick, which was 'played' by banging the device on the floor and bowing or, more accurately, sawing it with a serrated stick. It was his violins that he loved and he finished up owning thirteen of them.

Each year my father assembled the same group of performers to stage a concert at the Bagshot Hall a few miles north of Huntly. A number of farming families from the area were regular customers at The Crown and the evening's entertainment in the hall was a good public relations exercise for the hotel. The usual performers from The Crown, I am sure, took part for the love of it and free beer. For me it was the former. The format was the same each time with a short concert followed by ballroom dancing to music played by members of the concert group and then a fabulous country supper when the farmers wives produced endless plates of delicious farm cooked food.

I recall going with my father, at least twice, to the Bendigo gaol at Christmas to put on a Christmas concert for the prisoners. We took with us the same group of performers from The Crown concerts who did their usual stuff. There was some singing of Christmas carols, my sister came to perform some tap dancing and I sang, as always, 'Rudolph the Red-Nosed Reindeer' complete with antlers and red nose. The prisoners were very well-behaved and showed great appreciation at the end of the night. When my father completed his performance of 'Home Sweet Home' there was a long period of silence before the men applauded loudly and cheered.

It was Johnny Cash who said "There's nothing more honest than an audience made up of prisoners. They will let you know if you are any good or not."

A number of these men would later return to the Bendigo community after serving their sentence and retain fond memories of Reg Beck and his entourage who had come to brighten up their

Christmas while they were in prison. Some of them would call into The Crown for a beer.

Christmas dinner at The Crown was the most important meal of the year. The dining room was always full with around 60 people. Every table had a miniature Christmas tree as its centrepiece, complimentary dishes of lollies and nuts, and cigarettes standing in little glasses with ashtrays distributed for butts. It was the usual Crown silver service with Reg Beck as master of ceremonies and violin player entertaining the guests throughout the dinner with his customary variety concert performers.

Preparation for the event started at least three or four weeks before Christmas day, with the delivery of two or three geese to the hotel backyard where they were installed in a big old cockies cage and fed as much as they could eat until a few days before Christmas. Turkeys, like hams, were purchased fully prepared from the delicatessen but for some reason the geese were always delivered live. It was my job to keep the feed up to them until the day of execution when our resident axeman and hotel 'useful' Barney Fagan severed their heads. They were tied up in a large sack with only their head and neck poking through a small hole which effectively disabled them to enable a clean blow and prevent them from running around the yard in a state of decapitation. When I was old enough, I was employed as assistant plucker and gutter each year to earn some extra pocket money for Christmas.

About the same time as the geese arrived the cook started with the Christmas puddings. After steaming for more than eight hours, wrapped in large pudding cloths, they were hung from a rafter that traversed the kitchen. There they cured for the weeks leading up to Christmas.

A typical Christmas Day menu included an entrée of seafood cocktail (a couple of prawns in lettuce leaf with a dollop of mayonnaise served in a cocktail glass) and for the main course turkey, ham or goose (or all three if you wanted), roast potatoes and carrots, green beans, tomato and onion pie, cauliflower au gratin, cranberry sauce and lashings of gravy. There was, of course, no air conditioning back then so Christmas dinner went ahead in the middle of the day with a full complement of hot food even if the temperature outside was more than 100°F. It was always a damn sight hotter in the kitchen. For dessert, brandy sauce was served with the Christmas pudding (booby-trapped with threepenny and sixpenny coins) and covered with heaps of custard. Alternatively, you could have the usually popular wine trifle, or compote of fruit with ice cream. In those days before .05 laws much beer was drunk by the men while the ladies enjoyed their Sparkling Rheingold, Porphyry Pearl, Cold Duck and Pims No.1 Cup.

In the 1950s, nearly all the commercial premises in the central business district of Bendigo had substantial verandas abutting the buildings and extending all the way to the gutter. Many of them, including the Crown Hotel had upper-level access and some were still decorated in intricate Victorian style cast-iron lacework surrounds. At Christmas time it was a tradition to decorate the posts of the verandas with big armfuls of green eucalyptus gum leaf tip branches which gave the whole city a refreshing, festival appearance. Subsequent regulations from the City Council required building owners to demolish the verandas because cars parked on an angle had the habit of hitting the veranda posts. Now we have a mall in Hargreaves Street with no cars, no veranda posts and no gum leaf tips at Christmas.

As I grew older The Crown, during Christmas, gave me the opportunity to earn more pocket money through the increased availability of odd jobs. I enjoyed the activity around the hotel and looking back they were good days. But the downside was that not once did I ever sit with my parents for Christmas dinner. They were too busy. I never saw a real pine Christmas tree until I was in my teens. Until then I had only seen them in the movies or in comics. I thought the miniature Christmas trees that my mother purchased to put on the dining room tables looked like some new-fangled dunny brush. I began to resent the fact that my sister and I were not like other kids and we both developed a longing for a normal family life. As long as I didn't think about it I was okay, but when I did I got angry.

Chapter 6

THE KITCHEN

All roads led to the kitchen. Apart from being command central for the accommodation side of the business, it was a place frequented and traversed by all staff members from time to time. The kitchen was where you could always get a snack, complain about something or get free advice and direction. It was a generous space that catered for six workers when fully functioning—the cook, two kitchen maids, two waitresses and my mother. There was access from it to the dining room and to it from an external door or via the hotel office through a small area approximately 14 feet × 14 feet, designated "the little room", which apart from our family's bedrooms, was the only area set aside for our exclusive use.

The dominating centrepiece of the kitchen was a huge wood stove and oven complex. The hot plate surface extended some 12 feet or more and below that there was a fire box slightly offset from the centre, with one large double door oven on the right and too large double door ovens on the left. The entire front of the stove was built flush with the interior wall. Externally a brick wall had been built around it to accommodate its mass with a huge brick chimney extending above the second floor of the premises.

Above the stove's hotplates within the chimney arch, several hot and cold- water taps were plumbed along its full extent for the easy access of the cook. To the left of the firebox on top of the stove sat a large copper water urn with a tap that provided boiling water all day. The firebox had a hollow grate and a multi-tubular piping system on the sides through which hot water was produced for the whole hotel.

The system was augmented by a device called a 'Scalebuoy' that was claimed to treat water to remove and prevent scale, corrosion and other deleterious effects of water action on boilers, tanks and pipes. Invented by Bendigo man R. H. S. Abbott, the device contained mercury and rare gases under various degrees of vacuum and was alleged to throw off electrons which created radiation of various wavelengths in an electrostatic field that set up a negative charge that purified the water! It's hard to tell whether it really worked or not. At times the water got so hot in the huge external water tank that steam shot out of an overflow pipe on the top, making it necessary to draw hot water off into the kitchen sinks to reduce the pressure and prevent guests being scalded by steam shooting out of bathroom taps or showers.

This stove was a serious cooker. Two or three times a year it was 'polished' in its entirety with Zebra brand black lead. At the end of the stove on the right a steel door opening into the wall led to a wood bunker that was filled daily by the hotel 'useful' through an external trapdoor. The fire in the stove was never allowed to go out—winter or summer. The last thing my father did each night before he went to bed was to give the stove a final stoke. In the middle of the night the nightwatchman, Frank Roach, would throw on a couple of logs to keep it going and first thing in the morning my father would stoke it again. The availability of unlimited hot water through the stove allowed me to develop a habit of indulging in excessively long showers as there was never a helicopter parent hovering about to tell me to get out.

The second most important piece of equipment was the refrigerator, about seven feet high and ten feet long with six doors to separate compartments, one equipped with metal trays for freezing, making ice and ice cream. It was so big that when my sister and I at times played hide and seek we could hide in a compartment if it were empty. Upon reflection not such a good idea. The refrigeration plant was housed in a separate engine room outside.

For washing up there were two large industrial size sinks, one for pots and pans and one for crockery and cutlery with a dividing bench between them. Unlike other kids, my sister and I never had to do the washing up after a meal or dry any dishes. Big double sash windows above each sink provided ample light to the kitchen. In the middle of the room a large bench, about the same length as the stove, was operation central for the cook.

The rest of the kitchen was lined with cupboards and shelves for storage and included a gas stove. A commercial toaster that could toast six slices both sides at once had no automatic pop-up mechanism which meant you had to watch it carefully to avoid its full-on cook elements scorching forgotten slices resulting in thick smoke and even flames. Hot cross buns had the propensity to disappear into this monster to emerge as clumps of hard carbon. A hand operated bread cutting machine (that I once almost cut my thumb off with) and a chopping block made from the trunk of a tree at the end of the cook's bench plus an industrial exhaust fan to expel smells completed the kitchen fit out basics. There were no pastry or dough mixers or food processors. All such tasks were done with a manual 'egg beater' or by hand. For its day it was a well-designed kitchen with adequate lighting and ventilation and capable of performing under pressure.

Next to the wood bunker the back door provided access to the yard and a nearby gully trap. A separate external pantry was always full of big hessian bags with potatoes and onions, and other fresh vegetables such as cauliflowers, cabbages, celery, lettuce, peas, tomatoes, carrots, parsnips and so on—even an occasional bunch of asparagus, but never any sign of alien vegetarian lifeforms such as bok choy, kale, rocket, broccoli, fennel or even capsicum. These items together with houmous, haloumi, feta, avocados and an endless variety of other stuff was just not available in Bendigo. Olive oil was only used for earaches. Additional storage was provided in an old stable converted for the purpose in the hotel backyard. Here you would find bulk tea stored in large plywood chests, big jars of ground coffee (when available), large four-gallon tins containing a dehydrated vegetable mix for soups, shelves stacked with various cans of preserved fruit and vegetables, varied bottles of condiments and miscellaneous dry groceries.

The cook always had a large tin of cooking fat which seemed to be an essential ingredient for everything. Every leg of roast meat was cooked in a very large pan awash with heaps of melted fat. Into this also went the vegetables of the day such as roast potatoes, carrots, parsnips, onions and Yorkshire pudding when dictated by the menu. At the end of the cooking process fat was drained off through a sieve into another tin and then used again. The flavour of the harvested lard or 'dripping' depended on whether it came from roast pork, beef or lamb and was used by the cooks according to their requirements. Fish and chips tasted best cooked in beef dripping. I remember well one of the cooks providing my sister and I with after-school snacks of bread smeared with beef or bacon fat dripping quickly seared on the hot surface of the wood stove and sprinkled with salt and pepper. Nothing could quite compare with the delicious taste. During the war, beef dripping was canned and sent overseas for our troops.

The breakfast menu included cereal, porridge, eggs (every which way) sausages, tomatoes, baked beans, bacon, toast and a variety of jams. New cooks would sometimes bring their own specialty breakfast dishes with them to trial on customers. Things like sheep's brains, dipped in egg whip, dusted with breadcrumbs and fried in boiling fat or skinned and sliced sheep's kidneys fried in butter and served on toast after being drizzled with a beaten egg and roasted in the oven for a minute or two. Sliced liver rolled in flour and cooked to a golden brown in smoking fat could be served on toast or with eggs. Fresh fruit was absent, stewed or canned fruit available sometimes and prunes most days. Coffee was made by wrapping the grounds in a linen cloth which was tied off and thrown in the pot and boiled. There it sat all day awaiting a coffee order.

Every day big joints of lamb, beef or pork were roasted in the ovens. Roast mutton, a meat cut taken from older sheep, was cheaper than lamb and often appeared on the menu. Meat was thought to be a necessary source of protein and essential nutrients for working adults and healthy growing children. At the evening meal there was always a choice of two roasts, with corned beef now and then to break the monotony. A basic selection of vegetables accompanied each plate with exotics like Brussels sprouts and asparagus spears appearing rarely.

Standards of cooking differed back then. Vegetables were often cooked to the point of collapse. To stop them turning grey, some cooks added bicarbonate of soda to the water to help them stay green. Meat was cremated to remove any hint of pink flesh. If anyone asked for a rare steak, they would be given a long stare of disbelief. Chicken was generally too expensive and reserved for the occasional Sunday roast. Fish and chips were always available Fridays. Boiled smoked cod smeared with butter was popular. There was no such thing as alfresco dining and only the upper crust of society drank wine with meals.

Leftovers from joints served hot were then available for next day's lunch menu served as "cold meat with salad". Remaining remnants might then be turned into a third dish such as shepherd's pie by pushing meat through a hand operated mincing machine, adding some gravy, covering the lot with mashed potato and baking in the oven. A popular lunch dish was tripe (the lining from the stomach of a sheep or cow) served with white sauce seasoned with garlic, and onions served on toast with mashed potatoes on the side. It was a cheap dish, that survived well into the 1950s from the tough times of depression and war when people couldn't afford any kind of culinary sophistication and generally ate what was available. There was always plenty of bread, butter and jam on tables to fill up on and a jug of water to wash it down.

The dessert menu would include puddings such as bread-and-butter, tapioca or creamed rice and jellied fruit served with ice cream. Occasionally apple pie with custard or rhubarb pie with cream. Jam roly-poly sponge and upside-down golden syrup pudding served with a large dob of cream were two of my favourites as was steamed jam pudding with ice cream. The most popular all round desert dish was wine trifle. Prepared in a rectangular dish starting with a layer of cut sponge which was then drizzled with a generous amount of fortified wine (cheap sherry or port), then layered with a lavish quantity of custard followed by another layer of coloured jelly and another layer of cream which could be sprinkled with a substance which we called 'dead ants' made of tiny chocolate pieces. Served with additional cream or ice cream, it was irresistible.

Kitchen rubbish comprising vegetable peelings, leftover and thrown out food and all such things, that today would be regarded as compostable, was placed outside in a large bin made from a 44-gallon drum cut in half and with a loose-fitting lid. The contents were collected a couple of times a week by the 'pig man' at no charge and taken by him to his farm to feed pigs. He was a short and stocky, powerful fellow who never had any trouble lifting these big bins onto the back of his rustic old truck. He serviced several hotels in this manner and it was always a pleasure to see him leave and take away the malodorous smells and swarms of flies that accompanied him.

A day arrived when we had a plague of cockroaches. They just weren't there a week before and seemed to come from nowhere. It was near the end of winter when they adopted the kitchen as their headquarters. Attracted, no doubt, by the warmth. They became rampant and set up breeding colonies in every nook and cranny. After all staff had left for the day, they would run like rabbits along the wall cracks at the edge of the stove where grease had built up and under the ledge of the main workbench where they rippled in a constant stream. My sister and I used to catch them by applying a lighted candle along their highways causing dozens of them to fall down into a jam tin which we then emptied onto the top of the hot stove where they would pop and explode. At first the management adopted an optimistic attitude hoping that they would go away as quickly as they arrived. When that didn't happen my father eventually called in the pest controllers resulting in cockroach obliteration arising from the liberal application of then popular chemical killers DDT or dieldrin.

Although I received little control or direction on my diet there was always plenty to eat. In the common absence of my mother from the kitchen, I was able to pick and choose what I ate with the co-operation of the cooks. I had a basic objection to anything green, which has stayed with me for most of my life, so Brussels sprouts, cabbage and lettuce were ruled out wherever possible. Peas and beans occasionally. Seasonal fresh fruit was sometimes available. At dinner times I occasionally refused to eat anything until all the staff were gone and both my parents were in the closed bar drinking after hours, leaving my sister and I in charge of the office. I then could plunder whatever I chose from the kitchen stores. Sometimes I would open a whole tin of canned peaches and eat the lot, or have a heaped plate of ice cream, or grab a full tin of condensed milk and drink it. During the day I had access to as many glasses of raspberry or sarsaparilla with lemonade from the bar as I wanted which, together with my other dietary habits, led to regular visits to the dentist at an early age.

As my second set of teeth pushed up and loosened one of my baby teeth it would become irritating and sore. Under advice received from knowing adults I would then tie one end of a piece of string to the sore tooth and the other to a door handle which I kicked shut to yank the tooth out of its socket. I employed this procedure several times with success, motivated in part by the prospect of receiving a dividend from the tooth fairy.

Dietary habits eventually forced me to receive professional dental care. The dentist was on the same block as the hotel—just up and around the corner in Williamson Street. The man in the white coat who became the stuff of nightmares was grey-haired Mr Doherty, the antithesis of the tooth fairy. I was taken there once by my mother at a very early age and thereafter had to front up by myself. There was no chance of getting lost as it was only about a three-minute walk.

The attack on the senses began in the waiting room where the acrid smell of antiseptic and the grinding sound of a low revving dental drill wafted in from the surgery. Once in the chair, after rinsing your mouth with dreadful pink stuff that tasted like nothing else, a horrible cube of dry wadding was shoved under your back teeth to keep your mouth open while the exposed nerves in your decayed tooth were poked with a metal prod to confirm, from the elicited painful response, that either an extraction or filling was required. Then a huge gleaming silver coloured syringe with a gigantic needle in the end was produced and shoved into your gum. Upon completion of the procedure, you received a pat on the head from Mr Doherty and a lolly as you went out the door with the advice not to drink anything hot or chew your cheek, the numbness in which made it difficult to talk coherently for some time.

Chapter 7

MARKET TOWN

During the war, trucks were requisitioned by the military which resulted in a shortage of vehicles lasting well after the war ended. All production of private motorcars ceased during the war years and a government permit was required to purchase a car in the early post war years when they were in short supply. Together with the rationing of petrol until 1950 this caused many businesses to revert to the time-honoured method of horse-drawn carts and wagons for delivery and haulage.

Well into the 1950s in Bendigo, big Clydesdale horses with white faces and shaggy hooves could be seen pulling wagons loaded at the railway good sheds with building materials, bags of wheat, chaff, hay, barrels of beer and general goods for delivery. Carts drawn by horses were used by bakers, milkmen and grocers. Drays were used to deliver earth, sand and gravel. One last horse-drawn cab remained for a while stationed at the fountain, roughly near where the Cenotaph is today, with the driver waiting for a fare while his horse munched away at the chaff in its nose bag. It was the last of the horse-drawn cabs and it was not long before it disappeared.

Of necessity, the traditional horse-drawn night-cart still did its rounds until the end of the 1950s servicing the removal of human excrement from unsewered areas. The dunny man came once a week. He would lift the door at the rear of the outhouse and after clipping a special lid on the large and full tar-coated drum, called a 'dunny-can', remove it and exchange it for an empty one. The full can would then be heaved onto a hessian bag slung over his shoulder as he ran to deliver it to the tiered racks in his old grey dunny cart.

After the war and well into the 1950s Bendigo was still very much a market town. The stock saleyards were at the top end of Nolan Street where it formed a T-intersection with Charleston Road on the right and Strickland Road which joined it on the left, with the Fleece Inn and Newmarket Hotels opposite the saleyards in Strickland Road. Sheep were sold on Monday, cattle Tuesday and horses on Wednesday. On Thursday, chickens, ducks, geese and turkeys were sold at Curnow's poultry auction in the heart of Bendigo in Queen Street between Williamson and Mitchell Streets. On Friday Frank A. Hill & Co. conducted the pig market and auction in the laneway at the side of the Lyric Theatre that ran from Bath Lane into Charring Cross. On the corner of Mundy Street and Lyttleton Terrace (opposite the old YMCA building) there was a skin merchant that specialised in rabbit hides and back further in the same block towards the town, where the City Council offices now are, Cowlings produce store sold hay, chaff, chicken feed and other stock requirements to farmers. Further again along Lyttleton Terrace on the other side of St Andrews Avenue and directly opposite The Crown, Abbott Supply provided all kinds of hardware to farmers and a few doors further along again Northern Seed Supply was a stockist for all kinds of seeds. I regularly went there to buy millet for my budgies.

Some farmers still drove their horse and gigs or buggies into town on market day and they were often tied up in the backyard of the Crown Hotel with nose bags on while the owners went shopping. The large yard was fenced on two sides with a high brick wall showing faded numbers that had marked the stabling and stall areas for guests' horses. Five brick stables remained fully roofed but had been purloined for other uses. One of the most important duties of the hotel 'useful' was to make sure that any deposited horse dung was cleaned up. My father had a garden plot where he grew tomatoes so that was where it all went. Both The Arcade and The Belfast hotels that fronted what is now the Hargreaves Mall had livery stables at the rear, accessible via Queen Street, where farmers could park their gigs, buggies and horses undercover and have them attended to by the hotel groom/'useful'.

Beer delivered to The Crown in bottles was only available in 'long necks' which came individually wrapped in straw sheaths that were packed and delivered in the same sort of big brown paper bags that cement arrived in. The handling of these was fraught with problems and required great care to avoid breakages which, if they occurred, multiplied the problem instantly. Leaking beer seeped through adjacent bags in the stack causing them to disintegrate resulting in bottles escaping and causing more breakages and a terrible mess. The back of a wagon pulled by two slow and gentle horses was a good place to effect delivery of this volatile bottled substance.

The 'long necks' together with draft beer in big wooden barrels strapped with iron hoops to keep them together were delivered to The Crown by a ginger haired bloke of suspected Irish heritage by the name of Danny Regan. Eventually Danny retired his horses and drove a delivery truck for a period until he lost his licence for drink-driving. He then brought his horses and wagon out of retirement and reverted to his original method of operation to which his driving disqualification did not apply. He was one of Bendigo's last general carriers to continue using draught horses, along with renowned Bendigo timber and hardware firm Hume and Iser who retained their reliable draft horse teams hitched to large wagons well into the late 1950s before exchanging them for trucks.

Milkmen were probably the very last to give up their horse-drawn carts, with many of them continuing to use them well into the 1960s. Horses were trained to drive themselves on the verbal orders of the 'milko' while he ran alongside from house to house. They would stop, go or turn on command. The milk delivered to the back of The Crown in a horse-drawn cart was then carried by the milkman into the kitchen in his large stainless steel can and ladled out with pint or quart scoops into our big enamel jugs left waiting for him. The quantity delivered was detailed on the handwritten bill he left. Milk still had lashings of cream left in it when delivered and after a jug had been sitting for a day or two in the big hotel fridge you could sneak in and cream the top off to use at your pleasure.

In the streets, some watering troughs still remained for horses to drink from. One was in Lyttleton Terrace near the old weighbridge on the Mundy Street side of the Town Hall. Another was at the fountain in Charring Cross, with a couple more going up the hill to View Street. There were two more in Hargreaves Street and hotels such as The Bulls Head and the One Tree Hill still kept their water troughs for patrons' horses. Within a few minutes walk from The Crown there were two fully operational blacksmith shops. One in Lyttleton Terrace and another in St Andrews Avenue

6. The 'Milko' with his horse and cart, circa 1950.

where it was common to see farmers' horses harnessed to carts or gigs parked and tethered to the plane trees with their noses snuffling away in chaff bags. On my way to Gravel Hill School, I often stood and peaked through the doors of the blacksmith's for a few moments to watch them at work. In Mitchell Street a saddler's shop still operated where you could have harness made or repaired.

The rationing of petrol during the war was also responsible for a resurgence in the use of draught horses as a means of power on farms. After the war, commercial market gardeners continued to use them for some years. Around Bendigo there were people farming very small holdings who kept a single working draught horse to pull a plough or harrows to work up their block where they would plant tomatoes and other vegetables for sale and their own domestic use. I spent a number of weekends at such a place, Tommy Burke's block at Huntly, when I was 10 or 11 years old and he often employed me as an additional weight to sit on the harrows as it was pulled by the horse. A bloody dusty job it was too.

As well as the proximity of produce stores and blacksmith shops, The Crown was surrounded by four butcher shops. Facing the hotel, the first shop next to it on the right was Clarke Jeffrey's. On the left-hand side there was Laurie Eames butcher shop and, several doors further up, John's shop. Over in Lyttleton Terrace Lou Robinson had another butcher shop. They had a monopoly on the sale of fresh meat as supermarkets were unknown in the early 1950s in Bendigo. There were some delicatessens that sold sausages, saveloys and other pressed and preserved meats and poultry (even mutton birds) but generally not plain meat.

The floor of every butcher shop was covered in sawdust and the meat chopped on large wooden blocks that sometimes were just the trunks of trees. The smell of raw meat radiated from fresh unrefrigerated joints hanging from hooks on a sliding meat rack. On the instructions of customers the butcher, in his blue and white striped apron, selected and sliced a joint with knives from the large scabbard hanging on his belt. Every butcher sold tins of beef dripping and most manufactured their own saveloys, sausages and corned beef. At the back of the three butcher shops closest to The Crown were large metal cauldrons in which the butchers boiled meat for their products or melted down leftover bones and scraps to harvest the beef dripping fat. Customers purchased, the solidified dripping, for their cooking. At times the shops closest to The Crown created a malodorous effluvia from this industry that wafted up into the bedrooms on the second floor in the early mornings causing significant discomfort to the occupants and considerable annoyance to my father who then had to berate the offending butcher.

A further consequence to the neighbourhood arising from this practice was its capacity to attract mice and rats to the smell and any little bits of detritus ending up on the ground. Every butcher shop addressed this problem by having its own resident community of cats that went forth and copulated causing a multiplicity of moggies that began fighting amongst themselves. The cats became a problem, particularly at night, when marauding toms searching for new territory or marking their own, engaged with other toms in scratching and screaming matches that would wake the dead. My mate Dalla Purdon who lived a few doors up from The Crown, and I used to go on neighbourhood cat hunting expeditions with our Davy Crockett style hunting knives. Fortunately, we had no success. Nature itself addressed the problem with the arrival of cat flu from time to time resulting in a drastic reduction of the population.

The Crown dealt with each of the three butchers in Hargreaves Street. Every now and then my father would change shops as he believed it would keep them on their toes. It was never necessary to go to the shop and order. Each morning, except for Sunday, someone from the shop would call into the kitchen to obtain the daily order which was then delivered an hour or two later in a big cane basket carried by the butcher. They were all keen to have The Crown as a customer.

One man that didn't rely on a horse-drawn vehicle was the grocer. He arrived once a week in his small motor van wearing a white apron, a pencil stuck behind his ear and a notebook in his pocket. After leaving the current order he would seek and duly note down details for the next order. Grocery stores were largely confined to dry goods and seldom sold any meat except for processed items and were rarely licensed to sell liquor. They all had sawdust on the floor in the public area with shop assistants standing behind counters in white aprons or grey dust coats. Goods were wrapped in a brown paper bag or brown paper pulled from a large roll with a cutter on the front sitting on the counter.

Most things were bought in bulk and weighed and bagged by hand, including flour, rice, sugar, washing powder, biscuits, tea, coffee, tinned fruit and so on. Cheese was cut from big blocks, butter from big square blocks. Large tins full of biscuits were weighed to order and bagged up. Broken biscuits at the bottom of the tin were sold to kids in the know for a few pence a bag. Other containers were filled with dried apricots, sultanas and dates, while almonds, walnuts and Brazil nuts were squirrelled away in wooden drawers. If small items were required urgently during the week, I was often given the job to collect them from Cairns Grocery Store in Hargreaves Street a few doors up from Mundy Street. Vegetables and fruit were sold by separate green grocers. Bread also arrived in a motorised van each day from Jeffrey's bakery, delivered to the kitchen by the driver wearing a white apron carrying a large cane basket full of lovely hot and crusty loaves covered with a tea towel.

Chapter 8
PICTURE THEATRES

The Australian unemployment rate in 1950 was only 1.2 per cent. Elsewhere, 72 per cent of the world population lived in extreme poverty and 64 per cent were illiterate. In Australia, cinema audiences reached record numbers and church attendances started to decline. The Korean War began in June and the average annual consumption of beer for every man, woman and child in Australia rose from 76.7 litres to 103 litres. It was a good time to own a pub.

My parents, constantly involved in the running of the hotel, were too busy to consider such questions as whether I should be restrained or allowed freedom, whether if left alone I would stay safe, or where parental responsibility for development of my skills and interests or emotional well-being started and finished. In any event, there was no perimeter fence to corral me in the hotel. No door or gate that could be locked to prevent my exit. There was a large front door, three backdoors and a large driveway that I could escape through at any time. I could go wherever I wanted. Anyway, parental surveillance was not the issue then as it is these days. Kids just played and explored and parents didn't feel the need to know every little thing they did. While my parents allowed me to be free the truth was that they had no alternative. I had the opportunity to range freely around The Crown Hotel and Bendigo's CBD on a daily basis from a very young age and pursue my urge to play and explore as I wished. The hotel itself was like a playground, my own personal Luna Park, the CBD of the city was my frontier to explore and then I had Rosalind Park, The Fernery and the lawns around the Town Hall as wild country.

I started the decade in the prep class of Gravel Hill State School at the age of five, but had started to go to the movie pictures in the lead up to Christmas in the year before that. Bendigo had three picture theatres, The Plaza, The Lyric and The Princess, and all of them were within a few minutes walk from The Crown Hotel. As soon as could be arranged, I had been enrolled in kindergarten at the Baptist Church in Short Street and before long learnt to wander home from there back to the hotel on my own, enabling me to walk past both The Lyric and The Plaza theatres. Kindergarten was in the morning, so I could go to the pictures in the afternoon. For the first couple of times I was taken, with my mother's consent, by a staff member of the hotel who had taken pity on me. After that I was hooked. The two shillings to go was provided by my mother who quickly caved in to my whingeing and whining. It probably suited her to know where I was as I was always 'missing in action'.

The Lyric, with its entrance on high-street near the City Family Hotel, was my favourite although it was the least well appointed and had the nickname of 'the flea house'. Unfortunately, it was destroyed by fire in 1967. I recall going to the ticket box there and reaching up to the counter, which I could not see over, and saying "one please". The cheapest seats at front stalls were nine pence which left me one shilling and three pence to spend on lollies and ice cream at half time.

The program changed each week on Thursday with special matinees on Saturday, so in a full week with three theatres it was possible to see six different movie shows, each of which usually had a main feature and a support B-grade movie. On Sunday theatres were shut.

By the time I started in prep (which everyone called 'the bubs') at Gravel Hill, I had seen more films than any other kid my age in Bendigo. I just couldn't get enough of the movies. They occupied a lot of my time during school holidays and on weekends. I rarely missed the opportunity to escape from The Crown to the wonderful make-believe alternative reality of movie land. Just as today's mothers use TV to babysit their children, my mother used the movie theatre and was happy to pay the two shillings fee.

The Plaza in Mitchell Street was a mini 'Picture Palace', with plaster decorations painted to look like real carved wood or gold, and faux celebrity boxes on each side of the stage that, together with a vast red velvet curtain with full-length drops on the side and scallops on the top edged in gold braid, gave it the appearance of a genuine elegant theatre. It usually had the best film program. The Princess Theatre in View Street sometimes mixed film with live variety entertainment. Built in art deco style and outwardly unpretentious, it was clearly the best theatre in Bendigo with its entrance of wide steps leading to an expanse of glass doors. The ornate interior complete with orchestra pit, stalls, circle, gallery and private boxes seated up to 2,000 and the large stage could accommodate extravagant theatrical presentations. All the theatres were equipped with buckets painted red and filled with sand placed strategically near entranceways or doors and labelled

"Fire". I found out later that these had been installed as a wartime measure for the use of usherettes who had been instructed on how to use the sand on fire-starting incendiary bombs.

Saturday afternoon matinees, where few adults were present, were the most fun—just 300 or so unruly kids with most aged around 11 to 13. The show began with a newsreel followed by cartoons such as *Heckle and Jekyll, Tom and Jerry* or *Popeye the Sailor Man* or sometimes a short singalong clip with a ball that bounced across the screen and landed at the right times on a word that was part of the song. The entire audience was encouraged to sing and it was all designed to stir up enthusiasm. A serial shown in separate weekly chapters followed, such as *Superman, Batman and Robin* (filmed in 1942 as 15 episodes) or *Flash Gordon* with death ray guns. A short B-grade picture followed leading up to interval after which the main movie was shown. At the conclusion of the last film the National Anthem, 'God Save The King', was played and every child stood at attention. In 1953 it was changed to 'God Save The Queen' as we watched Her Majesty, Queen Elizabeth on film astride her favourite black horse Burmese. We were all drilled and instilled to honour the King and Queen at school.

This sober finish was in contrast to the mayhem that took place during the screening with kids throughout the theatre booing for the baddies and cheering for the goodies. This was easy to figure out in westerns, that seemed to consist of endless chases on horseback, because the baddies always wore black hats and the goodies white hats, except in the case of Hopalong Cassidy who was a goodie always dressed in black. If the film reel broke and the screen went blank the theatre would explode with catcalls, jeers and boos and everyone would yell out, "Put a penny in it!" as the projectionist tried to fix the problem and usherettes ran around with torches endeavouring to locate and illuminate miscreants.

Kids used to get up to all sorts of tricks such as, if you were sitting upstairs, throwing rolled up bits of paper (or even paper planes) into the light stream coming from the projection box, rolling Jaffa lolly balls down the aisle to create a clatter or throwing them at the plebs sitting in the front stalls below. If the uniformed ushers that policed the theatres apprehended a delinquent he was summarily removed from the premises. I recall being the victim of such rough justice at the hands of Plaza Jack, notorious senior usher, on several occasions. There was of course no appeal and in fact not even an initial hearing!

At interval, refreshment ushers dressed in cap and uniform appeared on each side of the theatre holding a large tray, suspended by leather straps around their neck, containing Dixie ice creams, chocolate and other lollies for sale. Some kids obtained a pass-out to slip down to the Cozy Corner Café near the fountain to buy fish and chips to smuggle back into the theatre in their armpit under their coats. Many others spent their time swapping comics, which they had brought with them, in the very first row of front stalls, being the area designated for that purpose by popular consent.

I was lucky to be born into what was known as The Golden Years of Hollywood. It was also The Golden Years of Westerns with more of them being made back then than any other time. I loved the world of B-grade westerns where Roy Rogers and his horse Trigger with be-whiskered sidekick Gaby Hayes, and Hopalong Cassidy and his horse Topper, were megastars. More than 60 *Hopalong Cassidy* movies were made and I saw a lot. 'Hoppy' was a clean-shaven, clean living very moral character who always rounded up bad men, usually after an exhilarating chase on his white horse Topper at the end, which was a staple feature of the series. Lots of shooting was involved in his rescuing of the downtrodden and exploited, but fatalities were few. There were

7. Plaza Theatre, Bendigo.
Photos by Lyle Fowles, Harold Paynting Collection, State Library of Victoria.

8. Princess Theatre, Bendigo.
Photos by Lyle Fowles, Harold Paynting Collection, State Library of Victoria.

'flesh wounds' and people were 'winged' in the shoulder but hardly ever any blood. If there was it was in black and white. Fistfights were clean by today's standards and you never had to make a quantum leap to figure out a plotline. Throughout the whole production Hoppy wore a congenial smile which he never seemed to lose. He was every kid's hero. In 1954 when I was 10, he visited Melbourne where 60,000 people turned up to see him drive a Land Rover around Albert Park. 3AW radio sold tickets for a broadcasting gig with Hoppy in a circus tent and 12,000 turned up. Other favourite movies included the daring adventures of The Lone Ranger on his horse Silver with his sidekick Indian mate Tonto, The Cisco Kid and of course every western film ever made by John Wayne.

Although I didn't know it at the time, I was being moulded and imprinted by many of the values of my wild west heroes who I saw on the big screen. An integral part of the drama in many westerns included a strong moral dimension in the lead characters who in the end were saved by their own resilience or the love of a woman, or both, as is displayed in the conflict in *High Noon* (1952) between Gary Cooper's civil responsibility and his love of a woman, Grace Kelly. It was a clear-cut, simple, constant world in which outcomes of bad and good were always ultimately tilted towards the latter with style, and where law and order were brought to places of chaos. I learned right from wrong, how to have and show respect, that lying and cheating were bad, how to suffer through disappointment and failure and work through it, and I gained valuable insights into fairness and unfairness.

There were kids who watched fire engines who wanted to be a fireman or who watched steam locomotives and wanted to be train drivers. When I watched westerns I wanted to be a cowboy hero. They could ride and shoot and fight and were brave and strong and always did the right thing. It was John Wayne who said,

"Nobody should come to the movies unless he believes in heroes." And I did. My mother bought me a facsimile Hopalong Cassidy outfit complete with black leather chaps, spurs, black leather vest, gun belt with holster, cap gun and black hat which I wore about the hotel with immense pride sneaking around the premises to jump out of doorways and arrest, or if necessary, shoot, the numerous bad guys and gals therein. My cap gun had the same action as a genuine semi-automatic Colt Lightning 45. When you pulled the trigger the hammer was brought back and the chamber rotated as it fired causing a 'shot' every time you pulled. While it was a more innocent time, my parents were happy to provide a device to keep me amused and out of other trouble. Later, as I got older, I abandoned the Hoppy outfit and practised walking like John Wayne.

While American films dominated our cinema screens there were still some great British films around in the 1950s. Some of the best were war films, like *The Cruel Sea* (1953), *The Dam Busters* (1954), *The Colditz Story* (1955) and *Reach for The Sky* (1956). Other popular shows included *The Lady Killers* (1955) with Alec Guinness and Peter Sellars, *The Bells of St Trinnian's* (1954) and *Carry-on Sergeant* (1958), and other *Carry-On* films. Epic films from America included *The Robe* (1953), *The Ten Commandments* (1956) and *Ben Hur* (1959). Popular Saturday matinee comedy duos included Dean Martin and Jerry Lewis, Bud Abbott and Lou Costello, and Bob Hope and Bing Crosby. Horror shows such as *The Creature From The Black Lagoon* (1954), featuring the sad eyed gilled man with webbed hands and feet, got a regular showing and always frightened the beegeezus out of the kids. I saw them all and more. Not because I had nothing else to do but because I wanted to. I loved to see the huge curtains fold back in front stalls to reveal the giant screen bursting into life with the moving searchlights and dramatic fanfare of the 20th

9. Young Mickey and Zel with her puppy, early 1950s …

… and 'Hopalong Cassidy' (Mickey) and friend.

Century Fox logo, MGM's roaring lion, Columbia's torch lady or the man with the gong from J. Arthur Rank films. And, because I could, as my mother always gave me the money to do so. I never gained the impression that she wanted to get rid of me but I think she was comfortable knowing where I was.

An important part of the cinema experience were the newsreels screened at the beginning of each session. Usually about 10 minutes duration, they included both serious and light-hearted stories from all corners of the world and Australia. Movietone, with their laughing kookaburras, dominated the Australian market that also included Cinesound, Pathe, Paramount and Universal newsreels. Every time I went to the pictures, I saw dramatic news clips of overseas scenes and events such as the post-war efforts to rebuild devastated Europe and Japan, the Korean War and its fatalities, tests for nuclear bombs and a variety of other things that many parents would censor from their children. Reporting on the post-war criminal trials for the Nazis at Nuremberg dragged on well into the 1950s and the newsreels in picture theatres often showed short clips of their terrible atrocities. In a great many ways these newsreels, together with the enormous variety of drama, comedy and other programs I saw, added significantly to my education. I probably had a broader understanding of the world at large than most children of my age.

I was in Grade 3 and only nine years old when I was enthralled by the movie coverage of the first Redex Car Trial in 1953. One hundred and eighty-seven cars battled it out over more than 10,000 kilometres watched by huge crowds along the route of mainly dirt tracks where cars collided with kangaroos or each other and rolled into ditches. The winner was a battered and bruised Peugeot 203. The event was so successful that it was run again in 1954 and 1955 when, in that year, out of the 176 cars that started only 63 made it back to Sydney after travelling 16,800 kilometres over Australia's roughest roads. By then I was aged 11 years and there was much discussion in the schoolyard at Gravel Hill on the subject of the Redex Trial and which were the better cars.

As I grew older, I became drawn in by the countless movies that portrayed teenagers and their families as well-adjusted and valuable community members embracing the virtuous values of middle-class respectability and increasingly envious of model romantic relationships I saw in the comedy movies such as *Roman Holiday* with Gregory Peck and Audrey Hepburn, *Pillow Talk* and *Lover Come Back* with Rock Hudson and Doris Day, *Operation Petticoat* with Carry Grant and Tony Curtis and love stories such as *A Summer Place* with Dorothy McGuire and Richard Egan and *April Love* with Pat Boone and Shirley Jones, and television programs which displayed model happy families. While such programs provided me a happy escape and imprinted on my psyche aspirational goals for the future, they also created great discontent within me arising out of the circumstances of my domicile at the Crown Hotel. All my sister and I desperately wanted was to live in a normal house with normal parents. Our happiness would soon be further depreciated with the realisation that both our parents, but particularly our mother, were drinking too much.

Chapter 9

THE PUB BAR

Shortly after purchasing The Crown my father, Reg, decided that the bar area needed improvement. To accommodate the additional drinkers he planned to attract, he needed more empty space where men could stand shoulder to shoulder enjoying vertical drinking during the arduous "6 o'clock swill". In Victoria, until the 1960s, pubs closed at 6 p.m. Men who had knocked off work could buy as many drinks as they liked before 6 p.m. so long as they drank them by 6:15 p.m. Five minutes before 6 p.m. Reg rang a loud bell and would yell out "Time gentlemen please!" This was the signal for any last purchases to be made within the next five minutes. In busy bars like The Crown, drinkers would be lined up four or five deep at the counter. As full pots of beer were planted on the bar and then handed back to drinking mates a quantity tended to be splashed around resulting in this daily ritual being labelled "the 6 o'clock swill". In an endeavour to outflank the turning off of beer taps, many patrons bought two or three pots at once to line up on the bar knowing that they had 20 minutes at most to down them. Nearly all drinking was done under the 'shout' system where say six drinkers would purchase a round of drinks for the whole party and the favour would then be returned consecutively by the other five. Anyone missing his turn at stepping up to the bar to buy was quickly reminded that "it's your shout mate!"

All drinking was done standing up, with 99 per cent of men smoking, throwing their cigarette butts on the floor and talking furiously. As the smoke caused visibility to reduce the volume of sound increased until at 6 p.m. Reg rang the loud electric bell again signalling the end of serving and the cry would go out once more, "Time gentlemen please!" In the next 15 minutes, barmen cleared the bar of all empty glasses telling drinkers, as they did so, to finish up. Then when 6:15 p.m. arrived my father would yell, in an ominous voice, "Time gentlemen please!" several times and leave the bell switch on continuously until the last man left.

Overcoming the handicaps of shortages of materials and tradesmen, Reg managed to get the remaining buttresses and walls removed wherever possible and construct a new larger island bar. He then threw out the lovely old big silver National cash register, with fabulous lever action buttons that pushed up little metal numbers behind the glass at the top of the machine, and installed two new ones. He ripped out the old beer pipes coming from the cellar to the bar which were made of lead as they needed to be flexible down in the cellar to bend and connect up to barrels. Until now earlier patrons of The Crown must have been getting a dose of lead poisoning, as even low levels of lead can cause brain and kidney damage. New nylon pipes, very high-tech at the time, were installed together with a new 'Temp Rite' beer-chilling system that chilled the beer just as it came out of the tap.

Reg made the most of these revolutionary improvements in newspaper advertisements he placed. The lead pipes were not wasted. Some were melted down to make fishing sinkers and others simply cut into short sections with a hacksaw to make different sized weights for cross lines to catch Murray cod. Lead was used in lots of things back then. Toothpaste came in enamelled lead tubes, petrol and most paints contained lead as did some cosmetics, and some kids toys were still made from lead. Even the floors of the upstairs ladies and gents toilets were lined with lead sheeting to prevent any possibility of leakage down below.

An important part of the specifications for the new bar included a platform raised several inches behind the counter. This not only gave the barmen a better view of the entire bar area, but also made them look considerably taller than they were when viewed by the patrons. Reg had a somewhat diminutive stature of just over five foot two inches and the elevated platform, together with the fact that he wore R.M. Williams elastic sided high-heeled boots, raised him behind the bar to a position where he could almost adopt "the traditional military advantage of high ground" to provide a useful base for crowd control. Behind the bar he always wore a collar and tie with cufflinked shirts and expanding metal armbands to shorten the sleeves and keep the cuffs clean.

The entire inside of the exterior wall of the bar room was tiled up to shoulder height and similar cream-coloured tiles installed around the front of the bar facing the drinkers. Countertops were covered with linoleum throughout and a new polished rubber compound floor covering installed in the customers area. The net result was rather like a large public toilet.

To smarten the place up, Reg installed a panel of three foot high mirrors above the tiling around the internal side of the exterior wall. He was very pleased, because not only did it make the whole bar look bigger, he could always see what was going on behind him when in the bar by looking at any mirror in front of him. The mirrors together with the fluorescent lighting he had installed and a large window fronting Hargreaves Street certainly brightened the place up. Upholstered stools were provided around the perimeter of the bar. On one wall he hung a taxidermied 80 pound Murray-cod (later to be joined by the heads of two 60 pounders). Behind the bar he installed, above the drinks rack, a collection of huge buffalo horns in due deference to the Buffalo Lodge of which he was a member. Below the mirrors he hung a series of large framed photographs of monster crocodiles that his brother, Roy, had sent him from Queensland. Above the mirrors he displayed the showcase containing the set of chrome plated various horseshoes that my blacksmith grandfather had won first prize with at the Royal Melbourne Show. Finally in the bar parlour he hung a large oil painting of 'The Bourke Street Merchant' which was a portrait of an old man in an overcoat selling wax matches. It was obvious than this was entirely a bar for blokes.

Reg Beck understood the need to establish authority and create control and order as the proprietor of a public house. Although small in stature, he had the self-restraint and strength of character necessary for the job. Customers who violated his set standards of behaviour were 'barred' for their breaches. He made it known that his position of authority enabled him to say who stayed and who left the premises. His personality and temperament with characteristics of congeniality, tolerance and sincerity equipped him well to calm situations down. His watchwords were "decorum", "decency", "politeness" and "civility". Male patrons were expected to act as gentleman in the presence of ladies and there was no swearing allowed in front of women. The bar area was entirely a male domain where women were prohibited. He welcomed regular visits from Salvation Army officers each Friday with their square wooden donation boxes they rattled in front of patrons who on making a contribution were given a copy of *The War Cry* newspaper. He refused to entertain the idea of barmaids serving behind the bar, including my mother.

Children were not allowed in the public bar area but could enter the ladies lounge in the presence of their mother. The exception to this rule were the children of the licensee who were, of course, subject to discretionary parental orders which might vary from day to day.

Regular patrons knew how they were expected to behave. Notices posted around the wall stated gambling was prohibited, service to underage persons was prohibited and that there would be no service to intoxicated persons. The latter rule was noted more in the breach than actual implementation with Reg's definition of "intoxicated person" being somewhat imprecise at times.

While he was working behind the bar Reg would not drink. The bar was his fortress and refuge of power which he refused to compromise. He would only accept a shout from a customer if he left the bar and entered the public area. He often expressed the philosophy (privately) that to be a good publican you had to suffer fools gladly. He was courteous and attentive to each customer, made it his best endeavour to avoid arguments with troublemakers, knew how to be diplomatic and tactful, was always friendly and good-humoured, a great storyteller and always careful about his personal appearance. As a result, he was popular with his customers and a damn good publican.

Under his proprietorship, The Crown quickly developed a reputation for a civilised place to drink with prompt and courteous service. The bar room was always kept spotlessly clean and glasses, bottles and beer taps sparkling. Above all else Reg understood the need to provide a first-class product for his customers. Before the commencement of trade every day, the beer pipes were disconnected from the barrels and washed out with detergent and clean water. When reconnected the first few glasses were discarded. He then spent money advertising in the paper and on radio that the beer at The Crown was the best, freshest and coldest beer in Bendigo. In fact, it was, and as a result trade increased substantially.

When Reg purchased The Crown in 1949, all supplies of beer were sourced from Carlton and United Breweries (CUB) and he continued to deal with them. CUB was the major brewing company in Melbourne and it held a monopoly on much of the beer trade throughout Victoria as a consequence of its program of buying out other breweries and acquiring a huge chain of tied hotel premises through which it enforced its price-fixing policy. As Reg owned the freehold of The Crown, he was free to fix his own prices and deal with any brewery.

At a meeting of Bendigo's hotel keepers in the late 1950s, it was decided by a firm majority to increase the price of beer sold in glasses over-the-counter by a small margin of a couple of pennies.

As soon as word reached CUB of Bendigo's publicans' outrageous attempt at independence, they began to receive phone calls from Mr Fogarty at CUB with advice to the effect that such conduct would not be allowed if they wanted to continue sourcing beer from CUB. One by one all the hotel keepers eventually caved in, except Reg who decided to sack CUB and change over to the Richmond Brewery. The little brewery with a tiger's head as its trademark had been set up in 1928 in opposition to CUB and was now the only other independent brewery in Victoria. Advertised to be "the most hygienic and wholesome of all beverages with a delicious flavour and 100% pure", its beer was a huge success from the start. *The Sporting Globe* newspaper reported on 4 March 1931 that hotels that had changed to Richmond Beer had made small fortunes as their trade increased by 400 to 500 percent!

Reg made a big deal out of the changeover, with advertisements he ran in the *Bendigo Advertiser* exclaiming the superior qualities of Richmond Beer and noting at the bottom of the advertisement that "The Crown was not under the powers of dictatorship." Such powers, of course, being particularly distasteful to a drinking public that had just experienced World War II. After running the advertisements for several weeks, the *Bendigo Advertiser* refused to include the reference to dictatorship. Speculation at the time was that their refusal was due to representations from CUB. In addition to price, CUB dictated the size and style of the glass beer was sold in. Reg wanted to introduce a beer glass smaller than the minimum size specified by CUB and had the last laugh when he transferred to Richmond Beer by introducing the glass and naming it a 'Fogarty'.

The advertising campaign of The Crown cranked up when the then popular oil company Esso ran a promotion program for their performance petrol featuring the cartoon logo of a big smiling tiger with the catchphrase "Put a tiger in your tank". When Richmond Brewery released their bottled 'Tiger' draught beer with its roaring tiger's head trademark, Reg ran a series of ads championing the no preservative, 100 per cent pure, flavoursome, Tiger Draught Beer and encouraging drinkers to come to The Crown and "Put a tiger in your tank!" They came in droves and they kept returning. Businessmen in their suits and ties and workmen in their overalls or other work clothes. The Crown was the only Richmond Beer pub in Bendigo and it became the city's best watering hole. Sales of bottled beer also took off. There were summer days when a truckload of long necks, now packed a dozen at a time in cardboard boxes with dividers, would arrive and be stacked along the interior external wall of the bar room, only to be sold out by closing time at day's end. The claim that Richmond Beer was absolutely pure, wholesome and delicious in flavour was born out by its sales. Additional part-time barmen were employed to handle the rush leading to 6 p.m. and I was even shanghaied into working behind the bar. The law allowed underage children of the licensee to do so.

After the specified licensing hours, hotels could only provide liquor to in-house guests and bona fide travellers, defined in Victoria as those who had travelled at least 10 miles in a direct line from their place of residence on the day on which the alcohol was consumed. My father was opposed to 'sly grogging' or trading after hours. Although this was one of his rules that he sometimes broke he kept it in principle, refusing most requests, with the bar doors always locked tightly after hours.

Reg bent the rules only for exceptional customers, one of which was Reggie Bennett, a hopeless local alcoholic, who often appeared at the back door of the kitchen on Sunday mornings around 11 a.m. with red eyes, the shakes, and no money, pleading for a long neck bottle of beer. He had a dreadful stutter and would say to me, "T t t t t tell d d d d dad to p p put it on the s s s slate Mick a a a and I I I I'll fix him up n n n n next w w w week." I would say, "Right o' Reg" as I knew him as a regular, and when, with my father's permission, I returned to hand him the bottle of beer in a brown paper bag he would always seal the deal with his signature phrase which was, "Sh sh sh she'll be a a a apples!"

My father took pity on Reggie knowing that the only thing that kept him going was his drink. Over the years he got worse. One Saturday, mid-afternoon, when I had been given the job of sweeping up the floor on the public side of the bar I noticed Reggie holding himself up at the counter and a pool of urine at his feet. He had pissed himself in situ. When I reported the matter to my father, he just quietly took Reggie by the arm and walked him outside, piddling as he went. At no stage did my father admonish him. Reggie was always a gentleman drunk. Had he been a loud, uncouth boisterous, foul mouth boozer my father would have had him out the door in a flash and banned him permanently.

10. Esso and Tiger Beer advertisements.

Chapter 10

MUM'S LADIES LOUNGE

My mother, Madge, was born in 1906 on 28 October, the day of St Jude the patron saint of lost causes. By the middle of the era known as the Roaring Twenties, she was in her early 20s. It was a time when values began to change under the influence of the cinema. Apart from being characterised by materialism, a preoccupation with entertainment and skilfully improvised music in the form of 'jazz', technical development of the motorcar, womens' fashions, consumer goods, booze and crime, there was also an uninhibited youth culture that fore-shadowed what would come in the 1960s. There was an attitude of bravado and a contempt towards the past. Young couples danced the Charleston with little inhibition in dance halls that sprang up all around the country. The hemline on dresses rose above the knee for the first time and flesh-coloured stockings became standard.

Women changed to short bobbed-cut hair, drank and smoked, went to the pictures where romance dominated as the theme, lipstick and make up became popular and they were labelled 'flappers'.

It was many years after my mother died that I first heard the word 'flapper'. I had asked my mother's older sister, my Aunt Anne, to tell me about my mother's younger life, which I knew little about. Aunt Anne was then a conservative mature lady married to a bank manager in Hobart, where she worked as a senior nursing sister in a local hospital. She said, "Oh, she was a bit of a flapper." I had no idea what the word meant. The definition I found in *The New Oxford Dictionary of English* told me more: "(in the 1920s) a fashionable young woman intent on enjoying herself and flouting conventional standards of behaviour." I imagined my mother comfortably fitting that description as a charming flapper, always a bridesmaid but never a bride as her birthday crept towards the 'tragic 30' mark.

The gaiety of the 'roaring 20s' ended abruptly in October 1929 when the New York stock market crashed. Australian unemployment climbed to 30 per cent and the carefree world of the flapper became just a distant dream. When working as a nurse in Sydney at the age of 33, just as the depression was ending and 18 days after World War II had started, she married on the 18th day of September 1939. My father was managing The Imperial Hotel at Castlemaine at the time, where the young couple took up residence for a short period before moving to Seymour, which had been my mother's family's home town since they moved there in her teenage years. At Seymour they took over the running of The Canadian Hotel where my father became licensee.

The American writer, F. Scott Fitzgerald summed up the Jazz Age in two volumes of stories called *Flappers and Philosophers* (1920) and *Tales of the Jazz Age* (1922) in which he widely used the terms 'jazz' and 'flapper'. His most famous book, *The Great Gatsby* (1925), told the story of the wild swinging, party throwing, bootlegging, desperate decade of the 1920s. His wife who was a novelist, painter and socialite had the unusual name of Zelda, which was the name my mother chose for my sister. Zelda Fitzgerald was described by her husband Scott as "the first American flapper". The two of them became emblems of the jazz age.

My mother, Madge, was a generous, caring, compassionate person and a marvellous hostess who took pleasure in making sure that a high standard of service and cleanliness was applied to the guests and hotel environment. She was responsible for supervision and management of the kitchen, dining room and accommodation areas and on a practical level had to make sure that the sweeping, scrubbing, polishing and washing carried out by staff left these quarters grime free and gleaming. She was in charge of the hotel office accepting prime responsibility for reception and accommodation booking with my father taking responsibility for all accounting, payroll and money matters. Lastly my mother took full responsibility for the management and supervision of the ladies' lounge making sure that service, hospitality and safety needs of customers were met at all times.

Madge was above all a social person who enjoyed company and was a first-class person to carry out these duties. She took pride in her appearance, attended the hairdressers regularly and always dressed impeccably. She made people feel welcome and relaxed and did her utmost to comply with their requests. But like all women in the 1950s she was not fully emancipated. It was the men who were considered to be the breadwinners and women were not paid the same rates or treated equally. Many of them, including my mother, did not drive a car and were not liberated to the extent they are now.

11. Young Madge Walker, 1933.

12. Madge married Reg Beck in 1939.

There was no air-conditioning in the ladies lounge or anywhere else. There was a ceiling fan for use in the summer and a wood fire for the winter. The place was sparsely furnished with polished hard rubber floor covering. There were no lounge chairs, just a series of roundtables with artificial timber Laminex tops and chromed metal legs. All tables were equipped with an ashtray and chairs had matching metal chromed frames with slung leather seats and backs. At one end a series of tall windows looked out over a laneway through louvre blinds and to the right was a door that led to that laneway through which ladies could enter and leave the lounge without suffering the embarrassment of going through the front door of the hotel. Service and drinks were provided to the lounge through a sliding window that gave direct access to the barmen and a view of the mens bar. Polite society held the view that it was unacceptable for women to drink in hotel public bars. Their drinking was confined to the loneliness of the ladies lounge where men were prohibited unless they were accompanying a lady. Although women were allowed to bring their children into the ladies lounge with them, this practice was frowned upon by society in general and my father in particular who did what he could to discourage it.

Each day when I came home from school I knew I would find my mother in the ladies lounge having a drink with one of the regular customers where she would be sipping a scotch and soda or brandy and dry. Her favourite spot was at the table near the door closest to the hotel office where she could sit and still hear the telephone or office bell ring. Some of these women customers became frequent drinking mates of my mother and I got to know them by name.

Lottie was a middle-aged woman who, in her younger days, might have been quite attractive but the passage of years together with the wear and tear of alcohol and cigarettes had already taken a shine off her face and her demeanour. However, she was always well dressed and relentlessly happy and pleasant. Every time we met, the standard greeting was, "Lovely day isn't it Mickey," which was more of a statement than a question. Her greeting was always the same to anyone she met in the hotel, hail, rain or shine, so that in the end she had the nickname "Lovely day!" She became one of my mother's regular drinking companions all of whom my father, Reg, disapproved of. He and Lottie, or Lovely Day, like other drinking mates of my mother, did not get on. He blamed them for contributing to my mother's daily drinking.

Lottie drove my father mad with her dithering and dilly dallying over what sort of a drink she would have. He would say, "What would you like today, Lottie?" And she would say, "I think I'll have a shandy Reg."

And as Dad reached for a beer glass she would say, "No, I have changed my mind, I think I'll have a brandy and dry."

After he had grabbed a brandy bottle and glass from the shelf and was about to pour the brandy she would say, "Sorry Reg! Put that back. I have changed my mind again and I think I would prefer a scotch and soda."

By this stage Reg was starting to lose it as he waited for the next order change and she said, "I know what I want, I think I fancy a glass of port!—Do you mind?"

The scotch bottle would go back and the port bottle would come out at which point Reg would say, "Christ Lottie, make up your bloody-mind!!"

One particular day Lottie came in and in answer to my father's query, "What will you have today, Lottie?" she said, "Oh Reg, I think I'll have a gin!"

BECK'S CROWN HOTEL

OPPOSITE CITY HALL, HARGREAVES ST.

FOR RICHMOND TIGER BEER

Richmond Bitter, Lager & Draught Bottled

Pint Lager Bottles 1/11

Leading Brands Wines and Spirits

Ladies: Use side entrance to Ladies Lounge for your bottle requirements

Free Parking   **Phone 3-4720**

13. An advertisement for the Crown Hotel placed in the *Bendigo Advertiser.*

"Well," he said "we have three kinds of gin. We have oxygin, nitrogin and Gilbey's gin. Which one will you have?"

"Well," she said. "As far as I'm concerned there are three kinds of turd, custurd, musturd and you—you bloody shit, and you can stick your gin!"

She then walked out in a huff but was back a couple of days later exclaiming to everybody, "Lovely day isn't it."

At a very early age I became so used to my mother's drinking habits that I was not aware of any problem. She was also a very heavy smoker. By the end of the war more than one quarter of Australian women were smokers. Smoke wafting out of the ladies lounge, joined with smoke coming from the bar to permeate throughout the hotel. Today most mothers wouldn't dare expose their children to second-hand cigarette smoke, particularly inside their own home. My sister and I were impacted by passive smoking on a daily basis from a very young age. Everyone smoked. Both my parents did so constantly. It was a time when smoking was advertised as a socially accepted and sophisticated thing to do. There was no mention of it causing cancer or being unhealthy in any way. It was allowed not only in hotels but buses, planes, trains and even in elevators and hospital wards. In some hospitals, cigarettes were sold at the bedside by ladies who came around with a tray selling lollies, snacks and smokes.

In The Crown there were ashtrays in every room, including the bedrooms. People's clothes and all soft furnishings reeked with the smell of cigarettes and pipe smoke. When I was working as a swab boy, wiping tables and cleaning ashtrays, I was also enlisted to walk around offering to light people's cigarettes. I didn't smoke then but often bought pretend cigarettes called 'Fags' at the lolly shop. They came in an imitation cigarette packet enclosing a stick of white confectionery with some red dye on the end to simulate the burning end of a cigarette. Later on in my early teens I would buy from the same corner store 'Turf' or 'Craven A' corked tip cigarettes in packets of 10.

In the 1940s and 50s tobacco was a major sponsor of radio and then of television when it started in 1956. Celebrities were paid to appear in ad campaigns to create characters like the 'Marlborough Man' with exaggerated fantasies of manliness and independence to attract smokers. In the mid-50s big tobacco companies like Rothmans and Philip Morris began promoting the merits of their utterly meritless filter-tipped cigarettes.

All this advertising and the desire to emulate adults who smoked constantly in films as well as real-life certainly had an effect on me. It was too easy for me to start as my mother constantly left a trail of half smoked packets of cigarettes wherever she went. All I had to do is sneak a couple of smokes to start with and then later a whole packet. I remember well some of the brands she smoked that I started with—Turf, Capstan, Players Navy Cut, Black and White, and De Reske.

There were plenty of places to hide and have a smoke. I was busted once when hiding in a cubby hut I had built out of old hessian bags on the narrow garden strip my father had in the backyard. The hotel useful observed smoke emanating out of the hessian and thinking there was a fire, pulled it away to discover me furiously fagging.

I think I was 12 when I had my first cigarette, because I was then still sleeping in the sleepout on the hotel veranda and had a secret hiding hole that I had dug in the wall to hide my stash of smokes. By the time I was in Year 12 at school I was completely addicted and never left home without a packet of 20 Peter Stuyvesant filter tips in my pocket. At recess at Bendigo High School my very good mate Tony and I would sneak out of the schoolyard into the adjacent Rosalind Park for a quick smoke.

Chapter 11

PRIVACY AND PARENTS

It was complicated being a publican's son. The environment of the hotel was entirely different to a private home. The Crown was always full of mostly strangers. You never knew what they would want or when they would appear. You were co-habitating with them at all times which sometimes made you feel nervous and uneasy. Most mothers told their children not to talk to strangers. I had a new lot of strangers to talk to every day, but I did meet a range of people. I got tired of seeing them and dealing with their standard patronising small talk and cross-examining questions such as "How old are you?" and "What are you going to be when you grow up?" and "How is school going?" and "What sport do you play?" and so on.

Hotels had a bad reputation in some families who thought people who patronised pubs were drunks. Society generally did not approve of children being in pubs at all. Parents would not let their kids come and play at my place because it was a hotel. My sister Zelda and I could go to our friends' houses but they could not come to ours. Unlike other kids, our parents never organised birthday parties for us. Part of the reason, I think, was that invitations extended were at risk of not being accepted. Such circumstances did little to advance our self-esteem, particularly in early teenage years. We felt inferior and embarrassed at our unusual situation. Living in a hotel led to a feeling of isolation from the rest of the community, a sense of worthlessness and rejection. I eventually got to the point where I felt more comfortable with adults than children of my own age. The Crown may have been the biggest playground in the world but in the end all I ever wanted to do was grow up.

Our backyard was a gravel car park where we were discouraged from playing games. Due to our parents being involved constantly with the running of the hotel, our interaction with them on a daily basis was mostly fleeting and we felt acutely the lack of attention that we were sure 'normal children' were receiving from 'normal parents' in a 'normal house'. We had a glamorised vision of a normal family life from what we had seen on the big screen at picture theatres. We desperately wanted to escape the environment and live like 'normal' children with parents who had the time to teach them games like football, and basketball. It was not that our parents were thoughtless, uncaring or selfish. It was just that they were enveloped by factors in our environment that they couldn't control.

Having staff available to service household needs meant that we never had to learn how to make a bed, or acquire other basic skills such as washing dishes or clothes, how to cook or set a table properly. Because our parents rarely ate at the table with my sister and I, we had little supervision on table manners, how to properly use cutlery or specific eating times. We had a window of opportunity of at least one and a half hours around each mealtime in which we could decide what time we would turn up at the kitchen for something to eat. Some guidance was given by our grandparents but there is no doubt that we would have taken more notice of our parents if they had been present. Growing up in a hotel did teach us a broad range of social skills such as civility and politeness, tolerance, and the ability to communicate with a wide range of different personality types that you would not normally come across in an ordinary household. But we also learned to distrust and be suspicious of people and I learned how to swear and be rude.

I got from my mother not enough of what I needed and too much of what I wanted. She always agreed to my request for pocket money but wasn't overly generous with emotional remuneration. There was little touching, hugging or outward show of affection in the family. When I got a little older, I enjoyed travelling by train to Melbourne with my mother and sister Zelda where we would then meet up with some of mum's friends at the London Hotel in Elizabeth Street. Sometimes we would go to the theatre. In 1952 when I was eight, she took us to see the production of *South Pacific* at Her Majesty's Theatre and we both loved those times with her.

Small change was not scarce in the hotel and all I had to do was ask to receive funds to go to the pictures or buy comics. Our parents didn't read to us much as kids and expected us to learn how to read at school. Comics were my introduction to the written word. I could recognise and interpret a visual image before I could read any words. Simple Disney comics based on Donald Duck, Mickey Mouse, Goofy and others were my go-to preference at an early age. While it was entertaining just to look at a story sequence of pictures featuring a familiar cast of cartoon characters, I quickly learnt to recognise and understand words in order to more fully enjoy the fantasy, adventure and humour. Dialogue contained in 'balloons' coming from the mouths of characters made the tale easy to follow.

I soon found that newspapers had comic strips and began to read them on a daily basis leading me, ever so slowly at first, into looking at and then reading other parts of newspapers. Comic strips were also in weekly women's magazines and I remember pouncing on my mother's to read the latest weekly serialisation of *Mandrake The Magician* as he "gesticulated hypnotically" to administer his powers.

There were psychologists and educators that tried to blame many social ills on the pernicious effects of comics on developing imaginations of children, arguing that they should read books instead of the cheap sensationalist trash that flooded in weekly from America to pervert the minds of Aussie kids. I wonder what they would have said about today's social media influencers, online games and TV.

For me comics were a delightful form of miniature entertainment and at the same time educational. I learnt to read from them and was not aware of suffering from any adverse effects. There was no television and secure in the knowledge that when I was given a comic I would, for a while at least, remain in the one spot when I read it, my mother rarely refused my request to purchase them. It was not unusual for her to give me 10 shillings or even a pound which meant I could buy at least six or a dozen comics at once, which I argued would be shared between me and my sister Zel. I knew though that she wasn't as keen on them as me and I always did the buying. She did enjoy our subscription to the comic newspaper from the UK *Chucklers Weekly* which, apart from containing usual comics such as *Jungle Jim* and miscellaneous other superheroes, included short stories from Enid Blyton's *Famous Five* series, games and even addresses for pen-pals. After the Disneyland characters and usual superheroes such as Batman and Robin, Superman, Superwoman and Superboy, my favourite comics included *Archie, Dagwood and Blondie, Dick Tracy*, with his two-way wrist radio that is now a reality, *Tarzan* and *The Phantom*. The comic book industry flourished through the 1950s with a vast array of titles including war comics and dozens of westerns.

Because The Crown was anybody's house, there was always a fundamental lack of privacy. The only place where we had our own space for privacy was our small bedrooms. Everywhere else, including where we ate meals in the 'little room', was traversed by either staff or guests. The latter changed on almost a daily basis. When we became teenagers, we felt keenly the intrusions into our personal space and our lack of ability to control that.

Until my sister was 14 and I was 12 even our bedrooms were far from private. We shared a sleepout annexed to our parents' bedroom and built on the end of the hotel's veranda that extended out over the footpath of Hargreaves Street. In a sense we were "sleeping on the street". The area was divided in half by a masonite partition that went only two thirds of the way up to the uninsulated fibro cement sheet ceiling. This provided two small rooms capable of accommodating single beds, a bedside table and half size wardrobe. An external door in my sister's room allowed access to the rest of the veranda but to get to her room she had to walk through our parents' bedroom via a permanent open space, that formerly fitted double French doors, and then my room. The entire sleepout was surrounded with head height opaque windows with intermittent sliding openings fitted with fly wire including holes to let the mosquitoes in.

I got the worst of this contrivance because also in the corner of my bedroom was a toilet with another half masonite partition that went only two thirds of the way up to the ceiling on one side and a 'shower curtain' on a rail for a front door. Consequently, not only did this reduce the size of my bedroom, but was also the source of intermittent flushings, other noises and dreadful smells when used by the rest of the family. My bedroom seemed to be an extension of the sewerage system. I felt as though I was sleeping in a toilet. But the worst of it was that I could hear clearly almost everything that went on in my parents' bedroom including lovemaking and arguments. As time went on there was more of the latter than the former. I remember hearing one night a screaming argument about 'infidelity'. I had no idea what it meant and next day looked it up in the dictionary, which said it meant "treachery, disloyalty, unfaithfulness, untruthfulness" and that fidelity meant "loyalty, faith, integrity, devotion, dependability". I was greatly troubled by this and spent much time speculating on what details might have led to this argument.

The sleepout bedrooms were freezing when Bendigo's winter frosts arrived. Standard equipment at bedtime was a hot water bottle, big woollen socks and an extra blanket on top of the bed. I would start by disappearing completely under the blankets for a while to breathe my own hot air to warm things up. Then, on surfacing I would try and wrap my head in the bedclothes only leaving my nose and mouth out. You would wake up with a nose feeling like ice and your warm breath making fog in the room. Sometimes frost would form overnight on the inside of the sleep-out windows. It was a noisy place to sleep. Bendigo was a major freight centre for the railways and the banging sound of rail trucks being shunted into place in the tracks seemed to take up most of the night. On still, frosty nights they always seemed louder through the thin fibro–cement sheet walls of our sleepout.

Apart from the usual street traffic there was the rubbish truck that served the central business district each morning accompanied by the clanging and clatter of tin rubbish bins and "stop" and "go" orders yelled at the driver by the garbos. Then, at 6:30 a.m., 7 a.m. and 8 a.m. the start work whistles and sirens of factories fired up. Each one had their own distinctive sound. Notwithstanding, I always found it fearfully difficult to get out of bed without repeated calls from my parents. Then, on Sunday mornings, the church bell duels between the Anglicans, Catholics, Presbyterians and Methodists, together with the bells from the post office clock that clanged every 15 minutes, made it impossible to sleep in on our veranda bedroom.

14. Beck's Crown Hotel in 1950s.
Mickey and Zel's bedrooms on the balcony, top right.

Chapter 12

GRAVEL HILL

I cringe when I recall my mother taking me as a small child to Matthew's Bros, an old-fashioned manchester, haberdashery and general clothing store in Hargreaves Street, to be fitted out for school. She sent me off looking like Little Lord Fauntleroy in new jodhpurs, a fabric covered straw pith helmet and polished black leather shoes with metal toe and heel tips. I was the laughing stock, quickly lost the pith helmet and refused point blank to wear jodhpurs to Gravel Hill school again! It was 1950, petrol was still rationed, the Korean War was about to start and while 64 per cent of the world's population was still illiterate, I was heading off to school at the age of five. My school in Mundy Street was No. 1566. It opened in 1875, was built of double-brick walls resting on Harcourt granite block foundations and was named after the gravel hill it was erected on. It was about only eight minutes walk from The Crown.

In Preps, or 'bubs' as we called it, each child was equipped with a 'slate' or small blackboard about A4 size and a box of chalks to learn how to draw and write. An important accessory to this device was your 'duster' made out of an old sock, stuffed with other old socks or rags, which was used to 'clear the slate' or rub out your mistakes. With repeated use the sock got chocked with chalk so that once a day we were all taken outside to belt our dusters against the granite foundations of the school to shake out the dust and breathe it in. Spitting on the school slate to clean it was a serious offence as it was feared that doing so could spread tuberculosis and whooping cough.

There was much repetitive learning as is in "D is for dog" and "C is for cat", but the teacher did read us nice stories and taught us some songs. My favourite activity was fingerpainting where we were given different coloured paints to create whatever on large sheets of paper. I recall that all my creations finished up in a brown monotone. I also enjoyed plasticine play where, when I was finished, I could smash everything flat. It wasn't long before the plasticine also turned into a brown monotone. The great achievement of the year was to progress from writing with chalk on your small slate blackboard to mastering the use of pencil on paper.

After the bubs, classrooms were geared to learning, not playing. They had their own peculiar, intimidating smell of oiled floorboards, chalk, ink and, in particular, kids, which together with an overlaying 'old' smell of the premises, books and learning, sedated you the moment you walked in. All rooms were rectangular with a blackboard the full extent of the wall at one end except for stopping short on one of the corners to accommodate an open wood fireplace. In front of the blackboard ran a platform elevated some seven or eight inches upon which perched the teacher's desk and from which the traditional military advantage of high ground over the enemy could be gained. Hanging from the wall high up in a corner was a loudspeaker connected to a PA system in the headmaster's office.

Lined up in rows before the teacher, to the back wall, were four columns of double desks each accommodating two students under a buddy system. Six desks in each column provided total seats for 48 students. Classroom numbers of 40 or more were common with the majority more than 30. A single flat plank in these ancient desks, inlaid with multifarious carvings, ink stains and other scars left by the successive generations of frustrated occupants, provided a seat for two.

15. Gravel Hill State School.
Photo by Laurie Burchell, State Library of Victoria.

There was strict separation of the sexes with girls sitting on the left of the class and boys on the right. Smart kids were seated in the back row and slower more troublesome ones in the front where they could be more easily thumped for getting things wrong. I never did get to sit at the back. Sometimes a boy would be sentenced to sit in the girls' rows as a penalty for a minor offence. Hinged desk lids provided a storage place for school bags, books, pencils, lunches and contraband. At top centre a single inkwell was provided for dipping steel nibbed pens to load with enough ink to write a couple of words at a time. This was a tricky business that required the loading of just the right amount of ink on to the nib to avoid ink splotches on your exercise book and your hand. Ballpoint pens were prohibited. The wells were filled on a regular basis by appointed ink monitors whose job was to manufacture the ink from powder mixed with water. The activity took place in the designated area of the school gully trap and involved a deal of intentional flicking and splashing of ink, always resulting in the monitors finishing up with blue hands and often arms as well. Naturally, the job was highly coveted.

All male teachers were addressed as "Sir," and female teachers as "Mrs" or "Miss". There was no air conditioning and, in the winter, the Grade 6 boys had to cut wood for the fire. In each class boys were appointed as wood monitors to fetch wood and keep the fire going until lunch break after which it was usually left to die out. In summer, the class rooms could be dreadfully hot.

The main school building was surrounded by asphalt yards segregated clearly into areas for boys and girls. In the assembly area at the back of the school children were marshalled into their class platoons at the commencement of morning and afternoon sessions and the end of recess breaks and then marched into their rooms to the sound of military marching music played through a loud speaker. On Monday mornings, after the Union Jack was run up the flagpole by two flag monitors, we were required, as we stood to attention in the assembly area, to chant with our hand on our heart, "I love God and my country, I honour the flag, I serve the King, and cheerfully obey my parents, teachers and the laws."

Combined singing of our anthem followed, which, back then, was 'God Save the King' (changed to 'God Save the Queen' after the king died on 5 February 1952). We then marched into class to the sound of two kettle drums played by Grade 6 boys. The flag monitors, chosen from Grade 6, after being trained in flag raising protocol, carried out their hoisting and lowering duties at the school flagpole every morning and afternoon.

While my first year in the bubs was mostly fun, my second year in Grade 1 with Miss Bennett was like living in a horror movie. She was a senior grey-haired lady who must have done her training at a teachers college run by Attila the Hun. She was an expert at putting the 'frighteners' on everyone, using fear as her main method of motivation. Each night we were given a list of words to learn and spell the next day, or times table to remember and recite, and upon the call of your name you had to stand and perform. Any error, not paying attention, fidgeting, or talking in class could lead to a whack on the knuckles, or a slap on the legs, with her wooden ruler. Tomfoolery of any sort resulted in a sentence to stand in the corner of the classroom facing the wall. The worst part of this punishment was the feeling of utter humiliation. I don't recall anyone teaching me before I went to school about numbers, letters or reading and I found Miss Bennett's class difficult.

A feature of the school year was the introduction of free silver capped one third pint bottles of milk for each child to drink at morning recess pursuant to a government program to address poor health and calcium deficiencies that had been found in a survey of children under 10. In summer the milk often sat in the hot sun for several hours after delivery before it was drunk causing it to curdle and go sour with the result that kids that were stupid enough to drink it vomited when class resumed.

The highlight of the calendar year was the 1951 Jubilee Celebrations for the 50th anniversary of the Australian Commonwealth. It was also Bendigo's Centenary. Cobb & Co. coaches rolled again in the city to celebrate the discovery of gold in Victoria. In Roslyn Park local youths dressed up as aborigines wearing only loincloths. With bodies painted brown and carrying spears, they ran beside the coaches while ladies dressed in Victorian period costumes were accompanied by men in top hats. Others dressed in national costumes from all over Europe added to the colourful performance. Meanwhile, of more important significance, the Murray and Loddon rivers flooded, the Menzies Referendum to ban the Communist Party failed and I escaped Miss Bennett's class by graduating to the second grade.

Increase in student numbers after the war necessitated the construction of temporary classrooms on lower ground fronting the railway line. Constructed from painted galvanised tin walls and roof panels, they were designated 'The Army Huts'. I have no idea whether they had any connection with the army but the one I was in for Grade 2 was strongly linked to lightning when it was struck one day with a God Almighty flash causing half the kids to fall out of their desks and the world outside to turn orange. I finished on the floor with other kids, all of us none the worse for wear. Some girls were crying. First aid was immediately applied to our post-traumatic stress by class teacher Miss Kennedy who took us straight into a group singing session. She was the antithesis of Miss Bennett, instrumental in restoring my interest in education and by the end of the year, at the age of eight, I had fallen in love with her.

Grade 2 was great as we were virtually quarantined from the rest of the school by a huge embankment on one side and, on the other side, fronting the railway line, we were constantly entertained by the traffic of steam locomotives choofing past pulling all types of freight and passenger carriages. Our designated playground included a real World War I field cannon, with some of the small mechanisms still working, that we used constantly in our wargames. The clay embankment behind our classroom was ideal for making tracks and garages for our toy model cars. This was "Boy's Own stuff!"

Later that year, 1952, Victoria began the launch of its diesel electric locomotive fleet. When one went past, all the kids would excitedly yell out, "Here comes a diesel!" and run down to the fence to watch in awe. The previous year had seen Victoria launch the last class of mainline steam locomotives in Australia. Proof that the steam era was left behind came this same year when the first jetliner started carrying passengers, the bikini was launched to the horror of my right-wing Presbyterian grandmother and the Victa rotary lawnmower was invented.

Every teacher was equipped with a strap as a standard issue, but I don't recall Miss Kennedy ever using one on kids. Miss Fraser, my Grade 3 teacher the following year (1953), was prone to use hers, which she called 'Charlie', rather frequently. During the previous year, H. C. Dent the editor of *The Times*, said much of what he had seen in Australian schools perturbed and depressed him. He found Australian education to be authoritarian, hierarchical and stereotyped. True to type, Miss Fraser always kept Charlie in a drawer on the right-hand side of her desk. One lunchtime two kids with more courage than I sneaked in and kidnapped Charlie who was taken to the wood heap and chopped up with an axe. His dismembered body was tossed behind the loudspeaker panel on the wall above a cupboard. His death coincided with that of another tyrant, Stalin, who suffered a massive cerebral haemorrhage. Miss Fraser never did find Charlie who remained missing for the duration of the year. Before long he was replaced with a new strap, Charlie II, which, if anything, hurt more.

What was really hurting the country in 1953 was the estimated 750 million rabbits when we had a population of less than nine million people. I was troubled by the news footage, seen at the pictures, on the spread of myxomatosis which showed rabbits with swollen heads and weeping eyes hopping around dizzily until eventually they toppled over and dropped dead.

The following year when I was 10 in Grade 4 my teacher was Mr Burke. 'Burkey' as he was known, had difficulty in controlling the class. His first mode of attack if anyone was talking, laughing, not paying attention or doing anything else he was not happy with was to throw something at them. Usually, it was whatever he had in his hand at the time and commonly a piece of chalk or a blackboard duster. He was mostly accurate and able to 'ping' someone on the head with a piece of chalk wherever they were sitting unless they ducked and then the person behind them copped it. He was a reasonable teacher and a good man but for some reason simply seemed to lack authority. A prodigious user of the strap, but he never seemed to put his heart into it. The boys used to run a contest to see how many 'cuts' of the strap they could score from Burkey in a week. Whoever got the most was king of the kids. Current studies have found that smacking children increases aggression, harms brain development, and does not improve behaviour. I can't help wondering how much smarter I would have been if I had been born in the 21st century. Polio outbreaks in Victoria this year caused extreme concern to teachers and parents.

In Grade 5 we had the same teacher as in Grade 3, Miss Fraser, who brought with her Charlie II. Educational emphasis continued to be on basic subjects such as reading, writing and arithmetic. Multiplication tables from once times one to twelve times twelve were again chanted by the whole class. We also chanted other critical things such as important poetry, and the names of countries comprising The British Empire and the States of Australia as the teacher pointed them out on a map. In 'Social Studies' we learnt, among other things, about the location of coalfields in England.

A couple of times a year school inspectors would arrive to observe and report on the principal, teachers and instructional challenges of the school. As students we were always warned that they were coming and that we should be on our best behaviour, it being inferred that it was us, the students, who were being inspected when in fact it was the teachers. Once a week we had religious studies and a black-and-white film session that seemed to mainly deal with aboriginal and Islander communities. We all thought they were boring compared with the movies we could now see at Bendigo's Golden Drive-In theatre that opened this year, 1955.

There was still no television and 'drive-ins' were a huge overnight success. You didn't have to dress up to catch a movie, parents with kids didn't have to worry about hiring babysitters or quieting noisy children and young couples could enjoy the show in the privacy of their car. While the Golden Drive-In only had one screen, it could accommodate nearly 700 cars, which on a blockbuster movie night, would be lined up along St Aidan's Road waiting to get in. Stories went around about kids being smuggled in car boots to avoid paying.

My schoolmate, Rob Iser, and I used to go to the drive-in on our pushbikes. We would pay the full fare and then pull up to a speaker as close as possible to the screen, and sit on the concrete block on the base while we watched the movies. There was a children's play area with swings and slides below the screen and on special nights there were pony rides.

The projection box, cafeteria and toilets were housed in an uninspiring, utilitarian brick blockhouse at an appropriate distance and elevation back from the screen. A switch, or button, on the speaker enabled you to turn on a little red light on top of the stand to catch the attention of refreshment vendors who moved around selling Dixie ice creams, drinks and lollies from trays slung from straps around their neck. In the very back row, utilities and trucks with armchairs on the back were allowed to reverse in. When the business closed the site was demolished and subdivided into housing estates with street names such as Goldwyn Court, Mayer Court and Hollywood Court.

By now, 1955, more than one million post-war immigrants had arrived, 70 per cent of them as assisted immigrants. My recollection, is that at Gravel Hill, 99 per cent of the kids were Aussies and I can only recall one foreign student. Mothers rejoiced at the news of disposable nappies being available for the first time and in Russia the Soviet Union finally released the last of its surviving German prisoners of war. Of the five million prisoners Russia had taken, it is estimated that only one and a half million survived.

I was 11 going on 12 by the time I was pushed on to Grade 6 in 1956. The year was a hard slog. Our teacher, Mr Dede (pronounced "Deedee"), was humourless and boring. He employed the obligatory strap with usual vigour but it seemed most of the boys had developed a philosophical acceptance of the device and had lost their fear of it. We were more afraid of failing to be accepted by our chosen secondary school and being kept at Gravel Hill to do year seven and eight in the 'Forms' where kids with 'learning difficulties' were sent. All outcomes would depend, we were repeatedly told, on our scholarly performance during the year. It turned out that some things we were taught were just not true such as Australia had few base resources such as coal, iron ore, oil and gas. I continued to struggle with arithmetic and anything at all to do with mathematics/algebra and, in my frustration, wrote "Get f….d!" across a page of my arithmetic book that I just couldn't understand, which resulted, upon its discovery by Mr Dede, in me being marched into the headmaster's office to receive six cuts.

Grade 6 was a big class with more than 40 students and no doubt a challenge for any teacher to manage that number of 11 to 12 year olds who were on the cusp of realising a new identity. Boys in particular were testing the limits. Ink wells were frequently sabotaged by miscreants stuffing them with blotting paper. The steel nibs of pens were employed as tattoo instruments, arrow and dart points or simply to poke the butt of the kid sitting in front of you. Small strips of paper were rolled tightly, folded into a 'V' and fired off with a rubber band strung between two fingers, when the teacher wasn't looking, to hit some unsuspecting kid on the back of the head or ear. On one occasion this practice caused chaos when the missile misfired and hit the blackboard close to where Mr Dede's hand was writing. In cherry season, boys sneaked into the classroom during the break to slip cherry pips under as many of the floor runners on the old wooden desks as they could so that when the teacher gave the order "Class be seated," the cherry pips fired off like a machine gun as everyone sat down.

One day a week, the whole class was forced to do gardening after recess for the rest of the afternoon. We all assembled at the gardening shed to collect tools where the bigger boys were issued shovels or forks for digging on the hardest jobs. Other kids were allocated to weeding, raking or general clean up tasks. So-called 'gardening duty' was promoted as part of our education but in fact seemed more like forced slave labour.

I am sure none of the kids in our Grade 6 heard the words "Good evening and welcome to television" when it went live on

16 September 1956. The sets were very expensive and reception of the signals then transmitted from Melbourne was terrible. Our only chance to see the Melbourne Olympic Games was in the newsreels at picture theatres. After lots of kids had seen the Olympic torch when it went through Bendigo, they were inspired to make their own from jam tins stuck on the end of a broom handle complete with a kerosene fired wick.

[Appendix 5 contains a list of Gravel Hill State School students who I think were in Grade 6.]

Chapter 13

KIDS AND HEALTH

Shortly after I started school at Gravel Hill, my parents decided that it was time for me to attend a regular Sunday School. Neither of them was outwardly particularly religious though they both acknowledged a belief in God, and had themselves been brought up in a Christian religious environment. Presumably they thought that what had been endured by them should be endured by me. It is likely also that the influence of my right-wing Protestant Dutch Afrikana grandmother, who lived with us at The Crown, had something to do with encouraging my mother to send me off for religious instruction. After having been delivered once in person by my mother to the St Pauls Anglican Church Sunday School in Myers Street I was thereafter sent out the front door of the hotel each Sunday in the direction of the church, only two city blocks away. It was kind of interesting at first with stories about Noah's Ark, Moses who started off in bulrushes and eventually parted the waters of the red sea, and Jesus who turned water into wine. I thought my father would have been interested in that.

I was very much less interested in being drilled with the basics of Church of England cataclysmic Christian doctrine, which I found confusing and troublesome. I was conflicted about Jesus as the son of God. If God was God and Jesus was God also, then were there two Gods? If so, which one was the boss? There was also the Holy Spirit and I couldn't figure out where he fitted into the hierarchy. Jesus' mother, The Virgin Mary, was also important and had some clout. Darned if I knew what though and there was Hell where the Devil was in charge. A hot place where the damned burned for all eternity. It seemed to me that there were too many of these characters wanting a piece of the action. The plot was exponentially far more complicated than any of the movies I had seen and I just couldn't follow it and found it depressing. Religious instruction was not helping my mental health.

After Sunday School, which went from 10 to 11 a.m., the kids were shanghaied by the Sunday School teacher to attend the full adult church service in St Paul's till midday which only compounded my confusion. I stuck to attending for several months only because, regardless of my pleading, my mother refused to let me off the hook. I hated the proceedings so much that I started to wag it and spent several Sunday mornings hiding by myself in the bushes in the gardens outside the Town Hall. Eventually, after my continuous whingeing and complaining, my mother relented. It was too late for my psyche which had been imprinted with the fear of God. For many years after, I continued to have a bet each way by saying my prayers each night.

The kids at Gravel Hill came from a mixed socio-economic group. While some were from well-off families, other pre 'baby boomers' born before the end of the World War II had experienced deprivation arising from being a member of a large family, sometimes without a father's support due to his death or inability to cope in a post-war environment. With several children and a husband absent or disabled and out of work, home-made clothes and hand-me-downs were mandatory and 'store bought' clothes for very special events only.

Some kids at Gravel Hill truly smelled badly. I clearly recall cases of serious body odour and particularly the smell of stale urine and I remember one kid who had green stuff growing on his upper front teeth. At times low-grade infections such as warts, nits, and impetigo went through the school. The latter was particularly infectious resulting in red itchy sores that developed blisters that broke open and led to clear fluid or puss which then formed unsightly yellow scab formations, often on the face around the nose or mouth. I know all about that because I had it. Our chemist gave me a green lotion to dab on that caused the scabs to go green. Very attractive. There were regular, albeit cursory, medical inspections. The staffroom was taken over by a visiting doctor who required all the boys to strip to their underpants and file past as he spent no more than a minute or two in the examination of each one, comprising a testicle cough test, followed by the order to, "Open your mouth and say aah." A nurse then took our temperature and did a quick head check to see if any nasty nits had taken up residence.

Toilet facilities were basic. The boys toilet was a brick rectang-ular block with roofed dunnies down one side and a roofless cement rendered brick wall urinal on the other. The dunnies had green doors that didn't lock, with toilet paper never guaranteed. The lack of a hand basin meant that if you wanted to wash your hands you had to walk across the schoolyard to the drinking fountain trough to do so. Nobody did.

Each day the boys competed to see who could piss over the wall. To do so was quite a feat but some of the six graders nearly managed it. Some kids were quite good at using their stream to spell out words or messages on the rendered walls. A common trick of the older boys was to sneak up behind a younger kid who was peeing and push him in the back to thrust him towards the urinal so that in endeavouring to save himself he had to put his hands out to prevent landing full-face on the wall covered in piss, in the process losing control of his penis which could then slip back in his pants causing him to wet himself. The pusher would then bolt immediately, leaving the crying and soaked little kid. A dastardly act that I never delivered but regretfully received more than once.

Polio, or 'infantile paralysis' as it was commonly called, attacked adults as well. Victoria had suffered severely from polio in 1937–1938 with more than 2,000 children and adults infected causing schools to be closed. The teachers at Gravel Hill made it plain to us that it frightened them. Worldwide it was killing over half a million people a year and crippled many more. To be handicapped in some visible way still carried with it social opprobrium. With varied sorts of treatment, some improved so that they could walk again with callipers on their legs. My close friend at Gravel Hill, Jon Rechter, had it in his right arm, which was severely withered and of little use. He could only move it by walking his fingers across the desk or using his other arm to lift it. His feet were also badly affected. He had contracted polio around four years of age before starting school and had been in an iron lung artificial respirator for "a long time". He started school one year behind in age compared to the other kids and became a competent sportsman, marking the football and playing cricket with only one arm.

Jon was an inspiration to me as I was fairly hopeless at sport. During one physical education session at Gravel Hill an exasperated teacher made the offhanded but accurate remark, "Beck! You have no ball sense!" The words lodged in my brain permanently thereafter. He was right of course, as I had little opportunity to develop ball skills on the crushed rock backyard of the Crown Hotel with my father constantly counselling me against such activities for fear of causing damage to parked cars or hotel windows.

In 1956 all the kids at Gravel Hill were filed through the staff-room to receive their Salk polio vaccine injection supplied free by the Commonwealth as part of a nationwide immunisation campaign. In that year, over 1,000 new cases of polio were notified in Australia. Eight years later, only eight were recorded. Records suggest that 70,000 Australians were registered as suffering polio, but the real number may be higher. It was through a combination of sheer luck and good management that I dodged the polio bullet.

I last saw my mate Jon Rechter nearly 50 years after we had left Gravel Hill school. It was at St John of God Hospital in Bendigo on 4 November 2005. I had received a call from his brother Peter to say that Jon wanted to see me. He was suffering from cancer and 'post-polio syndrome'—a recurrence of polio symptoms. While he was most articulate and it was a joy for us to reminisce about our old times together, I was horrified at his condition that was little more than skin and bones. After saying goodbye and getting halfway up the passage I cried like hell. He died the next day.

There were other childhood illnesses such as chickenpox, measles, whooping cough, German measles, diphtheria, tonsillitis and mumps. Most kids got most of them. One third of all deaths were caused by simple infection before penicillin became available. Australia became the first country to make it accessible to civilians when it began manufacturing in 1944 at the Commonwealth Serum Laboratories in Melbourne. Tuberculosis was also a big concern. In 1948 it was killing one quarter of all people dying between the ages of 20 and 39 years. Vaccinations were then introduced together with compulsory chest x-rays for all Australians to ensure early detection of the disease that progressively destroyed the lungs. It proved fatal once a person showed symptoms of coughing up blood, night sweats, wasting and general debility resulting in victims becoming pale, weak and emaciated. All kids were lined up and inoculated at school. I had my jab at high school so it would have been at least 1957. By the end of the 1950s tuberculosis had been brought under control.

Kids at Gravel Hill often had very ordinary lunches. Spam sandwiches were common. It was a cheap substitute for ham, allegedly made mostly from pork that came in tins with a doubtful pedigree and taste, and an unrecognisable texture and colour. Other popular sandwich fillings included jam, vegemite, mashed potato, bananas, chips, cheese, tomatoes, peanut butter and a paste that claimed to be made from fish. Beetroot seemed to be a common additive as its red juice was seen leaking on a regular basis out of the newspapers used as lunch wrap.

Those with money to spend could buy their lunch from the Eales Pie Cart parked near the front gate of the school in Mundy Street at lunchtime. We called it a 'cart' but it was really a motorised van loaded with all sorts of goodies such as meat pies, Cornish pasties, sausage rolls, lamingtons, vanilla slices (we called 'snot blocks'), cream buns, jam tarts, custard tarts, Boston buns and fruit buns. With two or three shillings lunch money you could buy much more than you could eat and there was no one standing over you to say what you could or couldn't have. The overwhelming power of money and free choice enabled kids, including myself, to simply buy one big Boston bun and eat the whole lot for lunch, or you could have two pies, or a pie and a pastie or just a paper bag full of cakes. As my mother rarely refused my request for money, I was a customer most days.

After buying lunch we would run down to the little shop opposite the butter factory in Mundy Street where you could still buy a single small lolly for a halfpenny (equal to 240th of $1). The glass topped counter was jampacked with all sorts of temptations from shop-made toffee umbrellas on a stick, cupcakes, and toffee apples plus the usual range of commercial lollies. Shop-made flavoured ice in little square cones for a couple of pennies were also popular. As a special treat, if I had enough money left over from the pie cart, I might buy an ice cream wafer or a two-in-one ice cream.

Chapter 14

TOUGH SCHOOL

C hildren in Bendigo's state schools normally graduated straight to high school or technical school from Grade 6. Gravel Hill was unique in that classrooms extended to years 7 and 8, but were made available only to male children with special learning problems. Students and teachers referred to years 1 to 6 as Grade years and years 7 and 8 as Forms 1 and 2. "The Forms" were established during World War II for boys deemed to be "unsuited for advancement to either high or technical schools." They had a wide range of mild to severe learning difficulties derived from a variety of causes, many of which were not properly identified or diagnosed, including genetic causes, environmental conditions in terrible family circumstances, psychiatric conditions, mal-nutrition, physical injury or a combination of some or all of those things.

The school rule was that The Forms students should not associate with the students in The Grades, who themselves were warned to stay away from The Forms kids. This suited the kids in the lower grades as most of us were frightened of the bigger kids and, from time to time, their strange conduct. Some were known to have a reputation for violence, a few being practised schoolyard bullies. Quite a few had speech defects and some drooled at the mouth. We, as young kids thought that they had "mental problems" and in the vernacular of the time were "not the full quid" or "retards". For the record it should be noted that at least one student of The Forms was clearly incorrectly sent there as he later went on to obtain a degree from Melbourne University.

Mr McGuinness, a notorious disciplinarian, was in charge of The Forms. He was the most feared teacher at Gravel Hill. A tall man, of medium build, who wore a three-piece suit and had black hair and black rimmed glasses to match. He had a loud, oppressive manner and either appointed himself as the chief disciplinarian of the entire school or that job had been delegated to him. He clearly enjoyed assuming primary responsibility for punishing any schoolyard infringements and would unhesitatingly haul in any child late for assembly, caught taking a shortcut by running up a school embankment, found riding a bike in the school grounds or involved in a scrap with another kid or swearing. All such misdemeanours and variations thereof resulted in a severe strapping.

He used a long thick strap which whooshed when it came down on each whack or 'cut'. Being late for assembly in the morning (that is late for school) incurred a penalty of two cuts administered as one on each hand. Likewise, if after the sounding of the school siren you were caught late running to class at lunchtime or at recess you would again be lined up for two cuts. Before delivering the strap, he would line the condemned offender up against a brick wall in the passageway and deliver his usual lengthy, excruciatingly agonising, sarcastic lecture condemning the appalling, woeful and ruinous behaviour that left him no alternative but to administer the punishment he was about to inflict. It was a mistake to hang your head and look down as this resulted in him chucking you under the chin and banging your head against the wall. It was his softening up procedure at the end of which many kids were crying, well before the punishment was delivered. Some kids pissed themselves from fear before the punishment began.

To receive your punishment you were required to hold your hand out at shoulder height, steady, while Mr McGuinness delivered a full roundhouse circular wallop aimed at laying the strap along the length of your arm as well as your hand. If, like me, you had prior convictions for misdemeanours the punishment could be doubled and instead of one wallop you would get two for a similar offence, or three for a further and so on. You were always given the opportunity to change hands to spread the pain. And it was very painful. Some kids believed that if you could spit on your hands beforehand it would lessen the pain. It was a mistake to try and reduce the impact by pulling your arm downwards as the strap descended because if McGuinness detected this (as he usually did) you were lined up for the two-for-one penalty. There was no doubt that he practised corporal punishment with great enthusiasm. The pain of the strap could last for several hours with bruises and welts extending from your hand up your arm lasting longer.

In defence of McGuinness, it was a time of different strokes from different blokes back then. In Victoria the punishment of flogging with the cat and nine tails was still meted out to prisoners as late as April 1958 when inmates of Pentridge prison, William John O'Meally and John Henry Taylor, were flogged with 12 strokes each. I was then aged 14 and in Form 2 at Bendigo High School.

It was not until 25 years later that corporal punishment was finally abolished in Victorian state schools in 1983.

I knew better than to tell my parents about any punishment I had received. I figured there was no point because I might very well get another whack or penalty for having misbehaved at school in the first place. Corporal punishment was predominantly meted out to boys, and the kids in Grades 5 and 6 seemed to get more than the younger ones. Perhaps they were naughtier.

The school bully that impressed me the most was Theo from The Forms. With black curly hair, olive skin and a mouth full of missing teeth, he seemed without fear and lacking appreciation of the consequences of his conduct. His reputation included the capacity to absorb any amount of punishment, as was evidenced by the number of times he was given the cuts by Mr McGuinness. When walking to school one day, Theo frightened the daylights out of me when he jumped out from behind a tree and ordered me to stand at attention in front of the trunk while he fired his catapult at me. I think he missed on purpose as a don't recall being hit by any of the projectiles but I did think briefly that I might die.

After that experience, the mere sight of Theo at a distance terrified me to the core. I figured after a while that the best way to handle him was to front up and say, "G'day Theo, how are ya'?" in the pretence that he didn't bother me. In a short space of time I became his little mate and he my ultimate default bodyguard whose services, fortunately, I never had to call upon. Without any warning Theo disappeared one day. The cause of his absence was allegedly due to him having thrown a steel chair at Mr McGuinness, the ultimate consequence of which was a sentence to reform school. After this Theo went on to develop quite a record.

Every spring, a day would come when developing hormones crystallised into some primeval urge that prompted the boys at Gravel Hill to select sides, pull up tufts of grass with clods of earth attached and go to war. Battles usually took place on the very lower-level of the tiered playgrounds away from the sight of teachers. No one ever got seriously hurt but plenty collected eye and earfulls of dirt. Participants accepted the danger of being caught and strapped as a reasonable risk for having so much fun.

On bright summer days magnifying glasses that kids brought to school to concentrate the sun and burn holes through dry leaves, were applied to the backs of hands as a test to see how long the pain of a burning hot dot could be endured.

In winter, when it was too wet to play the usual kick to kick footy, the Boys' Own game of British Bulldog was played in the shelter sheds. Not for the fainthearted and commonly resulting in injuries, it began with one player in the middle chosen to be 'Bulldog'. At the end of the shelter shed the other players assembled in a safe area. The aim was to run from one end of the shelter shed to the other without being caught by the Bulldog. It started with one player selected to make the first attempt to run across. If the Bulldog caught and held him long enough to shout "British Bulldog" then he had to join him in the centre and become another Bulldog. Then the others in the safe area had to rush across with the Bulldogs trying to catch as many as possible who, when caught, were co-opted to join the Bulldogs in the middle. The remaining uncaptured survivors would then rush back and forth until all had been caught except one who was the winner. The game involved tough physical tackling resulting in torn and grubby clothes and an investment of considerable skin in the game in the form of bruises cuts and grazes.

Gravel Hill school was tough and there were times that I didn't want to go. Instead, after going home to the The Crown for lunch, I would head off under the pretence I was going to school and deviate to the pictures. I could only do this if I had my own hard earned pocket money as I could not make a parental approach for finance to 'wag' school. Truancy was frowned upon and dealt with strictly. The local truant officer, Dick turner, was known to lurk around neighbourhoods to catch kids 'wagging' school. If you were caught, you would be hauled back to the school for punishment and your parents visited and given a lecture. You would then likely be threatened to be sent to 'Reform School' if the misdemeanour was repeated. All the kids knew about Dick Turner. I knew also that he was a customer at The Crown from time to time, an accomplished football commentator on local radio 3BO, and their lead broadcaster covering the game each Saturday.

16. Sam Tongway, Gravel Hill Headmaster.

Overall, I had a marvellous time at Gravel Hill and could not describe my experience there as miserable. While the approach of most teachers was to instil knowledge through discipline, they kept me entertained most of the time and managed to enlarge my knowledge bank and broaden my universe. We had two headmasters while I was there, the first one was Mr George, a mean little man who could swing a big strap. The second and best was Sam Tongway. Mr Tongway was Chinese and in those days it was most unusual to have a person of that ethnicity as principal of a state school. He was well liked and made an effort to learn the names of individual children, often meeting and welcoming them at the front gate of a morning. He had served with the Australian Imperial Force in World War I after which he studied physics and chemistry at London Imperial College of Science and Technology, Latin and history at Oxford University and then, on returning to Australia, graduated with a Bachelor of Arts from Melbourne University in 1921. We were very fortunate to have him at Gravel Hill.

Still, it was always a relief when the Christmas school holidays came around. It meant seven weeks of deliverance into freedom and adventure.

Chapter 15

TROUBLE

There is no end to how much trouble young boys can get into. Most of it was mischief such as pinching fruit, knocking on front doors or throwing stones on a roof and running away. But sometimes it was outright vandalism as when a group of us were overcome by an overwhelming temptation to upend an on-site toilet at a building location. My mate Harry and I committed a similar offence on a dunny at the Bendigo Gun Club where we had ridden on our bikes one weekend. I was correctly identified as the chief offender and dragged before the parental court of my father who, after writing an appropriate cheque for compensation, convicted, sentenced and punished me.

I only recall once suffering from serious corporal punishment from my father and that was when I had been caught red-handed climbing over the roofs of buildings adjacent to the hotel in the same block. He delivered serious lashings to my legs with a solid brass ruler which left visible marks for several days. This was not the first time I had been caught and I had been given several prior warnings in relation to the gravity of such conduct, which was not only trespass on other people's properties, but put my safety at risk. I believe now that his main motivation for such punishment was the desire to deter me from such dangerous conduct because he was concerned for my welfare.

My father preferred to put the 'frighteners' on me to keep me under control. One place that I recall from a very early age that I desperately wanted to explore was the hotel cellar. Unbeknown to me at the time it was a place fraught with obstacles including a large deep sump full of water in which a drainage pump operated 24/7. When the pump failed, as it often did, the cellar filled with several feet of water causing empty barrels to float about. Apart from stacks of beer barrels there were also cylinders of carbon dioxide, beer lines going to various taps upstairs in the bar, a very wet slippery floor and an incredibly steep staircase that led from a trapdoor behind the bar to the cellar. Not at all a suitable environment for a young lad to explore. Every time I pleaded to go down my father explained in the most serious tone of voice that it was an extremely dangerous place to be because a vicious crocodile lived there and it would eat little boys. He expanded the fiction in the most elaborate way explaining how every time he or the other barmen went down there, they had to give the crocodile something to eat so it wouldn't attack them. Each of the barmen were fully briefed to corroborate the story and in doing so added their own elaborations about the danger. The fiction was kept up for years and had the desired effect but the prospect of seeing the crocodile simply reinforced my intention to eventually descend into the cellar one day and find it.

More regularly the sentence for my misdemeanours was what my father called "a loss of points". Under his point system I was granted an undefined number of points for doing chores or just being good. I never knew how many. A loss of points meant in effect the withdrawal of privileges such as a cut in pocket money or payment for chores, or being grounded at the premises. Points could be redeemed if I elected to do extra jobs around the hotel. It was a good system because it gave me a chance to reinstate myself and, in that process, provided direct parental benefit. The downside was that it left me in a depressed state of self-esteem huddling under a cloud of guilt until the lost points were reclaimed, which could take some time.

When I got into trouble with my mother, punishment often followed swiftly. After the summons, "Mickey come here now!" and my immediate attendance, a whack around the legs with any readily available implement often followed. Devices used to inflict punishment included straps, wire coat-hangers, a fly swatter, wooden spoons or any readily available kitchen implements. The back of a carving knife was used to wrap me on the knuckles when I was caught pinching food from the plate-up table in the kitchen. None of it hurt much. I knew I was in real trouble if she threatened, "Just wait until your father comes out of the bar." Fortunately for me, by the time he did, she had usually forgotten all about my offending behaviour.

Given the environment in which I was flourishing, it wasn't long before I established a vocabulary of comprehensive swear words. I regret to say that they were used not only in the presence of staff but also, at times, directed at them in response to their legitimate concern relating to my increasing bad behaviour. While they often responded by threatening to wash my mouth out with soap and water, they seldom reported me to my parents. Anyway, I had learnt some of the words from them in the first place.

The adventure playgrounds for Bendigo kids in the 1950s were the remains of the city's old gold mines. The last two mines to close were The North Deborah and Central Deborah in 1954. I was 10 years old at the time and recall that there was a great deal of ringing of hands, gnashing of teeth and "umming and ahhring" among the general populace over the loss. There was still much evidence left of Bendigo's gold rush beginnings. The landscape displayed dilapidated steel towers, called poppet heads, that had provided winding gear for the lifts down into underground mines. Between Bendigo and Eaglehawk there were great mountains of grey battery sand and slate mullock heaps, bordered by pepper trees as memorials to the past. Abandoned engine rooms, boilers and winding gear left rusting in situ waited to be broken up for scrap. A great place for kids to get into trouble.

We used the giant dumps of mining spoil to slide down on sheets of old corrugated iron and dug into the sandhills to build cubby houses. A couple of times the sand dumps collapsed and kids who had been digging into them were buried alive. Abandoned mines and uncovered shallow mineshafts remained for kids to explore. After a heavy rain it was not uncommon to read a report in the local paper of someone's backyard disappearing down an old shaft that had not been properly sealed. We climbed down the circular shafts of the Chinese alluvial mines around the Whitehills rubbish tip hunting for the mud nests of swallows to get eggs for our egg collections. On one occasion we descended an old shaft off Peg Leg Road where we found a rusty tin with sticks of gelignite. We climbed out with several sticks then threw them down the hole and ran like hell. Nothing happened. We even dug our own 'mine' near a water race at the rear of my mates Rob Iser's, house until we were caught and it had to be filled in.

The best thing my parents did, metaphorically speaking, was to let me "wander off into the woods". Left to roam, I had to work out the best way to survive. In retrospect this was good for me. For anyone to reach their full potential they must face new challenges and dangers from time to time. On the edge of a dam, we found an old tin horse trough that we purloined and used as a canoe to put to sea in on the dam. The only problem was that it leaked like a sieve and we had to bail furiously to keep it afloat for any length of time. In the end we were beaten by exhaustion and it descended forever into the murky depths of Davey Jone's Locker.

We floated down water irrigation races on inner tubes and we went 'bird nesting'. The phrase was a euphemism for the practice of stealing eggs from the nests of native birds for our egg collections. In the Victorian era the hobby of egg collecting had been considered a respectable pursuit for refined gentlemen but by the mid-20th century its popularity had reduced mainly to schoolboys where it was still considered to be a reasonable hobby.

Boys would go to extreme lengths to add to their egg collections. Some became highly skilled at climbing very tall trees to claim species that were rare because they were hard to collect such as magpie, crow and hawk eggs. Small lightweight kids seem to have a climbing advantage and it was amazing to see how they could climb the thinnest of branches to secure their goal. Amazing too that there were not more injuries as it was a risky business. When descending, the safest place to put the collected eggs was in your mouth. Birds' nests were found sometimes in the most unlikely places like mud embankments, which housed diamond pardalotes and even crimson rosellas, wooden railway bridges and corner fence posts that housed eastern rosellas and concrete culverts, or old mines that were often the nesting place of swallows. We scrambled through the culverts and over the bridges and we waded into the reedbeds at the end of the Kennington Reservoir to obtain the eggs of water hens and we climbed every climbable tree that had a nest in it. We then met at fellow egg collectors' houses after school to trade and swap eggs. It was necessary to be on alert for forgeries based on bantams' eggs sprayed with paint flicked through fine fly wire with a stiff tooth brush. State fauna laws have since been tightened and those caught with native birds' eggs in their possession may now receive hefty fines.

Punch ups between Catholic kids and Protestant kids were not uncommon. Sometimes the kids from Gravel Hill waited in ambush at the McIvor Road railway bridge for the Catholic kids as they rode their bikes home from school so they could bombard them with clods of dirt from above to the chant of "Catholic dogs sit on logs and eat maggots out of frogs!" Having learned from experience that these Catholic kids were damn good fighters we would then run flat out. (I regret to say that I was involved at times.) They were nicknamed 'Micks' because many were of Irish descent and had surnames starting with 'Mc'. Protestants were called 'Proddies' or 'Proddy Dogs' when the same chant was fired back at them by the Micks. This disgraceful bigotry also extended to mixed marriages with relatives sometimes refusing to attend a wedding service in a church not of their denomination. Some kids were still being raised to hate Catholics or to hate Protestants. That was never the case with me. My father, who was a member of the Masonic Lodge and could fairly be described as a right-wing Protestant, used to always say that he preferred a good Catholic to a crook Protestant any day. The proof was in his customer base at The Crown, many of whom were Catholics and his good mates.

My mate Dalla and I built Formula One Billy Carts with wheels made from old steel jacketed ball bearing races that screamed on bitumen or concrete surfaces. Basic construction was an old wooden packing box bolted onto a hardwood frame with a central plank spine for the chassis extending out front for the turning wheel assembly made from a cross board pivoting from a bolt at the end of the plank. The ball bearing wheels were attached by hammering them on to shaped wooden axles, slipping a nail through a drilled hole and bending it as a pin to keep them on. Steering was achieved with a rope tied to each end of the cross board so you could turn it in the chosen direction. The result was a machine with a ground clearance of about one inch (2.5 centimetres), that, with almost frictionless contact, was able to reach amazing speeds at low profile on a hard surface. A breath-taking experience to the rider. Completely useless on gravel.

On weekends we would take our machines to Roslyn Park for a drag race down the very steep bitumen roadways leading from the lookout tower to the park below. The roads were different gradients but at the bottom of each one it was essential to do a sharp left or right to avoid ploughing into the park botanicals. This grim-faced ordeal could only be undertaken by someone made of the right stuff. Once you were underway a level of speed was soon attained that made it impossible to get off and you were committed to the do or die of rounding the corner at the bottom of the road. The trick was to turn your front wheels at the bottom of the hill before it ran out so that you slid sideways on your steel wheels with the hope of negotiating the corner in some style. It was a trick that I found very difficult to master. Before very long I gave the whole idea away having decided that I had invested enough skin in the game. I tried other things such as harnessing one of my dogs to tow me along on my Cyclops scooter until he took off in the wrong direction one day and wrapped me around a post. My most serious accident was when I ran into the back of a parked utility truck on my pushbike. At the time I was looking at my untied shoelace.

The Crown had interesting kids' hidey holes to explore and play in. There was the space under the stage in the dining room, the plumbing inspection room between floors, the refrigeration plant room, the washhouse, the back of the wood heap, a tiny courtyard behind the pantry, my dad's personal store sheds if I could get access, my grandfather's workshop, the linen press and a store area under the main hotel staircase.

The linen press and staircase store were intriguing because they harboured old suitcases and items long ago left behind by customers which were interesting to rifle through. The staircase store also contained big cartons of toilet paper, paper bags used for wrapping bottles, and seasonal decorations used by the hotel for Christmas and Easter. It was all good flammable stuff. My sister and I were told to stay out of the area but couldn't resist exploring it armed with candles to enable visibility as there was no electric light in there. We were probably called away at some stage as we left the candles burning and forgotten. Someone saw smoke seeping out of the wooden staircase and raised the alarm. The fire brigade was called but, pending their arrival, my father organised a bucket chain of men shanghaied from the peak hour rush in the bar to douse the flames. Two rows of men, one handing on full buckets of water and the other handing back empty ones to the water source, worked furiously and had the fire under control before the brigade arrived. If the fire had taken off out-of-control the wooden staircase could have formed a conflagration that was capable of consuming the entire premises. The only real damage done was to toilet paper and Christmas decorations plus a financial loss incurred in bar takings resulting from my father shouting several rounds of free drinks to all customers. Due to the fact that my sister and I were very young at the time we managed to escape serious punishment.

Trouble was not hard to find around The Crown. When I was around 12 years old my grandfather, the former blacksmith, assisted me in the manufacture of a large heavy-duty wire prong or frame to form the basis of a serious catapult (or "shanghai" as he called it). Once set up with an appropriate sling powered with suitable rubber propulsion it was a formidable device capable of firing a large marble or ball bearing a long way and doing serious damage. The law might regard possession of such a thing today as being a prosecutable offence.

When my older cousin Gary Beck (later Air-Vice Marshal) visited me at The Crown I was anxious to display my skill with the catapult device and gave him an exhibition of how I could easily take out windows in an old warehouse at the back of The Crown that I assured him was abandoned. Based on my guarantee he quickly joined in and shortly thereafter the irate manager of the premises together with a posse of his staff turned up at The Crown demanding arrest and prosecution of the offenders together with compensation. It turned out the premises were owned by the Gas and Fuel Corporation and used for storage of valuable gas stoves and equipment. I was rightly identified as the principal offender, the device confiscated and compensation settled with my father and his cheque book. We were lucky that the police were not involved. It took me a long time to win back sufficient points to recover from this episode.

Chapter 16

BARNEY AND DANNY

In the environment of The Crown, I often formed close relationships with staff members, particularly ones that lived on the premises. The job of 'useful' came with one bedroom accommodation that comprised a converted stable in the backyard. His duties included chopping wood for the main kitchen stove and, during winter, the five wood heaters in the bar and lounges, servicing those fires including cleaning and setting for the next day's lighting, supplying the kitchen with stock from storerooms, cleaning the gents toilets and the kitchen grease trap, attending to bar duties at peak time in the evening and shovelling up any horse manure in the backyard left by customers' horses plus anything else that the boss told him to attend to. In return he received the accommodation, three meals a day, a quantity of free beer and a wage.

Most 'usefuls' turned out to be not very, and didn't last long. One that did was Barney Fagan. Aged in his mid-to-late 20s he was a jovial character, five feet and an inch or two in stocky stature, with well-oiled black hair and a round face. He smiled with a mischievous grin almost constantly behind light framed spectacles with perfectly round lenses. He looked a bit like Lou Costello of Abbott and Costello fame. I think he tried to laugh his way through life to make up for what had been very humble beginnings. He worked at The Crown in the early 1950s when the basic wage was less than £8 ($16) a week and I was aged around five to eight years.

Barney proved to be instrumental in expanding my vocabulary. Girls and women were "sheilas". Men were "blokes" but I already knew that. Apart from basic swear words (he never used ones beginning with the letters 'f' or 'c') he explained such things as what it meant to be so cold that it would "freeze the balls off a brass monkey" and counselled me not to "flog a dead horse" when I kept getting repeated refusals from my parents to buy me a dog. Eventually I figured out what he meant when he kept saying he was a bit "under the weather" even on a bright clear sunny morning, but I couldn't understand at first his expression on really wet days that it was "raining cats and dogs". I understood more quickly that his rule "You scratch my back and I'll scratch yours" meant that if I did not dob him in then he would not dob me in. When I avoided trouble, he would say that "you escaped that by the skin of your teeth" which for the life of me I couldn't figure out as I could never find any skin on my teeth. He dubbed me his "little china plate" which meant "his mate", calling me "china" for short or sometimes "cobber" and the two of us became "as thick as thieves."

As a young child I followed him everywhere around the hotel doing my best to conscientiously help him with his chores, asking him hundreds of questions as we went such as, "What are you doing?" To which he would reply, "Making a wig wam for a goose's bridal!" I would be in his way until eventually he would complain that I was "getting on his goat" and to "put a sock in it" and in response to my further questions, "What's a wig wam? How do you put a bridle on a goose?" He would say "What do you think this is—bush week?"

Although often totally confused I learned lots from Barney. Not to stand too close while he chopped wood to avoid flying chips, how to properly stack a wheelbarrow, clean the wood fires and set them for lighting, sweep the concrete driveway, hose out the gents toilet and a repertoire of tricks you could play on the other staff members. My favourite, which I used for many years after Barney left, involved the delicate balancing of a jam tin three quarters full of water on the top of a doorway left slightly ajar so that when it was approached by someone from the gap-open side the tin emptied its contents on the unsuspecting pedestrian. The only problem was you were never sure who you were going to get so you had to stay in the vicinity to witness the event and then leave very quickly.

Barney and I mostly enjoyed each other's company but there was a limit to what conduct he allowed me to get away with. If he thought that I had "gone haywire" he would pull me up or in a worst-case scenario make me "face the music" before a parental disciplinarian so I could be "taken down a peg or two". If I was grumpy he would say that I "had got my nose out of joint" or must have "gotten out of the wrong side of the bed". I had no idea what he meant as my bed was always up against a wall and I could only get out of one side anyhow. Always he counselled me to be cheerful and positive, to be sincere and not "two-faced", to speak plainly and call "a spade a spade" and be "fair dinkum".

He was never unjustifiably critical and if I did something worthy would readily grant praise to promote my self-esteem.

His best assertion was, "There are no flies on you." I couldn't make any sense of this at all at first and always double checked for flies. I eventually realised that he was really saying that I was too sharp and quick for flies to make a landing, that I was smart and "on the ball". An expert at playing the fool and a terrible tease and conman, at one stage he had me convinced that I could go to the hardware store up the street and buy a left-handed screwdriver or a tin of striped paint. I followed him about like his shadow and if he went anywhere, I always asked where he was going to which he would invariably reply, "To see a man about a dog," or "I'm off to Woop Woop."

With my parents' consent he used to take me to mass at St Killian's Catholic Church on Sunday. I would sit on the crossbar of his old pushbike as he pedalled down and back from the church. Always the clown, he showed me when the collection plate came around, how you could, if money was scarce, pretend to make a contribution by clicking the other coins in the plate with your finger. After church we would sometimes call into his nearby sister's humble house, where I remember her Coolgardie safe where she kept milk for our tea. It was a rectangular box with fly wire mesh on the sides and a large water tray at the top from which sheets of hessian dangled through which water trickled by the process of wicking to keep it moist. Breezes on the hessian caused evaporation and cooled the food inside the closed box which also kept out flies and scavengers. As the water dripped it was collected and drained into a bucket which could then be poured back into the tray on top. Many people still found refrigerators too expensive to buy. We would then ride on the bike down to Lake Weeroona to feed stale bread to the ducks. On one such occasion I fell in the lake over my head and Barney, fully clothed, jumped in and reefed me out. He no doubt saved my life as at that stage I could not swim.

He said I was his right-hand man. He was, upon reflection, very important to me at the time. One day I woke up and he was not there. I can't recall whether he was sacked or just left. I do recall a feeling of very great loss.

After Barney there were several years where the performance of several 'usefuls' was judged to be close to useless by my father. Then along came Danny Morrison who had spent a considerable part of his younger life as a 'pug', which back then was Australian slang for a professional boxer. It was hard to judge his age as he had a face like the battered leather of a deflated old football which together with its deep folds and wrinkles and his habit of constantly gritting his teeth truly made him look a bit like a pug dog. He clearly had been knocked around a lot over the years and I suspect that the reason he clenched his false teeth was to keep them in. Crumpled and old for his age he walked with a bit of a shuffle but still kept a sharp mind and bright brown eyes behind which was the sadness and frustration of an old fighter whose time had passed. He seemed pleased to settle in to his converted stable bedroom and adopted The Crown as his home.

Danny had been one of a select group of young men who fought with boxing troupes during the 'golden age' of Australian boxing that lasted until the 1950s, when men fought in large tents at agricultural shows, carnivals and rodeos throughout the country. My father thought that a man like that might be handy around The Crown. The best-known troupe was Jimmy Sharman's but at least a dozen others operated from time to time, several appearing regularly at the Bendigo Agricultural Showgrounds and at the annual Easter Street Fair. Young men joined the troupes to earn a quid and have an exciting life. Many were aboriginal youths. It was a tough life for the boxers who fought in, ate in and slept in the boxing tent. At each stop, they had to unload the tent and set it up with ticket booths and equipment to get the show ready. Young men were drawn by the excitement of the carnival and the perceived status and power of being a boxer, as food and pay was basic.

When showtime came the boxers in their gaudy outfits mounted the platform outside the tent as a bell jangled and a drum was beaten. Behind them were painted canvas backdrops and large banners with the names of the fighters. The tent bosses, all able spruikers, would round up the crowd with cries of "Who'll take a glove?", "Bowl my man over in three rounds and I'll give you a fiver!" or "Come and do a round or two for a pound or two!" To add to the theatre, boxers were given names such as "The Black Bomber", or "The Birdsville Mauler". The gathered throng would be taken in by the performance and willingly come forward to part with a few shillings entrance fee. Each fight went for three rounds of three minutes which had often been choreographed and rehearsed by the boxers with their wily show man. As a regular patron of these tents, I witnessed this myself at the Bendigo Show when I saw a boxer swing a roundhouse uppercut haymaker at another to land smack on his testicles causing the receiver of the blow, who had protected his vital parts with both gloves, to jump close to three feet in the air!

Gravel Hill was a tough school and after seeing me come home once too often with a black eye or a blood nose, which for some reason caused my father great amusement, Danny took a shine to me and decided to teach me the rudiments of how to box. Having bought me a pair of boxing gloves he would kneel in front of me to approximate our eye contact level and tell me to punch as hard as I could. I rarely hit him as he blocked everything I threw, but every now and then he would stop me and explain what I was doing wrong and what I should do to fight better. He counselled me not to close my eyes if I saw a punch heading for my face, to hold my head up and never to duck it, which would simply be an invitation to my opponent to lay me out with an uppercut. I should swerve, or bob left, right or back to avoid punches with head up, gloves up, elbows in and eyes open at all times. If I landed a good punch I was to make sure I always followed up quickly with another good one. Having learned the theoretical basics, I was pleased that on several occasions, before I retired from the art of pugilism, I had the opportunity to lay out kids bent on the intent of doing just that to me. I remember one kid in particular that I planted with a sizeable 'shiner' that took weeks to go away. Unfortunately, Danny only taught me boxing according to the Marquis of Queensbury rules and alas, in the end I was to meet my 'Waterloo'.

For years my father had rejected all pleas to buy me a dog. He said that the hotel situated in the middle of Bendigo was unsuitable for a dog. That the backyard could not be fenced to keep it in. That it would be run over by patrons who park their cars in the yard, urinate on their tyres and defecate everywhere. That it would wander off and get lost and that it might bite people or bark at night and keep guests awake. That it would probably infect me and my sister with horrible diseases and complaints such as hydatids and worms, and deposit fleas in the hotel. Danny thought that none of these objections was sufficient to warrant my father's refusal and at the risk of incurring his wrath turned up one day with the most beautiful little fully pedigreed, black-and-white Cocker Spaniel puppy in a cardboard box which he gave to me.

I called him 'Dusty', and we were inseparable. Right from the start I admitted him to the hotel interior where he was eventually accepted by my parents and staff. We did get into serious trouble though on one occasion when I invited him to join me in the bath tub of one of the upstairs bathrooms. Cocker Spaniels are water dogs and he was having a ball jumping in and out of the tub with water splashing all over the place until eventually it leaked through the ceiling into the kitchen below resulting in a joint investigation by my parents to discover the source. We both got a belting, causing Dusty to shoot out the door dripping water everywhere as he ran down the passage followed by me in hot pursuit crying and wearing nothing except several red marks on my butt from a wire coat hanger wielded by my mother. Dusty never wandered off, soon got to know the time that I returned each afternoon from school and each day would wait outside the front of the hotel on the footpath until I arrived.

17. Young Mickey and Dusty.

Dusty was truly a good-looking dog. I had been a regular attender at the Bendigo Agricultural Show held each year in the grounds opposite the Bendigo Gaol in Park Road and was familiar with the dog show event. Danny and several other people at the hotel suggested that I should put Dusty in the show, assuring me that he was bound to win some sort of a prize. I was aged around nine at the time and lacking the offer of any assistance I managed to find and go to the Agricultural Society office, complete the required application and pay the necessary fee all on my own.

On judgement day I rose early and groomed Dusty within an inch of his life. Reaching the dog pavilion with Dusty in tow I found that most of the exhibitors had already arrived and tied their dogs into the numbered partitioned stalls. With the help of some fellow dog owners, I eventually found Dusty's stall where I tethered him securely, having first made sure that he had water and something to chew on. I then wandered off to look at all the other attractions at the show.

There was lots to see and I wanted to make sure I saw it all: from pigeons and poultry to horses, pigs, sheep, cats, budgerigars and canaries. In sideshow alley alone there were enough attractions to keep a young boy busy for hours. With money in my pocket earned from hotel chores I could ride the 'Octopus', see the Snake Pit, go into the Haunted House, have a ride on the Ghost Train, pop a few ping-pong balls into the smiling mouths of oscillating clown heads, and maybe even get into Jimmy Sharman's boxing tent. There were also wood chopping competitions where men, dressed in white singlets and pants hacked away with great speed at blocks of wood, other arena events and machinery displays. I knew Dusty was safe and felt sure that when I returned to collect him, he would have been awarded a prize. When I did return several people asked me where I had been and why I had not been there when the call came for me to parade Dusty with the other cocker spaniels on the judging ground. The judging was now over and Dusty had missed out because I had let him down. I had no idea that it was necessary for owners to parade their dogs to be judged. Everyone at the hotel had assured me that Dusty would win a prize of some sort. It was a long walk home with Dusty from the showgrounds to The Crown where I had to face Danny, my father and grandfather. I cried all the way.

My father turned out to be right in the end. Dusty was run over by the car of a hotel patron in the backyard. I had never before lost anything that I loved so much. The patron was a regular customer whose name I remember to this day. It's strange that I do not remember what happened to Danny Morrison. One day he was just not there. I had to get used to losing people who had played an important part in my upbringing and understand that I could not trust them to always be there.

Chapter 17

WIRELESS DRAMA

Every Saturday morning local radio station 3BO produced a live kids show sponsored by BCX soft drinks. BCX was a brand name of Bendigo Cordial Extracts. I was a regular attender joining an audience of kids in ages that ranged from mid primary school to mid high school. It was a popular show with maybe 30 or 50 of us standing up and jammed into a small upstairs studio in Pall Mall with radio announcers Russ Pilley and Dick Turner, also standing, conducting the proceedings.

Each show began with the whole audience singing:

Here we are again
Happy as can be
All good friends
And jolly good company
Never mind the weather
Never mind the rain

So long as we are together
Up she goes again
La di da dee da
La di da dee dee
All good friends
And jolly good company!

There followed various quizzes and competitions with complimentary bottles of BCX soft drinks handed out as prizes and then more songs. Children were allowed to give "Cheerios" over the radio to their parents or siblings and birthday calls would be made by radio announcers who had been tipped off by parents with 'Happy Birthday' sung if the birthday person was present in the studio. At the end of the show 'Here We Are Again' was sung once more and nearly every child left the studio with a free bottle of soft drink. It was corny but it was great community radio and the kids loved it. I was picked to give a cheerio to my parents in which I mentioned that The Crown Hotel had the best beer in Bendigo. They never picked me again.

18. Advertisement for 'Orange Sip' and an old valve radio, circa 1950s.

With no TV, the radio was the main source of entertainment. Radio drama in particular reached its zenith on old valve radios which we still called 'the wireless' until the early 1960s. As a child I was completely taken in by the soft tones of a story teller's voice or the banshee like screams of an actor coming from the speaker of a big old valve wireless. My imagination took me right into the scene of the story so it became totally believable. Most parents had control over the tuning knobs of the wireless. Mine were too busy for that. Zel and I had access to two radios, an old Phillips bakelite valve mantle radio in 'the little room' and a small AWA valve radio in our bedroom area. The programs we received were great entertainment to us as young children after school and while we were supposed to be asleep in bed when our parents were downstairs. Neither parent had a clue about what we were tuning into so we were never handicapped by their disapproval of programs.

One of our favourite after-school shows was *The Air Adventures of Biggles* which ran from 1949 until 1954, clocking up 970 episodes. Biggles was a heroic British pilot with a gentleman's demeanour who flew Super Marine Spitfires in World War II and was Commanding Officer of 666 Squadron, RAF, that fought in the Battle of Britain. Popular supporting characters included Algy who adopted the role of Biggles' second in command, Ginger with red hair as his close friend and Bertie, an eccentric former racing driver, who always wore a monocle and flew with a hunting horn. When the episode finished, the commercial break gave us an opportunity to quickly grab another lemonade from the bar and a handful of biscuits from the kitchen before settling into *The Adventures of Smoky Dawson* which during the 1950s ran for eight years. The show was a program of Australiana based on Smokey's outback travels and his skill with whips, ropes, knives, repertoire of folksongs and horsemanship with his much-loved Flash. Broadcast on 69 stations the show featured the adventures of Smoky with his faithful sidekick Jingles and their young friend Billy, fighting the evil outlaw Grogan according to Smoky's Code of the West. It was peppered with songs from Smoky, his moral homilies, sound effects from Smoky and adds for Kellogg's Cornflakes.

The best radio dramas came on at night when Zel and I were supposed to be in bed asleep and our parents were downstairs drinking in the locked-up bar. After the close of trade each day the bar staff, at the end of cleaning up, usually stayed on for a drinking session with my father. They were joined by my mother when the kitchen staff and waitresses left around 7:30 p.m. The reception office was left unattended but a bell, which rang in the bar, could be pressed to summon service. We were instructed to go to bed. Drawn by the prospect of listening to the radio, we usually did. There was seldom any supervised tuck in to bed or good night bedtime kisses from our parents.

The show that Zel and I loved and hated was called *The Inner Sanctum*. A spine-chilling thriller dealing with the supernatural, the program began with an invitation to gather around the wireless alone, turn out the lights and listen. It began with the sound of a creaking door, which had to be the lid of a coffin opening, and was punctuated with haunting organ music and other creepy audio effects. Like most of the good shows it played at 9 p.m. when we were supposed to be asleep. We often hid under the blankets to listen as most times it frightened us almost numb with fear. Several times Zel turned it off because she couldn't stand it anymore resulting in an argument between us. I usually won and turned it back on again as I jumped back under the blankets.

Another favourite was *Dossier on Dumetrius*. A gripping and highly addictive spy serial about an international criminal known as Dumetrius who escaped from occupied Berlin to London where MI5 discovered that he had murdered an officer in Berlin. The 104-part epic, chock-full of foreign intrigue, action and suspense, followed Dumetrius as he sought to kill anyone who could incriminate him while he pursued his quest to locate £1 million of stolen Nazi loot. An unforgettable scene in the show depicted one of the characters, found hanging from a light pole in London's dockland fog, being pulled down and used as a shield against gunfire. Regarded as an outstanding serial it was described as "possibly the finest suspense thriller ever heard on Australian radio".

D24 was a series based on fact, drawn from the files of the Victoria Police force and named after its communications department *D24*. It was an authentic program that worked closely with the police to tell their personal stories and follow the way they worked, spoke and acted, but highlighted only the positive side of police life. Scripts had to be checked and approved by police before going to air with the explanation that "names, place names and dates have been changed to protect the innocent".

Victorians loved it and the series ran for 10 years. Each episode was introduced with the words:

> *From the files of the Victoria Police Department, for the first time, come these true stories of unceasing war against crime. Of day and night vigilance that protects our life and our property and the nerve centre that is the police information bureau—D24.*

A program called 'The Strangler' caused listeners to angrily complain about the "horror and sadistic violence" it contained. A magistrate in the Children's Court described the episode as "disturbing, alarming and detrimental to children". Zel and I had almost certainly heard it as we rarely missed an episode. The producers responded by saying that: "It was a fine piece of radio, with a very strong lesson for children and parents." I don't recall any of these programs teaching us a lesson. I do recall being scared stiff and hiding under the blankets again. I am sure though that somewhere out of the radio came some of the ideas that moulded our values and ambitions.

Nightbeat was an Australian version of a very popular US radio program of the same name with the same theme music and introduction. Each episode began with the words "Hi there … This is Randy Stone … I cover the night beat for *The Daily*. Stories start in many different ways—this one began …" Along with *D2* and *The Inner Sanctum* the program became one of the most successful self-contained radio series produced. Randy was a laconic, tough, streetwise reporter who worked the night beat reporting on human interest stories where he encountered criminals, eccentrics, the down and out, distressed children, the police, and troubled souls. The stories he reported on were occasionally humorous or sentimental but mostly full of scary suspense, crime, thriller themes and emotion. Each episode ended with Randy at his desk with the sound of his typewriter clicking away till it stopped and he shouted "Copy boy!" To call the junior messenger to deliver his story to the editor. Zel and I loved the program.

Sunday night radio was boring as it defaulted to mainly religious programs. The most entertaining of these was Herbert W Armstrong's *The World Tomorrow* an evangelistic religious propaganda program that became very popular. At times it verged on the hysterical and presented like a lunatic fringe religious sect. Zel and I often listened to it. After the national anthem 'God Save The King/Queen', transmission closed each night at 11 p.m.

Radio serials remained popular in Bendigo well into the 1960s because poor television reception and its high costs, due to complicated aerial arrangements, meant TV had lesser impact on radio than in metropolitan Melbourne. Even when Bendigo got its own television station in 1961 the expensive sets and antennas kept the medium out of reach for many people. Eventually, all the serials were designated as "old-time radio" and disappeared to be replaced by popular music and talk back.

Chapter 18

THE QUEEN, MURDER AND CUBS

On 2 June 1953, the Coronation of Queen Elizabeth II took place at Westminster Abbey, London. A documentary feature film of the event, *A Queen is Crowned* narrated by Laurence Olivier, was screened around the world and nominated for an Academy Award. It was one of the many movies I saw that year at the age of nine. My recollection is that I got more enjoyment out of *Calamity Jane* starring Doris Day and *Roman Holiday* featuring Gregory Peck and Audrey Hepburn.

After the war, the British monarchy was more popular than ever. At the time of the Queen's visit in early 1954 there had been no royal visits to Australia for more than 20 years and the visit of Queen Elizabeth II was the first ever of a reigning monarch. Her arrival was seen as a profound moment in our history. A million people had lined the streets of Melbourne for the first royal parade with the tumultuous cheering of the crowd described as "like the roaring of the sea".

For Reg Beck, the proprietor of The Crown Hotel in Bendigo, nothing could be more important in the months leading to the Queen's visit than to make sure he put on "a good show". With the monarchy at the peak of its popularity it was a perfect opportunity to advertise The Crown Hotel. Reg was certain that the royal procession for Her Majesty would proceed straight up Hargreaves Street past The Crown and continue on through what is now the Hargreaves Mall. After the coronation he had hung a large framed portrait of Queen Elizabeth II over the faux feature fireplace in the dining room. On the front of the hotel, he now tied large alternating Union Jack and Australian flags on each of the veranda posts and between each post covered the entire veranda in red, white and blue material of bunting scallops with large red, white and blue rosettes in the middle of each scallop. He was sure Her Majesty would be pleased. The balcony of The Crown would be the place to be on the day of the royal visit.

In anticipation of the huge crowd, Bendigo Council asked people living on the route of the royal progress if they would allow the public to come in and use their toilet on the big day.

On 5 March along the processional route, which unfortunately did not go past The Crown, the adoring crowd was estimated to be 100,000. An almost unbelievable figure given that the entire population of Bendigo and district was only around 37,000. Rural families had travelled long distances from all over Victoria to attend the event, some 2000 coming by train. It was later estimated that of Australia's population of nine million, seven million people had managed to see the royal visit personally. They waved their red, white and blue flags and other paraphernalia at the royal couple as they flashed by on their way to the Upper Reserve where I and the other kids from Gravel Hill, spellbound from the prevailing excitement, had been waiting and waiting in the hot sun with all the other 9,000 kids who had been bussed into Bendigo from schools all over central Victoria. Eventually they appeared standing up in a Land Rover that threaded its way through the throngs of children, marshalled together yelling "Hooray", waving more red, white and blue flags and jumping up and down at the same time. I managed to get a clear view of them for not more than a few seconds.

19. "LONG LIVE OUR QUEEN", Bendigo fountain, 1954.
Photo by Allan Doney, National Trust of Victoria, Bendigo Branch.

Since then, no visit of an international dignitary, pop star, sporting team or anything else has come close to the popular impact of the 1954 Royal Visit. A central component of the school curriculum in the 1950s was the acquisition of respect and knowledge for the constitutional monarchy and teachers saw it as their duty to ensure that their pupils saw the Queen and understood who she was. We were taught about the accoutrements of royalty and had to learn about the orb and sceptre and the mace and different crowns. The Upper Reserve, where a total of 50 to 60,000 people had gathered that day, was given the more prestigious title of The Queen Elizabeth Oval.

My father made the most of the Queen's visit by placing advertisements in *The Bendigo Advertiser* stating that Beck's Crown Hotel in Hargreaves Street welcomed Her Majesty and Prince Phillip and celebrated their visit to the City of Bendigo. Everyone was invited to visit The Crown Hotel and raise a glass to toast the Royal Couple. After the procession had passed, spectators piled into every bar, lounge and parlour of the hotel.

Precisely one month later on 6 April 1954, under the headline "Bendigo Murder", the Bendigo and Melbourne newspapers reported the story of a Mrs Beck of Hargreaves Street, Bendigo, who had been arrested by police for the murder of her husband with an axe. The same surname and same residential street led people to wonder whether the licensee of Beck's Crown Hotel had been done in by his wife. Whether in fact my mother had chopped my father up with an axe? It had only been a month since there was a run of newspaper advertisements in *The Bendigo Advertiser* by Beck's Crown Hotel, Hargreaves Street supporting the Royal Visit. There followed some very strange and awkward telephone calls enquiring when my mother answered if she had killed Reg? I can only imagine what her answer might have been. And, when my father answered, the caller expressing surprise, and relief, that he was still alive, and, when I answered, not knowing what to say to me. When I went to school, kids asked me if it was true that my mother had killed my father with an axe and the teacher, Mr Burke, was most unusually kind and supportive.

The full details revealed that the victim was Ivan Edward Beck, 30, quarry worker who was found battered to death in bed at his home, a small weatherboard house, in Hargreaves Street.

The accused, Dorothy Beck, 31 year-old mother of four, subsequently pleaded not guilty to murder saying that she had hit her husband with the back end of the axe while he was asleep in bed because he had assaulted her and threatened to cut her throat. After a short three hour retirement, the jury, obviously impressed by her testimony, found her not guilty of murder but guilty of manslaughter. His Honour, Mr Justice Barry, was apparently equally impressed as he only gave her five years jail.

I was attracted to the junior scout group, Cubs, by the uniform. I had recently seen so many uniforms in newsreels and movies with the Queen's Coronation, her Australian visit and the Korean War. I thought I looked important with the woggle that held my distinctive green and red scarf, special sock tops, and the cap with gold stars plus the insignia and badges you could collect to go on your shirt. I became the commander of a cub-pack gropup of six with the title of 'Sixer' that entitled me to wear two stripes and issue orders to the other five members of the group. The head of our cub group was Miss 'Akela' and we were based at the 4th YMCA Scout Group in Mundy Street. I looked forward to the weekly Tuesday after school meeting that involved games, storytelling and our chanted promise to Akela that "Akela, we'll do our best, etc," after which we would salute. The environment engendered positive self-esteem with a code of conduct that we should serve God, act in consideration for the needs of others and do our best not only for them but for ourselves in the development and use of our abilities. It was good stuff for me and my self-image, providing me with valuable alternative experience outside of school and the hotel surroundings.

Every year Cub groups participated in a fundraiser called 'Bob a Job' which encourage the kids to door knock the streets to offer to do jobs for a shilling. Money raised was handed into the local cub group and a competition held to see who would raise the biggest sum. Jobs varied greatly. A shilling was good payment for a small task such as sweeping the veranda but hardly enough if you were put to work chopping a pile of wood. Weeding the garden, cleaning windows or even hanging out the wash were common tasks. Basic painting jobs like oiling the fence with sump oil or painting a shed or chook house with whitewash usually paid better money. It was good education for the kids who learnt that some people were more generous than others and some jobs easier than others. I recall my toughest job involved chipping grass with a shovel in a huge backyard which took most of the day. I finished up with serious blisters on my hands but with a pocket full of 'real money'.

In 1956, at the age of 11 years, I went on a day trip with the Cubs to the Pan Pacific Scout Jamboree at Clifton Park, Victoria. The jamboree drew in 17,000 scouts from 53 countries to live collectively for two weeks in hundreds of tents erected for specified and dedicated purposes. I had never seen so many different races of people before in my life. Led by Akela, our little group of cubs from 4th Bendigo wandered in complete astonishment through the amazing complex of canvas and other buildings built by scouts from diverse countries, all displaying their national flag and many erected with branches of Australian gum trees obtained from the adjacent bush. The scouts had lashed together twigs and branches to form all sorts of endlessly useful items like shoe racks, dish drainers, stools, benches, tables and elaborate ornamental gateways.

I was amazed at the public toilet which was simply a long trench dug into the ground surrounded by a hessian enclosure. Seating was provided by a system of planks over the trench with toilet rolls tied at equidistant spaces along the planks to designate the space where you could sit. There was no roof, so if it rained you got wet and I recall that it did as there was a great deal of mud throughout the entire jamboree park. It was a 'privy' in name only as privacy was totally lacking. The advantage was that you could easily strike up a conversation with your neighbour as you sat on the planks emptying your bowels over the long drop. I imagined the scouts at morning peak hour yelling out "bombs away" at the point of critical release.

I think the reason that I was conscripted into joining the Saturday morning YMCA junior athletics group was due to the fact that the head of the local YMCA, Tom Tweed, was a customer at The Crown and a friend of my father who I believe thought that it might provide some extra external discipline and structure in my life. Dressed in white shorts, singlet and sand shoes we met on the lawn opposite the old YMCA in Mundy Street where we engaged in calisthenics, leapfrog, tumbling, running games, wrestling and playing rounders and tunnel ball. Upon reflection it was a bit like a replay of the Hitler youth movement, but I enjoyed it at the time, at least for a while. I didn't enjoy the YMCA camps at Axedale where we had to sleep on straw palliasse mattresses which caused me to suffer serious hay-fever and a wheezy chest.

Chapter 19

COOKS AND STAFF

The relationship between the hotel proprietors, my mother and father, with the staff was never one of strictly master and servant. It was, if push came to shove, but I recall numerous examples of deep attachment, loyalty and mutual respect between the employees and my parents. A line of command essential for smooth management and discipline required my father to be in charge of the bar staff and my mother the kitchen and house staff. In the kitchen, the cook assumed dictatorial powers over the kitchen maids and waitresses and, in the bar, the full-time barman was the overseer. There were no full-time night staff but a contract nightwatchman, by the name of Frank Roach, called in each night to check the premises and stoke the kitchen fire.

Frank was a portly, jolly soul with a strong Irish accent who always had a pocket full of peppermint sweets that he offered to anyone he met as he walked the central business district of Bendigo with an ancient bicycle that he pushed more than he rode.

The bicycle was equipped with a kerosene lantern that was bolted onto the right-hand side of the front axle. Back then, batteries were much weaker and short-lived and lights on a bike were generally operated via a dynamo wheel that turned when pressed onto a tyre so that they only worked when the bike was moving quickly. The kero light worked all the time so that at night miscreants could always see Frank, even when walking and wheeling his bike, and could clear out before he arrived. An outcome that I think Frank much preferred. He regularly patrolled shops in the central business district at night, checking that doors were locked and slipping his calling card under the door as proof of his attendance.

At The Crown Frank had a key to the kitchen door and open access to tea and refreshments when he called. On one visit he found the lights on well past midnight and burst into the premises with his 38-revolver drawn to discover me studying for my end of year exam. Over a cup of coffee, I begged him to show me his gun, which he eventually agreed to do after removing the bullets. I discovered it had a broken firing pin rendering it useless as a weapon. He had never attempted to fire it in all the years that he had it. I don't think he had even pointed it at anyone except me and I doubt that he ever repaired the firing mechanism.

Frank was probably one of Australia's last 'lamp lighters'. Originally an occupation involving the igniting of gas streetlights, it was, by Frank's time, confined to electrical switches. Shops that had illuminated street signs or windows commonly had the manual switch to turn them on and off positioned high above the doorway and could only be operated by someone with a hook on a long stick. This was Frank's job at dusk and dawn. He was a highly recognisable figure as he shuffled between shops dressed in his heavy overcoat, felt hat and bicycle-clipped pants, holding his long light stick and pushing his old kero-lit bike.

Hotel cooks, sometimes known as 'dough bangers' but never as chefs, came in many classes, shapes and sizes and went away just as often. One, a wizened faced undersized character, was an ex-jockey with a below the knee wooden leg into which he had carved a cavity where he kept his money. It seemed to irritate him after he had it on for a while as when he went to the bar for a drink during his afternoon break, he often took it off and put it on the counter. On the job in the kitchen, he was always slipping in and out of the pantry to check on something or other. When he finally left, we discovered hidden behind the vegetable racks a huge stash of empty hip flask bottles for nearly every kind of alcoholic spirit.

Another cook, Mrs Higginbotham, had 21 children. Apparently, there were several sets of twins. Her husband was an invalid pensioner who walked around with a constant look of surprise on his face. They all lived in a humble mudbrick cottage with basic additional outbuildings close by. Sometime after she left The Crown, a fire went through and burnt the place down. The people of Bendigo then raised funds to build a new house for them.

Then there was Mary, a devout Catholic who seldom smiled and attended church each morning before work at 7 a.m. She was a conscientious worker who spent much of the time during the day praising and thanking God and condemning the conduct of other staff sinners and myself who I think she thought was the Devil incarnate. She was not happy in the hotel environment and didn't last long.

One of my favourite cooks was Hoppy Hopgood. She was a big buxom middle-aged lady with a red face and constant energy and joviality. She introduced me to such culinary delights as bread fried in mutton fat sprinkled with salt-and-pepper, which became a standard order of mine when I came home from school. She and her husband both loved the bush and fishing and, after my constant pleading, she eventually managed to get her husband, with my father's approval, to take me on a fishing trip to the Loddon River at Bridgewater. We came home with a bag of small redfin and the trip was so successful that Mr Hopgood invited me to join him on a trip to the Edwards River in New South Wales. We travelled there in his little Singer utility with his tiny flat bottomed galvanised iron punt shoved in the back. Much of the road was hardly more than a single strip of bitumen at best and whenever an oncoming vehicle came towards us, we had to veer to the left with two wheels on the dirt and two wheels on the bitumen. The problem with the Singer was that it had a very much delayed reaction after you turned the steering wheel. For a few seconds nothing happened leaving you with a feeling that you were about to have a head on collision and then suddenly it would whip over to the left. This was a disconcerting experience with Mr Hopgood yelling at the Singer, "Come over you bitch! Come over you bitch!" Due to a combination of his exhortations and luck we arrived safely.

After a day's fishing we finished up with a fabulous catch of redfin, yellow belly and bream that we kept in a creel in the river until the end of the day. After cleaning the fish and feeding their entrails to a family of water rats that gathered around, we then strung all the fish on a single wire between two trees. Mr Hopgood explained that it was going to be a frosty night and that as he had no icebox this would be the best way of keeping the fish. When I enquired about putting up the tent, he had brought with him he said that we would just lay it on the ground and sleep between the canvas. Next morning the fish on the wire were frozen stiff as a board and so was I. It was the coldest night I have spent in my life.

Tommy Thomson was a heavyweight ex-navy cook with arms covered in tattoos. He had a big pot belly, light grey dishevelled balding hair and a puffy face with disorderly teeth and bloodshot eyes. He had little interest in sophisticated cooking but had made a fair study during his lifetime of drinking heavily. Each morning, after breakfast was over, he lined up at the bar at 10 a.m. for morning 'tea' comprising his first pot of beer for the day. As soon as lunch was over and the kitchen sorted, he would head for a stool in the bar where he remained for as long as he could before he had to return to organise the evening meal. Always a happy inebriate you knew he was really drunk when he started to sing 'Popeye The Sailor Man', singing "I am what I am and that's all that I am, I'm Popeye the sailor man!"

Tommy had many faults, was a rough cook, smoked prodigiously while stirring, kneading or carving so that remnants of tobacco ash fell into the food as a matter of course, but was a likeable person. My father enjoyed his company and claimed that he made the best scones he had ever tasted. My mother, on the other hand, was less impressed with his unrefined and artless skills. She had sacked him several times for various culinary indiscretions and each time she did he would plead to my father to be reinstated who, in these instances, acted as a Court of Appeal. On the night of Tommy's final dismissal, the dining room was full of guests and the kitchen in full flight. One of the several meat choices on the menu that night was corned beef, and as Tommy began to carve it, he broke out into a chorus of 'Popeye The Sailor Man' as he swayed and wobbled over the kitchen bench, carving knife in hand. As the slices came off half inch thick at a time, the corned beef spun off the carving board and landed on the floor. My mother shrieked with horror, and Tommy, undeterred, picked up the beef, plonked it back on the bench, and continued to carve. About three slices later the beef again hit the floor. "Bloody hell with the thing!" he said as he chased it around the floor trying to pick it up. Finally retrieving it to the bench and continuing to carve, the inevitable happened once more. For the third time he again lost his grip with the meat spinning onto the floor. "Oh, bugger it then!" he said, as he got down on the floor with the corned beef and started to carve it there. Within about 10 seconds of that Tommy was defrocked of his apron and out the back door. A subsequent appeal to my father for reinstatement failed. On finding out the gravity of the offence, he had to say, "Sorry Tommy, you've done your dash this time."

Many of the staff were very good to me and my sister, sometimes assuming de-facto parental care, responsibility and direction for us in the absence of the physical presence of our parents who were no doubt in the building somewhere but not currently with us. Employees who took us under their wing and took a caring interest in our welfare provided a degree of emotional security and made a significant contribution to our upbringing, instilling principles such as civility and politeness to everyone at all times and always to say "please" and "thank you". I often found myself in league with them if they had caught me being naughty but said, "Don't worry I won't tell on you." I also learned a lot through talking to staff from their down-to-earth humour and wisdom. Sometimes kitchen staff, who I got to know well, invited me back to their place during their afternoon break or at weekends. There was little Sally Sullivan with thick lensed spectacles who had talking pet galahs, Mrs Boyd (known as 'Boydie') who had ducks and geese and got me to crawl under her house to hook out unhatched duck eggs that had gone off, and Mabel Burke.

Mabel started as a kitchen maid at the hotel and then became the cook but was much more than that to me. She became one of my de-facto mothers and an important one. A medium built plump and cheerful lady with a bespectacled round rosy face, she giggled and laughed her way through life. Nothing was too much trouble for Mabel and she never had a bad word to say about anyone. Always positive in outlook and with an answer to all problems she was above all else a person of great strength. Each weekday she rode her very basic pushbike seven miles (11.26 kilometres) from Huntly to Bendigo at 7 a.m. in the morning to work at The Crown and then back home again after 7 p.m. when the hotel evening meal had finished. This she did in the dark in winter and on Bendigo's famously frosty winter mornings. She had weekends off and, when returning on Mondays, would often be sporting a black eye received from husband Tom who was a dreadful drunk. He worked at the Country Roads Board during the week coming home on weekends to drink constantly.

With my parents' consent, Mabel often invited me to her house on weekends. My presence there may have helped to curb Tom's aggressiveness. The house on several acres was a time capsule from the past and I loved going there. There was no electricity and no plumbing. An old valve console radio ran on a 12 volt car battery until it went flat and then had to be taken to the 'Independent Garage' at Huntly to be charged. Any water used had to be drawn from tanks collecting rain from the roof. The toilet was a dunny can some considerable distance away from the house. Kerosene lamps provided the only lighting including a hurricane lamp to go to the toilet at night. The tin bath in the bathroom was seldom used as it had to be filled with buckets from the tank and hot water boiled on a wood stove. The inside of the house was lined with wallpaper over hessian that on a windy day bellowed in and out. Tom kept a draught horse and a cow. The horse he used to pull a single furrow plough to prepare the ground for tomatoes which he grew and hoped to sell. The cow supplied their milk and butter, which Mabel magically produced from the cream in a small wooden churn she turned by hand. There were ducks in a dam, chooks and peppercorn-trees, a dog and sparrows and bird nests and in all it was just a fantastical place for a hotel kid to be. On her tiny little black woodstove in a tiny little kitchen Mabel produced some great meals but I particularly loved the egg and bacon hot iron jaffles which were always on at breakfast.

Then, one day Mabel was no longer at The Crown. Yet another important person in my life had gone.

Chapter 20

SMOKY CITY

Gas was generated at the works in Bridge Street from black coal sourced in New South Wales and transported to Bendigo from Melbourne by rail. The process required the heating of coal in the absence of air in enclosed chambers called retorts at a temperature of over 1500°F. This vaporised or decomposed organic substances in the coal, driving off volatile products including coal gas, coal tar sulphur and water. The gas produced was then passed through a condenser to extract the 'tarry matters' and then a water 'scrubber' and 'purifiers' before being stored in a big gasometer in readiness for the distribution system. The cooked and purified coal produced a top-quality by-product fuel called 'coke'. The process created a dreadful stink that everyone agreed was Bendigo's worst industrial smell until the discovery of commercial natural gas in 1965 in Bass Strait signalled the end of the old gasworks.

In late autumn come winter, the sweet smell of boiling tomato pulp from Rosella, White Crow, Kia Ora and other canneries producing nine million cans per annum of tomatoes, paste, soup and pulp, combined with the gasworks stench together with smoke and particulate pollution from backyard incinerators and heaps of burning autumn leaves smouldering in street gutters. Rubbish was something to incinerate if you could and if you couldn't you gave it to the council who would then try to burn it at the tip. An incinerator in the backyard was fun and functional. Everyone had one and given enough accelerant they could pretty much burn anything. This malodorous mix was then further augmented by multiple domestic wood fires, many burning low-grade coal in the form of briquettes.

The Crown ran five briquette heaters to warm the bars and lounges. Household technology was still rudimentary with wood-burning stoves common as were wood-heated coppers in lieu of washing machines. Many bathrooms still had woodfired chip heaters to supply hot water and the whole country continued to run on coal-fired steam locomotives pumping out smoke and carbon until the last of them retired in the 1960s. Cars using lead-based petrol pushed out far more smoke and particulate per vehicle than today and nearly everyone smoked cigarettes, pipes or cigars.

During autumn and winter in particular Bendigo was 'Smoky City'. It was particularly noticeable on cold and frosty calm nights when visibility was sometimes reduced and made much worse if there was any fog in the mix. The most gut-wrenching smells emanated from a street which the kids called 'Pong Road', known today as Beischer Street, East Bendigo. It was lined with pig farms and led to what was then known as the 'Blood and Bone Factory' which processed animal carcasses into fertiliser, and an animal hide tannery.

Sunday was incineration day at The Crown. In the backyard near the wood heap there was a large 44-gallon drum set on house bricks with holes punched in the side into which during the week all manner of burnable detritus was deposited. My job was to set fire to it and then once a month clean out the ash and shovel it into my dad's trailer with whatever other garbage I could find, which would then mean a trip to the tip. These regular excursions were often the only one-on-one times I would have with my dad most weeks and I greatly valued them. The tip was always an adventure with piles of smelly, flyblown refuse, cast off items that you might recycle, and rats. Lots of people who knew my dad would come up and want to talk to him every time we went there.

Once a year, a collective conflagration in the form of Bonfire Night contributed to Bendigo's air pollution. Planning often started months in advance. Officially the big night was 24 May, Queen Victoria's Birthday, also known as Empire Day and later Commonwealth Day. Guy Fawkes Night on 5 November was also celebrated but 24 May was more popular and, being in the wintertime, safer. Any kind of flammable material was piled up on the many available abandoned mining dumps and vacant house lots. Kids would go from house to house to ask if there was any old timber or rubbish that could be contributed to their bonfire.

It was a great opportunity for households to have an annual clean-up and all sorts of stuff from old mattresses, rubber tyres, sump oil and garden rubbish finished up on the bonfire. Parents aided and abetted their children by helping to build bonfires with rubbish from the household while the kids were at school. Sometimes the bonfire would grow magically overnight due to anonymous deposits by men with trailers. A schoolmate of mine had one of the best bonfires because his father was the manager of Beaurepair Tyre Service in Hargreaves Street and always donated a quantity of tyres to the heap. As the night got closer those who had better bonfire stacks were in danger of having their pile 'scragged' by kids conducting night-time raids to steal stuff for their own bonfire. This threat was taken seriously to the extent that some bonfire owners posted guards in attendance to well after dark. For several years, the Bendigo City Council conducted a large civic bonfire celebration that attracted substantial crowds but this was soon given up due to increasingly onerous health and safety regulations, insurance and legal issues.

In the lead up to the actual night, pocket money was used to purchase as many firecrackers as possible. There were no restrictions on their sale and they were available from many shops including small corner stores. The best place to go was the Chinese precinct in Bridge Street which by this time had been reduced to a row of brown, dingy buildings and seemed to be mostly deserted with boarded-up shopfronts and wonky verandas huddled together on the side of the street closest to the old showgrounds. It took a degree of bravery to go there as most kids had been warned away from that quarter by their parents. The shops were dark and had a strange smell of incense about them. One shop remaining open sold the cheapest and best firecrackers in Bendigo including huge sixpenny bungers that had the ability, when lit and placed under a metal bucket, to blow it high into the air. Saving your crackers for the big night was a problem as the temptation to fire them off before was overwhelming.

Fancy crackers included Roman Candles, Catherine Wheels, Jumping Jacks, Rockets and Flowerpots which squirted liquid fire in red green and orange. They were often unreliable and dangerous with many a blue paper wick just burning to its end and fizzling out only to suddenly fire off when someone approached for closer inspection. Tiny little poppers called Tom Thumbs tied together with a string cracked and popped all over the place when you lit them and were great for terrorising girls. Really serious and dangerous explosions could be created by tying a whole bunch of sixpenny bungers together to get one big boom. Penny bungers were chucked all over the place and you never knew one had landed behind you until too late. A good trick was to place a lit single bunger under an empty jam tin and then quietly disperse so that you were well out of sight by the time the tin exploded. You could frighten the begeezus out of a crowd of spectators by lighting a Catherine Wheel on the ground so that it took off out of control. All the kids loved sparklers, which were relatively safe to run around with and make sparkly patterns in the dark. Throw Downs which exploded when you threw them at the ground were more popular with the boys. Bonfire Night was still very much a community event where parents gathered to keep their eyes on the kids and the bonfires so that sometimes neighbours met each other for the first time. As the night wore on and the flames went down potatoes were produced to roast in the coals.

Although exciting, the night was a dangerous place to be with its dirty smelly smoke, searing heat windblown sparks and crackers going off all over the place. It was a nightmare for the local fire brigades which remained on alert for escaping flames and ambulance drivers standing by to treat burns. Of course, accidents happened. Skyrockets in particular had the capacity to create fire a considerable distance away from where they were lit when they lobbed into dry grass or other flammable material.

There was no limit to the stupidity of some kids when it came to the dangers of dealing with crackers. Some used them to blow up letterboxes—but I never did. Instead, I built a cracker gun from a short length of galvanised pipe with a screw thread on one end. A large bunger was inserted with its wick dangling out the thread end eased through a small hole in a metal cap then screwed on the pipe. For a handle I used a piece of cut off old broom dowel that

I attached with a single screw to a metal hose clip, which in turn was wrapped around the pipe and tightened. With the cracker in the pipe, it was first tamped down with a newspaper wad, a missile inserted (usually a ball bearing or a glass marble) and tamped down again with another wad. Now, ready to fire, all you had to do was light the wick hanging out the back and point the barrel in the direction of your target as you held on to the old dowel handle. This was a fraught process. I found that while it had the ability to drive a ball bearing through a sheet of galvanised iron at some ten paces, its lack of accuracy meant that you were lucky to hit a target. After a while the broom handle loosened so that the barrel could rotate 360 degrees. I was firing my last shot in the air when the barrel swung around and pointed at my head. As I ducked the cracker went off and shot a missile into the ground behind me. It was not the only bullet I've had to dodge but I did give the idea away after that. I have mused, several times since, that if my reflexes had been less acute, whether the coronial finding would have been misadventure or suicide.

Chapter 21

THE BLACKSMITH

When my father bought the Crown Hotel in 1949, my grandfather, Alec Beck, moved in with us to reside in the humble accommodation of a former horse stable in the backyard converted into a small bedroom. The nearest toilet was nearly 20 metres away down the driveway and the hotel laundry or 'wash house', located in another former stable, was used for his personal shaving and washing needs. For a proper bath he had to go up the back staircase of the hotel to the first level bathrooms which he did once a week, on Saturdays, whether he needed it or not.

Alec Beck had been born in 1874 into a family of 11 children raised on the goldfields at Chewton, near Castlemaine, where his father was a miner. The house had dirt floors and he and his siblings didn't have proper shoes until they were around 13 years old. This he told me many times. When he was six years old the first telephone exchange in Australia opened in Melbourne in 1880 with 44 subscribers. Not until he was 79 years old, in 1953, did the number of subscribers reach one million. By 1981 there were five million. It is estimated that there are now at least that many broken or obsolete mobile phones lying in drawers throughout Australia.

Alec was a tall man, probably 5 feet 11 inches in the old measure, not overweight, and would have been strong and good-looking in his younger days. He only wore shirts equipped to take a hard stud collar that he invariably left off, even at times when he wore a tie, which did look really strange on his bare neck. Sleeves were always cut off just below the elbow. A vest with a gold pocket watch and chain plus a 1950s hearing aid were always an essential part of his attire. His deafness was a consequence of his occupation that involved the constant clang of a blacksmith's hammer shaping hot iron on the anvil. His stable bedroom suited him as it was right next to his workshop, in another converted stable, where he pursued his hobby of gunsmithing.

Although Alec couldn't read a word of music, he was an accomplished fiddle player with a substantial repertoire of Irish jigs and Scottish tunes, but never claimed to be a violinist. With a tin whistle he was proficient and could readily blow a fine tune and was also a competent oral whistler able to perform very acceptable renditions of his favourite tunes over a range of notes. Whistling today is far more functional. You might hail a taxi with it or call your dog back, but no longer is it used as a pure form of entertainment.

Grandfather Alec was the hotel fix it man if anything was broken. He could turn his hand to almost any repair, from broken chairs, and mop head and axe handle replacements to fixing a hole in worn out saucepans with a rivet plug. There was never a power tool to be seen in his workshop.

He derived his greatest enjoyment from renovating and tinkering with shot guns that he bought and sold. Old stocks were polished to a gleam, worn barrels sanded back on the ends and then re-blued/blackened until they looked new. If barrels were loose on the stock due to excessive wear, he tightened them up on the anvil with a solid whack or two on the connecting lug with a ball-peen hammer on the end of a large punch. He often called upon me to hold the barrels and lug square to the anvil's edge while he swung the hammer. Several times the police called to enquire whether he had a gun dealers licence to which his standard reply was he was not a dealer and that shot guns were just his hobby that he bought and sold in the constant quest to eventually find one that would fit and suit him perfectly. The police accepted his explanations. Gun laws were slack back then. He loved the game of buying and selling and clearly got a real kick out of getting the best deal which he always described as having "exchanged a black cat for a white monkey." When he died, he owned 21 shot guns including some outstanding examples such as a Purdy, several Greeners, Webley and Scott, Hollis, Merkel and Krupp. A special public auction was held just to sell his guns.

I called him 'Daddy Beck' and he called me 'Cocky' because he reckoned I was. On a daily basis I spent much more time with him than with my father who, if not in the hotel bar, was usually at his desk in the office. In the workshop with Daddy Beck, I learned skills that remain with me to this day. He taught me how to use hand tools properly, the basics of different metal qualities, and every now and then little shortcut work tricks that he called "wrinkles". He instilled in me the importance of having a good work ethic. He often said, "If a job is worth doing, Cocky, it's worth doing well."

Most meal times he joined my sister and I in the accurately named 'little room' where we ate and where he always drank his tea from a saucer. An enthusiastic tormentor rather than just a simple tease, he would offer to myself and my sister a lolly from his pocket or a piece of fruit from the table and, when we went to accept it, would withdraw his hand and place the item in his mouth and laugh. We fell for his trap many times. He also had the annoying habit of spreading the broadsheet newspapers that he was reading at the table (*The Argus* and *The Age*) so that it took up an inordinate amount of space. Resolving to get even with him, one day I struck a match at the bottom of the paper while he was reading. It went up with a woosh as I ran out the back door. He also had a habit of going to sleep in his chair at the table and always wore a hat when he dozed off. We carefully placed pieces of orange peel around the brim so that when he woke up, he was peeled upon.

Daddy Beck's turn to get even with me came on the day he first took me shooting. I was only 13 at the time and he had equipped me with a single barrel Harrington and Richards that had a well-deserved reputation as a kicker, loaded with a 12-gauge overpowered shell. The first shot I fired at a flock of crows knocked me over flat on my back where, according to Daddy Beck, I was joined by the crow I had hit that had "folded up like a book". He dined out on that story, retelling it for the rest of his life, but the experience put me off shot guns forever.

Daddy Beck was a highly accomplished player of draughts (or checkers) having honed his skills in the game when he was the licensee of the Imperial Hotel in Castlemaine. There, he challenged customers on a daily basis to play for a free beer or one double the current price if they lost. They mostly lost but so too did he as when he engaged in a game, he ignored serving other customers to his financial detriment and the utter despair of his wife and my father. He undertook the job of teaching me how to play which consisted of beating me in every game week after week until in the end I picked up the board halfway through a game and flung it and the draughts to the other side of the room. He just laughed and said, "Steady up Tiger!"—which was one of the nicknames he applied to me. He often told me to "steady up" or "not to go like a bull at a gate". My tantrum paid off as after that he took the time to explain winning moves to me and teach me properly. In the end there comes a time in the life of every boy that makes him want to beat his grandfather outright. I finally achieved that as I got older and so did he.

20. Grandfather Alec Beck, known as 'Daddy Beck', the Blacksmith.

The Blacksmith had many stories to tell of his younger days. Stories of how, when he was a boy, he and his mates put tobacco juice from a smoker's pipe on frogs' tongues to watch them die and how they would put two cats in separate sacks tied at the top and then sling them over a clothes line to watch them fight through the hessian. He showed me the lead shot that he still had in the back of his hand from receiving a shot gun blast from the owner of a cherry orchard where he had been thieving fruit. He told me how he, as a kid with his mates, tormented the Chinese miners, boasting that they would hide and wait until they saw a 'China man' coming along with two full baskets hanging at either end of a yoke and then run out and grab the baskets to spin them in a circle resulting in the poor man winding down to the ground with his goods in a heap. Then, of course, they would run. Other times they would hide in the bushes along the creek and wait with their catapults until they saw a Chinese man returning to his dwelling with a bottle of gin dangling from a string in his hand that they would then fire stones at to break.

As a blacksmith he also bought and sold horses. He told me of one in particular that he had sold to a doctor for his wife and daughters to use in the family gig, a simple one-horse two-wheel self-drive vehicle. After six months the doctor returned the horse complaining that it had developed a habit of 'jibbing' or simply refusing to go and that it had been spoiled by his wife and daughters with sugar and carrot treats and too much affection and not enough discipline. He wanted to trade it in on another horse, so my grandfather said to leave it with him and he would send a message when he found a suitable replacement. The horse still had its shaggy winter coat on and the first thing that my grandfather did was give it a close clipping and trim its mane and tail. Then, harnessed in a gig, the re-education training began with an old chain in the foot well as a persuader. Every time the horse jibbed, a firm wrap on the rump with the chain got him going again.

After a week or two of training it was only a matter of rattling the chain with your foot when you said "Gee Up" and the horse took off without hesitation. A message was then sent to the doctor advising that a 'new' horse had been obtained that would prove to be very suitable to the ladies. After an inspection and trial run, the delighted doctor was thrilled to repurchase his 'new' horse. But, as the story goes, after six months had expired, he was back again with the horse complaining that his girls and wife had again spoiled the animal and he would like to trade it in again on yet another new one.

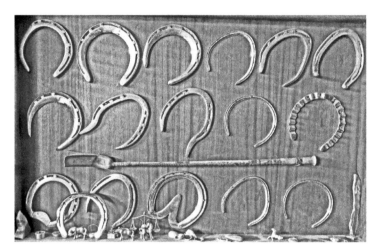

21. Grandfather Alec Beck's horseshoes.
First Prize at the Royal Melbourne Agricultural Show 1905,
"Best Display of Horseshoes".

Both my father and grandfather were crack shot shootists and regular competitors at the Bendigo Gun Club live bird shoots held at Epsom on Saturday. The previously trapped birds, including sparrows, starlings, pigeons or galahs, were placed in several boxes arranged in a semicircle about 20 yards or so from the gunner. When ready the shooter would yell "pull" and an operator would tug a cord to release one bird which, if shot, had to fall within a specified area or be deemed a lost shot. Dropped birds would then be retrieved by youths who ran out, picked them up and returned them to a collection area. At day's end shooters who had made kills of pigeons or galahs could collect them to take home for the cooking pot. My father won a silver cup for shooting "six sparrows straight" and my grandfather was awarded one for shooting "15 starlings straight". I still have the cups in my possession.

As a young spectator I went to the Bendigo Gun Club shoots with my father and grandfather on a number of occasions and at the end of the day was rewarded with the 'privilege' of assisting with the plucking and gutting of the shot pigeons and galahs in preparation for the hotel cooking pot. All birds were kept for family consumption and never included on the hotel menu. After cleaning and stuffing with breadcrumbs, herbs and onions they were roasted slowly in a saucepan with beef dripping and a few rashers of bacon for an hour or so and were delicious. But you had to be careful not to swallow or bite on any lead shot that had been lodged in the flesh. In 1956, when I was 12, Victoria was the last state in Australia to abolish live bird shooting.

Daddy Beck said I was the cheekiest boy in Bendigo, and later the cheekiest in Australia but finally promoted me to the cheekiest in the world, saying that no one could give more cheek than me. He said that I would never make good or be any good or come to anything and I was not "worth my salt". But he was the first person to buy me a wristwatch. It had the brand-name 'Lip', which he said suited me as I gave plenty of lip. I found out many years later that the watch was from a French company that in 1954 had 1,500 employees and made 300,000 watches a year. The one he gave me was a copy of a T18 model that had been gifted to Winston Churchill in 1948 by the French government in recognition of the services provided by Britain to France in World War II.

He spoke in a language that belonged to his time. When stating the road distance between two places he would often add his distance estimate of "as the crow flies" which was closer. It took 15 years, he said, to become a competent blacksmith and "know the ropes". And if I got the sulks he would say "Cat got your tongue?" As he got older and found tasks that had been easy for him to do as a young man but were now difficult for him, he would complain that he was "getting too long in the tooth" but used to be good at it when he was still "wet behind the ears". He gave me lots of advice, much of which I didn't understand at the time such as, "Buy straw hats in winter Cocky!" And "Keep your hat on" when I wasn't wearing one. I understood when he told me to "Cut out that tomfoolery". I disagreed with him when he said "You've got too much to say Cocky. Children should be seen and not heard!"

Chapter 22

HOUSEWORK AND RADIO HITS

It was impossible for my parents to keep tabs on me. While at any time I could walk out of the hotel and explore Bendigo, within the bounds of the hotel itself it was difficult to pinpoint my whereabouts with 34 rooms (24 upstairs and ten downstairs) plus the balcony, backyard, driveway and auxiliary nooks and crannies in service areas and outbuildings. I had to amuse myself as there were no other kids to play with apart from my sister who was 18 months older than me. Anyway, she was a girl and we shared few interests between us as growing children.

Annoying the staff or playing tricks on them was usually good fun and they seldom complained. The upstairs housemaids were easy targets. It was the practice to send the hotel linen to the Good Shepherd Laundry run by the nuns at St Aidan's Orphanage and each day a large rectangular cane basket was filled with the linen ready to be laundered. It was great fun to wait until housemaids were not looking, jump in the basket, close the big cane lid and hide under a white sheet. Next time the maids lifted the lid to throw in more linen I would, while covered with the sheet, launch myself like a leaping apparition with a blood chilling scream from the bowels of the basket. While they squealed in response, I very quickly scarpered down the passage still covered by the sheet. A variation on this theme was to hide in a wardrobe of one of the bedrooms that they were to do next and, at an opportune time, make strange groaning or whining noises or just jump out and frighten the bejeesus out of them. Power points were limited back then requiring vacuum cleaners to operate from long extension leads. It was all too easy to flick the switch and disappear. After a short break to allow memories to fade these misdemeanours could be repeated again with equal effect.

Interaction with the housemaids was not entirely a one-way street. They had their own way of seeking revenge such as 'short–sheeting' my bed. A procedure that required the top sheet to be folded in half so that when you got in your legs could not get past halfway down. To fix the problem you had to dismantle and rebuild the bed linen. Discovered at the end of the day when you jumped into bed, it was an annoying and irritating problem.

While the hotel linen and towels were sent to a commercial laundry it was still necessary to have on-site facilities to wash bar swabs, kitchen tea towels and the family's domestic laundry. One of the old stables in the backyard had been converted to a 'wash house' with a concrete floor, triple concrete wash tubs, and an electric copper for boiling everything in. Once the water in this device, about the size of a 44-gallon drum, came to the boil, whatever clothes that were in the copper were poked with a stick by a housemaid and stewed for as long as it took to clean and sanitise them. The hot steaming items were then hooked out by the same stick into one of the adjacent concrete tubs filled with cold water to wash out the boiling wash water. Clothes were then transferred to another tub for final rinsing and 'bluing' with little bags of 'Reckitts Blue', containing indigo, which was supposed to make white things whiter. At each process, heavy wet clothes, bar swabs and kitchen towels had to be lifted and wrung out. The housemaids then lugged baskets full of washed clothes to the line strung out between poles in the backyard with a prop in the middle to keep it all off the ground.

There was no such thing as a washing machine on the premises but there was a then-revolutionary, strange appliance called a 'spin dryer' sitting in the end washtub that was driven by a high-pressure jet from a water hose. Many women still used a mangle to squeeze water out of wet clothes as they were fed between two rollers. My mate Rob Iser caught his hand in one, leaving him with a serious scar. Eventually a 'Hills Hoist' was erected to hang out the washing and I soon discovered I could hang out on it too as it spun around. One day the centre post broke and the whole outfit came crashing to the ground on top of me. I lost a few points that day. Laundry work remained an arduous business.

The residential accommodation trade at The Crown was an important part of its business. When the first motel opened at Oakleigh, Victoria in 1956, the year of the Melbourne Olympic Games, Reg Beck reckoned that they would be a short-term fad, that people wouldn't stay in them because they couldn't get a drink, they were mostly on the outskirts of town away from shops and people wouldn't like the idea of eating breakfast in their bedroom. Hotels were then providing nearly all the accommodation needs of travellers and my father couldn't comprehend that this might change. As time went on and the accommodation trade at The

Crown declined, he became concerned. The residential amenities of the hotel were starting to look a little tired and were clearly not of the same standard provided by the motel industry. The Crown had no ensuite bathrooms, in fact no plumbing at all in the bedrooms. There were common use bathrooms and shower recesses, toilets floors were lined with lead sheet, bedding was in need of an upgrade and the bedrooms in need of painting.

The decision was made to supply hot and cold running water to all the bedrooms with the installation of some 20 hand basins, mirrors and accompanying tiling. This was a major undertaking requiring the installation of many yards/metres of piping in and sewerage out. Additional power points and bedside lights were installed and each of the bedrooms repainted. A bulk purchase of new mattresses and foam pillows was made plus new chenille bedspreads that came at a bargain price due to their strange colour of a cross between pink and orange which my mother dubbed "porange."

All the internal painting work was done by my father. He had originally completed an apprenticeship for doing the fine line work on horse gigs and buggies, and signwriting, and had worked at times as a painter and decorator, becoming quite skilled in the art including wall paper hanging. His signwriting was also more than reasonable. He would start his painting in the mornings, knock off in mid-afternoon to serve behind the bar and then often resume his painting projects late in the evening after the bar and kitchen staff had left. The problem was that by then he was often "three sheets to the wind" to use the nautical term, and continued to sustain himself with sips of whisky from a glass every time he descended the scaffold for something. He used this technique when painting the kitchen after hours. It was a major undertaking. The inevitable happened when he was high up on a scaffold that collapsed while he was on board with a bucket full of paint. He later boasted that the reason he suffered no injuries was due to the fact that he "rode the plank to the ground".

* * *

When I was 13 and my sister 15, we were still sharing the dreadful semi partitioned fibro cement sheet bedrooms on the hotel veranda. I clearly remember this because the Russians had launched Sputnik, the world's first satellite, on 4 October that year (1957) and I vividly recall watching its arc in the clear night sky through the fly wire on the window next to the toilet in my bedroom. When we were finally allocated our own rooms, they were at the end of the passageways next to the male and female toilets respectively. Although not the best location the move was incredibly important to both of us as now, for the first time in our lives, we had our own secure private area. I think it was especially important for my sister who was now approaching 16. It had been wrong for us to be kept in a general dormitory area in close proximity to our parents and selves for so long. For almost ten years I had put up with the rest of my family crapping in the half partitioned off toilet in the corner of my bedroom. I'm sure Zel was embarrassed using it when I was present in my room.

Requests for us to have our own radios were refused because we might disturb other guests. This seemed unjust to us as we always had access to the radio in our old bedroom set up. It felt like a kind of penalty for getting our own rooms. The radio had become an important part of our lives. It was like having our own personal portal through which we could escape the reality of the Crown Hotel into a world of fantasy. We were now at the age where we were enjoying popular pop music and being cut off from that felt like a real deprivation.

I resolved to save up my money earned from jobs around the hotel to buy my own radio and finally selected an operational unit from Mac McQuean's second-hand shop next to the Suitex Factory in Pall Mall. It was only the electrical guts from an old console radio that Mac had purloined the veneer housing from to use in his cabinet making skills and nothing more than a basic metal chassis with old-style vacuum valve tubes sticking up here and there that lit up when you turned it on. But it did have a separate huge cone loudspeaker that offered high-quality sound. There were times that I cranked it up full bore to get revenge on the world. Eventually I overdid it and it just went "Poof!", expelled a cloud of smoke and died. Until then it served me well.

It was not until 1958 that radio stations started to play the 'Top 40' popular music radio hit programs based on the American format. Local station 3BO took some time before it followed the trend and, in the meantime, listeners were left with replays of hits from the 50s. Guy Mitchell became popular with his first hit 'My Heart Cries for You' in 1950, reaching number one in Australia, followed in the same year by 'Sparrow in the Tree Top'. For the rest of the 50s he had a string of successes including 'My Truly Truly Fair', 'Pittsburgh Pennsylvania', 'Feet up, Pat Him on the Po Po', 'She Wears Red Feathers', 'Sippin Soda', 'Singing the Blues', 'Pretty Little Black-Eyed Susie' and 'The Roving Kind'. I thought they were all great.

Perhaps the most popular singer from the early 1950s was Johnny Ray who became a success with the release of his songs 'The Little White Cloud That Cried' and 'Cry', on a bakelite 78 rpm two-sided single which sold over two million copies. He was a sensation with his heart wrenching vocal delivery becoming the prime target of teen hysteria in the pre-Presley days, causing female fans to make sounds halfway between a scream and a moan when he actually cried singing some songs. He was dubbed 'Mr Emotion' and more hits followed including 'Please Mr Sun', 'Walkin' My Baby Back Home', 'Somebody Stole My Gal', 'Such a Night' and 'Just Walkin' in the Rain' which topped the Australian charts for 36 weeks in 1956. In March of 1955 when he arrived in Sydney, his young female admirers started a riot. He was the first of a long line of performers hated by the old and loved by the young.

My most indelible recollection of music in the 1950s and early 60s is that it was fun and enjoyable. This was most obvious in the early 'Doo Wop' rhythm movement with exquisite vocal harmonies exemplifying rock 'n' roll at its most innocuous, silliest and quaint. The genre was characterised by nonsense syllables often forming the backbone of vocals. Phrases such as "Doo wop, bop-bop dip-dip", "Bomp-a-bomp-bomp-bomp, buh-dang-a-ding-dong", "Wah wah, shoop shoop", "Dooby dooby doo" and "Yip-yip-yip-yip-yip-yip-yip-yip," were common. This was early rock 'n' roll at its funniest. I just loved it and soaked up as much as I could as it poured out of my old valve radio. A good example is the song 'Blue Moon' by the Marcels.

Chapter 23

FISHING TRIPS

My father had a boat and a tent and all the fishing gear you could imagine. As a young child I begged him to take me on his fishing safari trips which would last up to a week or more. He always refused my pleas saying that he would not do so until I had learned to swim properly. He had a reason for his rebuff.

Before my father bought The Crown in 1949, he took my mother and my sister and I on a long trip north and west of Deniliquin in NSW to visit his friend Lindsay Howe who was managing Murgha Station, a 56,000-acre sheep property along the Edwards River. Although only around four years of age at the time, I am told that as we drove along, I somehow opened the suitcase on the back seat between my sister and I and, unbeknown to my parents, slipped out through the back quarter vent windows the underwear and most of the clothing for the entire family. I apparently found this very amusing as the various items fluttered off into the saltbush and roadside drain.

After arriving at Murgha Station, Lindsay Howe decided to take my father and I for a quick boat trip along the Edwards River. When I was up the pointy end of the boat I suddenly fell in and disappeared and bobbed up again just as I went past Lindsay, who was driving the boat at the stern. He lunged out and grabbed me by the hair to pull me back into the boat, clearly saving my life in the process. This episode led to two consequences. Having frightened the daylights out of my father, it would be a long time before he would agree to me being in a fishing boat again with him. Second, Lindsay Howe took an abiding interest in me thereafter. I have heard it said that saving someone's life connects you to them forever. After you have done that, they belong to you. As I grew, he became to be a very important person to me and for more than the remaining 50 years of his life he was known to me as 'Uncle Lin'.

Finally, my father agreed to take me fishing with him when I convinced him I could swim. Full on preparation for his fishing safaris would start weeks before departure. Instructions were given to me to catch as many carp from Lake Weeroona as possible to use as bait. They were small fish and not the European species that eventually became a pest. At the hotel they were put in a 44-gallon drum with a water hose trickling in and out of overflow holes to keep them fresh and lively until departure. We then visited farms of hotel customers to drag dams with a huge dragnet equipped with lead weights on the bottom and corks on top. A strong man was needed on each side of the dam pulling top and bottom ropes through the water to operate the net. When the net was beached at the end of the dam, I helped collect yabbies for bait. I kept them in water among branches of gum leaves in the concrete wash troughs of the hotel washhouse until departure. They were then put into hessian bags with gum leaves and dunked in the river when arriving at the campsite. It was my job also to explore the stormwater drain system at the back of the hotel in search of tiger worms for bait.

22. Reg Beck and Lindsay Howe.

Packing seemed to take forever. There were two large steel trunks, one for tucker and the other for cooking utensils. A table to eat off, a table to cook on, folding camp seats, folding camp stretchers and bedding, a gas fridge, carbide lamps, Primus stoves, a heat pot to warm the tent, a canvas floor for the tent, the tent itself and its poles, ropes and pegs, a washstand for ablutions plus various supplementary pieces of paraphernalia too numerous to mention. Then there was the boat, outboard motor and fuel, fishing gear comprising rods, reels, lines, lures, nets and the bait. A shot gun and rifle had to be checked and cleaned. Beer, rum, scotch whisky, and lemonade for me, to be loaded.

My father always spent a great deal of time making sure that our old wooden trailer was perfectly balanced. If it was "light on" the trailer might rattle loose, lift off the tow ball and disengage resulting in the loss of trailer, its contents and the boat on top. If it was "heavy on" then it might interfere with the handling of the car, even causing the front wheels to lift up slightly. When driving my father had an annoying habit of putting his foot down to accelerate and then lifting it again resulting in a kind of go and slow progression. On one of our trips when my uncle Alf was with us in the front passenger seat he looked to the right and said, "Christ Reg, that looks like your trailer passing us!" When we looked to the right, our trailer with boat on top perfectly balanced, was overtaking us. It eventually slowed down and stopped in the grassy verge on the right-hand side of the road. No damage was done and we soon hooked up and continued on. In future my father put more emphasis on connecting the trailer and less on balancing it.

Our tow vehicle was my father's 1949 straight-eight Packard. Due to the volume of cargo we carried on these trips, the large back seat was removed to accommodate provisions. Being a publican, it was his practice to load multiple boxes of one dozen bottles of longneck beer, not just to drink, but also to give to the owner of the property where we were fishing in appreciation for allowing us on the river. The back of the Packard, with the seat out was deemed to be the safest place for this precious cargo along with myself. Instead of a seat I was given a box of beer to sit on. At the time I had a miniature fox terrier dog called Patch that, regardless of my repeated requests, my father had refused to allow to accompany us on fishing trips. He had the usual excuses, that he would chase farm stock, would get lost, would drown in the river and would generally be "a bloody nuisance". I decided to take Patch as a stowaway on a trip and created a secret space for him amongst the beer boxes in the back seat. Before I smuggled him in, I made sure he had something to eat and drink. We were heading up to Wendouran Station, 90,000 acres on the Billabong Creek near Moulamein in NSW, and had just crossed the Murray at Echuca when Patch started to fart. Both Uncle Alf and my father sitting in the front seat thought that the other one was to blame and at first attempted to ignore the acrid smells. While he was only a little dog, he sure could drop some doozies. Eventually my father said, "Jeezus Alf, did you just drop your breakfast or what?" Alf replied, "Christ no Reg, it was not me it must be you!"

23. 14-year-old Mickey with Patch, and Patch and his pups.

This response just engendered joint laughter between the two of them as each disbelieved the other. Similar banter and accusations continued between them as Patch continued to fart until we reached the Pretty Pine Hotel north of Deniliquin where it was decided that we should stop for a break. I thought that Patch was clearly in need of one too and let him out of the car. It was now my turn to laugh as my father went ballistic. Patch was a huge success as a camper. He came everywhere with us in the boat where he had his own special spot at the pointy end and often slept overnight on the foot of my father's camp stretcher bed. His behaviour was almost impeccable and in future he came with us on every trip.

Prior to arriving at our campsite, we would call at the closest town with an ice works and buy several large blocks of ice. At the camp a hole was dug and lined with gum leaves before installing the ice blocks upon which were laid long necked bottles of beer and my lemonade before covering the lot with more gum leaves and then a canvas tarp. It was amazing how long the ice lasted.

On my first trip, my father had purchased an ex-USA army tent from disposals. It was like a circus tent, round in shape with a single centre pole and low side walls. Its main problem was its weight. It was very heavy-duty canvas and took ages to erect. I think he only used it that once. As it was a new purchase he announced, after the consumption of several beers that he had to 'cure' the tent. This performance was aimed at repelling the legion of mosquitoes at night and swarms of flies during the day. The method required a fire being lit in a small oil drum and when it had settled down to red-hot coals, adding a quantity of cow manure and green gum leaves. A handle on the drum enabled it to be taken into the middle of the tent on the end of a shovel where it was left to pour out volumes of smoke while the tent was closed up. After an hour or two the tent was opened up so the occupants could resume residence. The only problem with this procedure was that it was not just the tent that was 'cured' but everything in it including everyone's bedding and clothing. It did keep the mozzie's away for a bit but the tent now had a 'pong' problem that I thought also needed curing.

My father's next tent was a 12 foot × 12 foot light canvas design that was much easier to erect. Like all tents at the time, it came without a sewn in floor and each of the corners had to be laced up separately around the poles. It was therefore much less than windproof. For the comfort of the occupants, my father included an old carpet square approximating the tent measurements to use as a floor.

On a duck opening trip to Barren Box Swamp in NSW we found, arriving late, that all the good camping spots had been taken up by the shooters, forcing us to erect our tent on a sandhill. The wind blew a gale during the night but failed to wake up my father and Uncle Lin who had been suitably anaesthetised through the consumption of copious quantities of then cheap De Bortoli flagon wine. Eventually the crack of shot gun blasts before the crack of dawn woke them to discover that there was sand everywhere. It was on the bedclothes, in our clothes, in the dishes, in the butter and sugar, in the water and all over the table and chairs. Even worse, it seemed someone during the night had sneaked in and stolen our carpet floor. A closer inspection revealed it was buried in sand. So completely was it covered that on de-camping we found it difficult to exhume and elected to leave it in situ.

Our camp cooking was done on three Primus stoves set on a homemade table with screw out galvanised pipe legs. After the stoves were preheated with methylated spirits a hand pump created a mixture of pressurised kerosene and air that vaporised into a gas with the heat. You had to pump them every now and then to keep them going but they gave out a substantial heat equivalent to a modern gas camp stove and you soon got used to their friendly hiss.

A pressure cooker was a vital part of the culinary equipment, especially when it came to cooking galahs. After cleaning and dressing, the recipe required "shoving an onion up its arse" before tossing it into the cooker with some bacon, carrots, spuds, more onions and pepper and salt. After a splash of beer, it was then sealed up and sat on the Primus until the safety steam valve blew off the cooker. It made a hell of a din when it did, often catching the beer-fogged occupants of the tent by surprise causing a scramble for the exit. Some brave soul then had to approach the Primus to turn off the heat. The cooker was then left to sit for a while to allow the pressure to go down to release the seal and access the contents. Upon examination it was discovered, more often than not, that the galahs had disintegrated leaving only their skeletonised carcasses as evidence of their pre-existence. The rest was a delicious soup.

At night, we lit the camp with carbide acetylene gas lamps. The gas was created by the reaction of calcium carbide with water. A cylindrical container with a screw top had an outlet pipe with a burner to allow a jet of gas to escape. A lump or two of calcium carbide was placed in this container and the top screwed on. It was then placed in a second cylindrical container holding water. A tiny hole in the first container allowed a small amount of water to find its way in and moisten the carbide which gave off an acrid, pungent smelling acetylene gas through the burner hole. Lit with a match, it fired up a bright white light. To turn it off the inner container was simply removed from the outer one holding water and it went out by itself. My father often sent me across the road to Abbott Supply in Lyttleton Terrace to buy the carbide on his account before we left on a trip.

Carbide could however be dangerous stuff. If the burner was faulty or too much carbide or water was added explosions could result when the pressure of the gas generated had to get out somewhere. Gas sneaking back out through the tiny hole below water in the inside container was sometimes ignited by the flame of

24. Reg Beck getting ready to fish and caught with beer in hand!

25. Reg, Uncle Alf and Mickey with two 60 pound (27 kilogram) Murray cod
from the Murray River at Hattah-Kulkyne Lakes National Park, 1958.

the burner resulting in an extremely startling loud bang not unlike a gunshot causing anyone in the tent to duck for cover. There were cases of exploding carbide lamps causing death. My father was always very careful with the lamps and counselled me never to interfere with them.

We even had a carbide lamp mounted on the front of our 12-foot bond wood boat when we used it to go around our cross lines and gill nets at night. My father had an amateur gill netting licence that entitled him to legally fish in designated waters with a limited length of netting. We used this system in the billabongs and lagoons around the Gunbower Creek with great success catching many big redfin or English perch (to give them their proper name) and English tench fish. At night I occasionally caught an Aussie catfish fishing from the bank with a line. Cross lines on the other hand were, as now, illegal back then. Consisting of long lines across or along a river or lagoon, with baited hooks on short lines dropping down every few yards/metres and baited with big yabbies or carp. They were meant to catch large Murray cod. We seldom had any success with this system probably because many of the big Murray cod had already been hooked out of the rivers by that time, due no doubt in large part to the use of cross lines.

There were still a few big fish left. One of our best trips was to the Hattah-Kulkyne National Park on the Murray River, home to the internationally significant Hattah Lakes wetlands. We camped on a large bend of the river underneath majestic river red gums harbouring a rich variety of bird life ranging from ring necked parrots and rosellas to Major Mitchell cockatoos, honeyeaters and tiny wrens and swallows. I was 13 going on 14 at the time and my school mate Rob Cook had come with us together with my uncle Alf Rasmussen from Castlemaine and, of course, my father Reg.

The scream of white cockies woke Cookie and I at sunup one morning and we soon agreed that we should leave the two old blokes to sleep off their hangover while we went fishing in the boat. We had permission to drive the boat ourselves as long as we went upstream so that in the event the motor conked out, we could float back to the camp with the current. We had trolled a large aeroplane cod spinner for some 30 minutes when, as we were going around a big horseshoe bend, Cookie who was holding the braided hand line connected to the spinner screamed out in pain as he was nearly pulled out of the boat. Thinking that he had hooked on to a log I immediately de-throttled the motor and threw it into neutral. Then the real fun started.

"I've got a fish, I've got a fish—it's a big bastard!" yelled Cookie.

"Give him line," I roared as the line went slack anyway due to us drifting down stream and the fish swimming upstream.

"Awrr, shit I've lost him!" he howled. "No, he's here, I've got him again," he screamed.

Then this huge cod appeared at the side of the boat. To us it was enormous and quickly assessed as being too heavy for one of us to lift. I remembered that my father had a blacksmith tailor-made fish gaff stowed in the boat which I grabbed and hooked the fish in the gills. It took the two of us, with Cookie hauling in on the line and me on the gaff hook, to drag the monster into the boat. It was more than half our size and later weighed in at over 60 pounds (27 kilograms). The whole episode from hooking to landing had taken a very short time due to our frantic excitement. The fish, still fresh and now in the boat, started flapping so madly that it was lifting itself off the floor of the boat. Worried that it was going to jump out of the boat we decided to secure it by sitting on it together as we drove back to the camp flat out. About a quarter of a mile from the camp we started yelling very loudly "We've caught a fish!" and kept it up until we arrived.

At the camp uncle Alf was saying to my father "That's nice Reg, the boys have caught a fish. If it's big enough we can all have some for dinner". When they saw it, they couldn't believe their eyes. For several days it was tethered on a rope in the river at the end of a big log and then cleaned and salted when we were ready to go home. In Bendigo, after one of the local butchers dealt with it on his bandsaw, it was taken to the Garsed Street freezing works until ordered by the cook at The Crown for serving in the dining room. The head of the fish was preserved, mounted and displayed in the bar of The Crown.

After returning from another trip my father was unloading all the gear from the boat as it sat on its trailer in the shed, when a very large brown snake shot over the side and disappeared through a hole in the galvanised iron shed wall into the adjoining premises, which was a pet shop. The building was owned by my father and leased to the proprietor Bill Allen. Reg went straight around to his shop and explained to the disbelieving Bill what had happened. The snake had entered the small backyard of the pet shop through which you had to traverse to access the toilet for the premises. Entry was through a door leading from the walkway then known as 'Dispensary Walk'. Bill and Reg gingerly opened the door to peek into the yard and saw the snake disappearing down a small hole in the concrete at the corner of the toilet.

My father had just brought back from the bush a large extremely venomous brown snake that he had let loose in the central business district of Bendigo. This was a problem. There were no registered snake catchers around at the time. Reg and Bill discussed various options ranging from pouring boiling water or petrol down the hole, which they discounted as a bad idea, to sit and wait on point duty with a loaded shotgun until the snake came out—if ever. Nobody knew where the hole led to. What if it came out in the pet shop? I knew Bill sold pet mice so I suggested that one of them should be securely tethered a short distance outside the hole in the hope that the snake would be hungry enough to come out and swallow the mouse. Bill organised the tether and Reg stood by with a shovel to dispatch the snake. Sure enough, the snake came out and swallowed the mouse still tied to the tether, somewhat delaying its retreat and providing an opportunity to go whack with the shovel. End of snake. Very relieved father and pet shop proprietor.

Chapter 24

CHARACTERS

In the 1950s there were a number of poor or disabled people living in Bendigo. They were not numerous but they were noticeable at times and some were very poor. It was not uncommon to see returned soldier customers in the bar of the Crown Hotel on crutches and minus one leg. The leg of their pants folded at the knee and pinned behind. Proper prosthetic legs were expensive and scarce. Others were distinctive because of their different disability whether physical, intellectual or both.

There was Kenny Kev who had squinty eyes behind very thick lensed glasses who always turned up at the Kennington Oval to act as boundary umpire when junior football teams played there. He was appreciated by the teams and did a good job returning the ball. Bendigo Brian was a likeable young man who had a clubfoot and lived at the Sandhurst Boys Home. Kerosene Kate, with a disability that was possibly alcohol-related, could be seen pushing an old pram around the town. It was Bayonet Bill who strode around the town in a big felt hat that all the kids were frightened of but I never heard any real evidence that corroborated their fears. I think it was just his name. They were also frightened of Scobie who seemed to live in an old railway carriage at the Bendigo East tip. He had a habit of scaring the daylights out of kids by jumping out from hiding places and yelling out, "If I don't get you the devil will!" Then laughing as the kids ran away. He did this to me once causing self-diagnosed, temporary serious juvenile post-traumatic stress disorder. Bill Peech used to come into Bendigo in his horse and gig, get very drunk and most times go to sleep in the gig as his faithful steed took him home in the direction of Epsom. Occasionally, Bill played up and I remember one occasion when he started fighting the tram pole in the middle of the Pall Mall Road outside the courthouse.

From time to time The Crown had a number of long-term boarders. Some stayed for years and during that time I got to know them fairly well and they all, to an individual greater or lesser degree, had some effect on my upbringing and input into my beliefs and values.

There was a gentleman, and I use that term sincerely, by the name of Percy Carne who worked full-time at Matthew's Bros drapery store in Hargreaves Street. He was a tall grey-haired, well-spoken man who wore a suit every day of the week. Perc lived at the hotel for years when I was a small boy. He told me how he had fought at Gallipoli and had been one of the lucky ones who survived. He described how he and his mates rigged their rifles on makeshift stands so they could fire them by looking through a periscope to avoid sticking their heads above the trenches and how, when they retreated, rifles on similar stands were jury rigged with a billy can full of water with a tiny hole in the bottom so that when the can drained the released weight resulted in a counterweight pulling the trigger and firing the gun. His story became three-dimensional on one of my explorations of the linen store when I discovered a large old brown leather suitcase belonging to Perc containing his Anzac uniform complete with leather leggings, slouch hat and medals. The contents of that suitcase had a unique antiquarian fragrance of a distant bygone era that was mildly intoxicating. I shall always remember it.

Sundays at The Crown were mostly dull, boring, tedious and tiresome. The bars were shut, the shops were shut, there were no people in the streets and hotel staff numbers were halved. I always knew where I could find Perc on Sunday mornings. He would be across the road sitting on a brick buttress in front of the children's library soaking up the sun. With sleeves rolled up, his shirt neck undone, this was one time he did not wear his suitcoat. I often joined him myself for a dose of the sun and a measure of Perc's wisdom. He constantly counselled me to stop swearing, warning that if I didn't control it now, it would become a habit that I'd be addicted to and wouldn't be able to stop. I had by that stage developed more than a basic vocabulary in the vernacular. I doubt that I acted on his advice immediately but his words remained with me. Many years later in life, after Perc had passed away, I discovered that he was gay.

Mr Griffiths and Mr Picard were two characters who lived in separate parts of the downstairs flat at the rear of the hotel. Their names were John and Jack, but to me and my sister it was always "Mr Griffiths and Mr Picard". Mr Griffiths was the owner of a British Humber Super Snipe Limousine that he parked under cover in the backyard. A beautiful English car with leather seats and walnut dashboard, it was his pride and joy. A small, pipe-smoking, meek and mild man with grey hair, glasses and a liking for brownish tweed coats with trousers and tanned shoes to match, it seemed he was trying to represent the embodiment of an English gentleman.

In truth, he was the epitome of the Walter Mitty type and a very ordinary ineffectual person who constantly told fantastic stories of his personal adventures. He told tales of his wartime adventures and visits to countries all over the world. It was impossible for it all to be true and I speculate that much of it was based on the last book he read. However, he and his friend Jack Picard were very good to my sister and I and on numerous occasions took us to the drive-in theatre sitting in the luxurious back seat of the Humber Super Snipe.

Mr Griffiths and Mr Picard were another two who assumed the role of de facto parents from time to time for my sister and I. I have often wondered why but I am grateful that they did. Maybe they pitied us or maybe they just enjoyed our company. When Jack Picard left, he gave me a beautiful antique silver pocket watch and also a wristwatch he had owned. Every time one of these people who I had formed a close relationship with at The Crown left, I went through a grieving process and got angry and cursed whoever it was that left. Eventually I accommodated myself with accepting the idea that, in the end, everyone vanished but I never did get used to it.

Arthur Norman was one of the long-time hotel guests who spent a great deal of time with me when I was still a student at Gravel Hill State School. He was employed in the office at the Bendigo Ordnance Factory and each day, after knocking off at 4:30 p.m, would hurry back to The Crown where he worked as a part-time barman in the lead up to the 6 o'clock swill. When my father noticed his skill as a piano player, Arthur became a vital part of the hotel concert group and an important part of the accompaniment to my father's violin playing. The two of them, with their similar interests of music and fishing, got on extremely well and became close friends, often going away on fishing trips together.

26. Reg, third from right, centre of attention on public side of the bar.

27. Arthur Norman and Reg Beck, Easter 1957.

Eventually, as I got older, I was allowed to join them and, as my father's confidence grew in my bush survivability skills and willingness to follow Arthur's directions, he allowed me to go with Arthur on weekend fishing trips. Leaving at 5 a.m., we would drive to Lake Charm near Kerang where we would wade into the water up to our waists and cast spinners around dead trees all day to catch redfin. They were good fish, in the days before carp invaded, weighing up to three and four pounds in the old measure, and we always brought home a bag- full. On other occasions, Arthur would take me out to the Campaspe River to spin for redfin from the banks.

My mother always took the trouble to make sure there were fresh flowers in the ladies lounge, bar parlour, foyer and dining room of the hotel. Each spring when the wildflower season arrived, she shanghaied Arthur Norman to take Zel and I on bush expeditions to pick wildflowers. Back then it was not illegal. We would head off in my father's old circa 1930s Chrysler up the back road of One Tree Hill and return with a car full of mosquitoes, grevilleas, wattles, hardenbergers, gum tips and whatever else we could pick. The old Chrysler had a wind out windscreen that, when employed, was very effective for blowing out the mozzies on the way home. It had a beautiful chrome leaping impala radiator mascot and was described as "six wheel equipped" because it had spare wheels mounted on the running boards near each side of the engine.

The part that Zel and I liked most was that you were able to gain access to the boot from inside the car by lifting up the back support, which was hinged at the top. If we knew our father was going somewhere in the car we would ask if we could go too. He would often say no so we resorted in the end to smuggling ourselves in the boot via the back seat access. We would wait until he had travelled a considerable distance before we popped out and said, "Hi Dad!" The trick worked on many occasions and he would then agree, albeit somewhat begrudgingly, to take us on the rest of his journey. There were times that he became quite angry and returned back to The Crown to discharge his stowaways.

One of my favourite long-term tenants at The Crown was Bruce Campbell who stayed there in the 1950s. He was a flight instructor working for Richard (Dick) Arthur who ran a flying school at the old Woodvale airstrip between Epsom and Huntly. Bruce was a short fellow with a greying moustache, sparkling blue eyes and salt-and-pepper hair that was starting to get a little thin on top. I soon found out that he taught people how to fly aeroplanes and I used every opportunity to cross examine him about all the details. I pestered him so much that eventually he took a shine to me and, with my father's permission, regularly took me on short rabbit shooting expeditions out to Sedgwick, after he had finished work, in his dreadful old severely battered Holden utility. As we got to know each other better I started pleading with him to take me up in his Tiger Moth aeroplane. For a long time, he refused but eventually relented having first obtained the approval of my father.

The Tiger Moth was a 1930s design British biplane trainer aircraft. Around 1,000 had been assembled in Australia from parts sent from the UK with most delivered to the Royal Australian Air Force to be used in pilot training. Powered by a four-cylinder 120 hp engine its maximum performance was around 175 kilometres per hour with a cruising speed of 108 kilometres per hour. Its double wingspan of 8.94 metres was longer than the length of its fuselage of 7.29 metres and both were mostly covered with fabric which contributed to its lightweight of only 506 kilograms empty. The fuel tank of about 86 litres was built into the top wing just above the head of the first pilot and drained down to the engine via a flexible pipe. The two open cockpit seats were in line, with communication between instructor and student via a speaking funnel protruding from the instrument panel in the cockpits and then into flexible tubes that went directly to the ears of both occupants through a headset. The Moth had the reputation for being a robust, generally docile little machine but required definite skill and concentration during aerobatic manoeuvres which, if botched, could easily cause a stall or a spin. It had to be started by hand, landed on two wheels with a 'tail dragger' at the back and had no brakes. Pilots were advised not to use full power for more than one minute at a time to avoid damaging the engine.

28. A Tiger Moth aircraft like Bruce Campbell's.
Source: *Alamy Australia Ltd.*

Of course, few of the above details were known to me at the time. I think I was then about 12 or 13 years old. I had seen pictures of Tiger Moths, knew that they were double wingers and had an open cockpit, but that was about it. Bruce was very caring with me as a passenger and kitted me out with World War II face goggles and a leather flying cap that was too big. Before adjusting the headset to clamp over my ears he gave me a fairly comprehensive pre-flight briefing that later proved to be lacking on one important point.

After strapping the safety harness around me over the thick warm clothing he had warned me to wear, the propeller was spun by a ground staffer, the engine exploded (I thought) with an enormous roar and we taxied off down the grass runway to the take-off point testing the transmit and receive capabilities of the tubing intercom as we went. Then it was up and away!

I felt like I was really living the 'Air Adventures of Biggles'. I had pleaded with Bruce to do some aerobatics and particularly put in an order for several 'loop de loops'. After doing a very big circuit of the airfield he then turned to line up with the grass runway and did a very slow barrel roll. This was amazing. One minute I was upside down looking at the earth and then the other way around. He then yelled at me, "Have you got your feet on those floor paddles?" (The paddles move the tail rudder to steer the aircraft.)

"Ah, yeah," I said.

"Well," he said, "Then get the bloody things off now!"

We landed very shortly after that. I never did get to experience a 'loop de loop'.

Chapter 25

JOBS

I was always keen to earn pocket money. I knew from one of
my schoolmates at Gravel Hill that a paper round returned a
good income. Ken Gouge had a bike equipped with a hessian
saddle bag slung over the top bar of the frame into which he piled
an amazing number of newspapers on each side. The papers were
prevented from spilling out by an old bike tube, running from the
headpiece to the seat piece, acting like a giant rubber band to keep
them in. Ken would get up at 5 a.m, collect his stock of papers and
pedal off to do his round with knees sticking out almost at right
angles to allow for his cargo. After it was delivered he would turn
up for school on time. The morning newspaper delivery boys had
the toughest job in Bendigo's frosty winters and could be easily
identified by the chilblains on their ears.

In the afternoon, after school, newsboys sold the late edition
of *The Herald* at busy intersections. The city boys were allocated
their own corner where they developed their peculiar individual

call to attract attention of purchasers. Something like, "Eeee yo heero heero hero!" Translated, this was meant to mean, "Here is your *Herald*, your *Herald*". Another kid a block away could be heard yelling out his own distinctive call. They all had an arm-full of heavy newspapers shoved into a sling hanging from their neck from which a leather bag for change also dangled. In winter they were mostly dressed in heavy ex-army disposal jackets and caps to stay warm. It was front line salesmanship with newspapers thrust at potential customers as they walked past, some of whom said, "keep the change" as they paid. Their best tips came from men drinkers in hotel bars where the newspaper boys were the only juveniles allowed in, apart from the children of the licensee. It was a tough gig but some did well if they had customers who regularly tipped.

I pleaded with my father to have a paper round or to be a newsboy but the answer was always "no". I think he thought it was demeaning for himself and me to have such a job. Newsboys were often from poorer families and had a reputation for being cheeky and not the best of character. He was not about to let me join this rough cohort selling newspapers on the street. Over the years, the number of paper boys declined markedly due to the disappearance of afternoon newspapers, employment laws regulating child labour and growing parental paranoia relating to the safety of children.

As I grew older my father provided legitimate ways for me to make money around the hotel. Under his instructions, the kitchen cooks were told to pour all waste fat into an empty kerosene tin where it solidified. When it was full, my father and I would take it to the skin and tallow merchants in McIvor Road where I would get paid a few shillings. Butchers always needed newspapers to wrap the customers meat orders after a first wrap in white paper. With the delivery of morning and afternoon newspapers for customers and our family, there was always plenty of out-of-date ones for me to pile up in bundles and sell to the butcher shops for a penny a pound weight.

In lieu of allowing me to be a paperboy, my father provided me with an endless list of jobs around The Crown and paid me well. My training in the hotel business began as a swab boy which required me to mop up any spillages of beer and other liquor on all the tables in the ladies lounge and bar parlour, and emptying, wiping clean and returning ashtrays to the tables, and returning abandoned empty glasses to the bar area. In this capacity I was employed only on especially busy days such as during Easter, Christmas, Bendigo Cup day and Grand Final day. The job specified that I be dressed in long black pants, shiny black shoes and white shirt with a bow tie. Under no circumstances was I to take drink orders or wait on tables. I figured that, like most rules, this last condition might be best observed in the breach when I was offered a substantial tip by a nice old lady to carry her tray of drinks back to her table. Alas, as I approached the point of delivery, I lost the lot, drowning the expectant customers in beer and spirits and showering them with shards of glass. Yells and screams of abuse followed me as I instantly panicked and fled the scene of the crime. I don't recall ever being a swab boy again after that. I can't recall whether it was because I resigned or was sacked.

Sunday morning, when hotel staff were in short supply, was my busiest time. First job was to stoke the kitchen stove and clean out the ash box and flues, the latter of which took quite some time as you had to get down to ground level to gain access via small trapdoors to underneath the ovens and scrape out the ash with a special tool. Next, I had to clean out the grease trap. This device was a series of connected rectangular brick tanks built into the ground outside the kitchen. Waste water from the kitchen sinks had to pass through them before reaching the sewerage outlet. Brick baffles within the trap slowed the passage of water allowing the flotation of fats, settlement of solids and the flow of clearer water in between to the sewerage outlet. Over time, the settled solids and floating fats accumulated and had to be removed manually. I performed this weekly task with a scoop made from a small saucepan connected to a broom handle. The solidified fat scum on the surface had to be removed first in order to access the solids on the bottom. The procedure created such a foul stench that I often dry retched. It was a job I always did before breakfast.

Then, during the winter, I had five 'Warm Ray' wood heaters to service. Three in the bar, one in the ladies lounge and one in the bar parlour. Each had to be cleaned of ash, set with paper and kindling for relighting, and wood racks next to them restocked with trolley loads of wood wheeled in from the wood heap in the backyard.

After hosing down the front footpath, paying particular attention to any urine stains, my next task was to clean the gents toilet in the laneway comprising a urinal and two WC stalls with elevated cast-iron chain pull flushers. Replenishing with 'toilet paper' in the form of old telephone books, if available, or squares of cut up newspaper hung on a nail, was also required. A task simple in its description but often challenging in its execution. The location of the toilets in the hotel laneway meant they were open to the public 24/7 and you never knew what you might find.

The main cleaning implement was a high-pressure hose but I learned from experience that this should only be employed after the removal of any non-hoseable items with a broom and shovel. One freezing cold winter morning, around 7 a.m., when I tried to open the door of one of the cubicles, I heard a loud clunk as it hit something. When I peered around the door, I saw a bearded man in a navy-blue overcoat lying on the concrete. I said, "Hey! Wake up," and gave him a poke which disclosed to me he was as stiff as a board. I then noticed that he had a wooden leg! That was what the door had hit. All this information was a bit too much for a circa nine-year-old to take in at once. I bolted around to the back door of the kitchen yelling repeatedly all the way, "Dad! Dad!—There is a dead man in the dunny!"

A subsequent cursory forensic inspection of the body by my father, comprising a solid kick in the ribs, revealed that it was not dead but severely hung over from drinking methylated spirits from the bottle still in possession. We eventually stood him up on his peg leg and, with advice that the police would be called if he didn't leave the premises, managed to send him on his way. I will never forget the vision of this bearded old bloke, in his shabby navy overcoat and porkpie cap, hobbling off on his wooden leg. I had truly believed he was dead and was relieved that my father had managed to resurrect him.

I was 12 years old before my father put me into service behind the bar. As the son of a licensee, I was exempt from the usual law prohibiting juveniles in licensed areas. I began at first as a glass washer and after completing that apprenticeship graduated to serving patrons. In the end I enjoyed the frantic pace of the 6 o'clock rush and managed quite well with beer, stout and shandies but often struggled when serving through the slide window to the ladies lounge with drinks such as gin and tonic, brandy Alexanders and sherry.

I quickly learned that liquor had different effects on persons of different dispositions. Men who normally spoke with regular conversation could express themselves with amazing pro-fanities. Some with limited education could suddenly fully understand science, politics, law, religion and arts. Others became argumentative and pugilistic and a few were even overcome by the need to sing. Customers could be appreciative, generous and warm-hearted or demanding, rude and arrogant.

For my regular jobs, I was paid well in cash. I can't remember precisely how much but I always seemed to have plenty of money compared to other kids. In addition, my mother gave me extra amounts for such things as school lunches, going to the pictures, buying comics and so. All I had to do was ask and she gave.

There were other jobs I did without pay that my father awarded me points for under his merit system that he used to reward or penalise my conduct. If I did something wrong, he would say, "You have lost 10 points for that" or whatever number he thought appropriate. On the other hand, if I had done something he approved of as being good or worthy he would say, "You have got 10 points for that." If a fishing trip was coming up at the end of the year he might say that he would take me if I earned 100 points in the meantime.

I still found further sources of revenue. When I was given the job of cleaning and restocking with bottles the bottom of the lower shelves under the bar, I discovered a veritable treasure trove. When my father built the elevated floor behind the bar to give him the traditional military advantage of high ground over the customers, it resulted in the bottom shelves under the bar being relegated to below floor level where the area became a receptacle for a considerable quantity of coins dropped by barmen serving customers. I claimed the first one I saw under the principle of 'finders keepers' arguing that it had been long abandoned. Judgement having then been made in my favour, I used it as a precedent for every coin I discovered thereafter, and there were plenty.

Soft drink bottles then had a deposit paid on them at purchase that was refunded when you handed back the empty. It didn't take me long to figure out that I could grab half a dozen or so empty bottles from the stack in the backyard and head off on my bike to O'Connell's soft drink factory, the hotel supplier, a short distance down Hargreaves Street where I could cash them in for a refund. From memory every bottle had a sixpence refund on it so half a dozen would have netted me 36 pence (three shillings) which to me was real money. I then hit on the idea that I could increase my return exponentially if I traded in soda siphons, which had a much larger refund deposit of around five shillings per siphon. When I turned up at O'Connell's with a couple of empty soda siphons, I was cross-examined on the spot as to how I had come to possess them. Mr O'Connell formed the view that I was lying when I told him that my father had given them to me to get refunds on and performed a citizen's arrest while he phoned Reg. I lost a lot of points that time.

Chapter 26

DAVE AND GEORGE

avid Harry Harris and George Samuel Harris were brothers who lived together in a small bluestone cottage surrounded by slightly undulating open farm land of an indeterminate acreage, on the left-hand side of the road just before you got to Axedale. Dave was a few years older than George. When I knew them, they were both in their 80s and lived the life of hermits with very few friends. One of their friends was my father, who in his very younger years had received his first violin lessons from them.

As a young child I first met George when he came to the back door of the hotel kitchen. He presented to me as a big man, covered by an old army coat, wearing a felt hat pulled down over his head with long straggly grey hair protruding and a large moustache, but otherwise with a clean-shaven face, albeit weather-beaten and age marked. My father had arranged with my mother for George to have a free meal at the hotel when he came to Bendigo but, due to his appearance, she would not allow him to sit in the dining room and made him eat in the kitchen.

While George's pants, coat and hat were ingrained with dirt, that was just the start. The clothes under his coat were rags. Everything seemed to be held together with safety pins used to hold pieces of cloth, patching up holes, as substitutes for lost buttons and in lieu of sewing torn material. One thin and worn-out cardigan with large holes in the elbows was covered again by another with larger holes. A basic canvas shoulder bag blackened with age and grease, and a plain rustic walking stick completed the vision of a shabby and decrepit old man. However, from my mother's point of view one last thing was the dealbreaker—George had some home-made metal teeth in the front of his mouth. (There was a precedent for this, Stalin's Martial Konstantin Rakassovsky had metal teeth which replaced those he lost to interrogators when Stalin purged the Red Army in 1937–38.) George and his brother Dave also had a very distinctive smell arising from their living conditions. Nonetheless my mother, who always found some good in everyone, made George extremely welcome, providing personal attention to his needs.

When my father visited George and Dave every three or four months and brought them provisions I often accompanied him. The brothers had a quince orchard down near Axe Creek from which they sold the annual crop to the Bendigo Preserving Company and I was co-opted by my father to help pick the fruit each year. Zelda joined our visits once but refused further invitations.

I enjoyed visiting George and Dave as it was like entering a different universe compared with The Crown. Their bluestone blockhouse was a simple square shape like the ones I used to draw in prep class at Gravel Hill with the front comprising two windows with a door in the middle. It was not a jerry-built dwelling, had a galvanised iron roof with a ceiling throughout and inside there were two bedrooms, a 'lounge' room with a big fireplace, a storeroom and kitchen with a rear door. That was it. There was no electricity, no plumbing, no bathroom or internal toilet. Each room had double-hung sash windows and a wooden floor laid throughout the premises with no further covering.

When the last of the brothers, George, died my father was appointed the executor of his estate with everything being left to the Bendigo Benevolent Home for the aged. I attended the property subsequent to George's funeral with my father and the lawyer handling the estate to take an inventory of goods and chattels and on that occasion had the opportunity to closely inspect the property.

Each bedroom had iron framed beds with old-style wire mattress supports but no sign of anything you could call a mattress. It seemed to me there was just a pile of rags where a mattress should have been, covered by hessian sacks opened up and stitched together with a bag needle. Pillows were made up from calico bags stuffed with more old rags. The total lack of linen meant they never had to address a change of it for their beds. They had said they couldn't see the sense of undressing and dressing and always went to bed in full marching order.

Furniture throughout the premises was sparse, ancient and rough. Some of it looked home-built with basic tools like a saw and an axe. There was no stove in the kitchen and all cooking was done in an open fireplace over a blazing wood fire where iron pots, buckets and billy cans, hung on hooks at the end of blackened chains dangling down the chimney. On one visit Dave asked us to stay for lunch saying that he had a large hare on the boil he could share. To prove it he shoved a toasting fork into a tin boiler hanging over the fire to hook out the hare complete with unskinned head displaying floppy ears, glazed white eyes, whiskers sticking out and teeth bared. Fortunately, my father, offering some lame excuse, declined the invitation.

The kitchen table, with legs that stood in large tin dishes of water to stop the ants crawling up, was large enough to seat six people but was bush built and made out of rough timber. It was clearly higher in the centre, where a large kerosene lamp sat, than around the edges, which my father claimed was caused by the build-up of dirt in the middle and the edges being worn down through repeated chopping and cutting over the years. On the right-hand side of the fireplace, in the corner closest to the external door there was a pile of rubbish on the floor consisting of old bones, jam tins and whatever else was deemed to be appropriate. An old gum tree branch hung from the ceiling which the brothers explained was intended to provide a resting place for the flies to keep them off the food. There was some crockery but most utensils comprised tin or enamel pannikans, pots and dishes that were washed outdoors in a tin dish on a bench where Dave and George also performed their basic ablutions. My most abiding memory of the kitchen is that it was black from years of accumulated smoke from the fire. There was a shelf and cupboards up one end but I don't recall any Coolgardie safe.

Outside there was a water tank and a huge woodpile but no sign of a clothesline. An external toilet refuge built from old rusty recycled galvanised iron sat over a hole dug in the ground. At the appropriate juncture the shelter was moved and placed over a new hole from which some of the excavated earth went to top off the one fully stocked. The toilet was too far away to use at night which explained the presence of chamber pots under the beds. External sheds were sparse and of simple construction framed with bush timber and saplings and tied together with fencing wire with any ridge pole supported by a forked branch stuck in the ground. They were roofed with old galvanised iron, partly nailed but mostly wired on.

Fencing around the property was mainly wooden post and rail construction, now in a dilapidated state. There was a stockyard or corral of similar build near the house where I witnessed a fight between two bulls that was broken up by Dave when he jumped in with them to punch them consecutively in the ribs to distract them. He succeeded, causing them to direct their attention to him, almost catching him before he dived through the post and rails to safety. Dave and George had a few cows but I never saw any horses. A little yard for chooks was never occupied as the chooks always hung around the back door of the kitchen for scraps. I suspect that they largely had to fend for themselves although I do remember seeing in their pen a feed trough made out of a hollow log cut in half with a piece of tin nailed at each end.

The most frightening and horrifying part of the place to me was where the brothers kept their dogs and cats chained up. The several dogs lived in large hollow logs to which they were chained with very heavy link chain. When you walked anywhere near them, the dogs would fly out of the logs barking mad with teeth snapping to be checked only by the length of chain which finally stopped them. Their fearsome charge frightened the daylights out of me. At the front of their 'kennels', the limits of their tether, worn bare by constant pacing, were fouled with dog excrement and the remains of rabbit fur and bones. In another location several cats, tethered in similar circumstances by chains to hollow logs, flew out to hiss, spit and claw at you if they were approached.

For their entire life Dave and George had learned to depend on their own resources. They had been strong, sinewy, tough men, capable of walking astonishing distances and used to being exposed to all weathers. With the few sheep they ran and some cows, beef cattle and chickens, plus the rabbits and hares they trapped and galahs and cockatoos they shot, they had plenty of meat for the pot. With milk from the cows and eggs from the chooks plus cash from the sale of quinces to The Bendigo Preserving Company, they had a better than subsistence existence. Tea, sugar, flour, potatoes and a few other vegetables and kerosene for lighting were bought with the cash. They were both smokers, made their own wood pipes from cherry trees growing in the orchard and grew their own tobacco, a crop that had been harvested in Axedale as early as 1864. They had never owned a motor vehicle in their life and neither of them could drive. A telephone had never been connected to their house.

With no paths around the cottage except for a few bricks at the back door, living in dirt surrounds with no proper bathing facilities was conducive to the accumulation of dirt within the dwelling and to Dave and George themselves. On an occasion when George was admitted to the Bendigo Base Hospital my father said that the nurses had told him George was so dirty, they couldn't find his navel. With no electricity, radio or newspapers they were not subjected to advertising propaganda that suggested that in soap and water there was "self-respect". They already had that in spades anyway and clearly seemed largely unconcerned about what other people thought of their looks. However, when going into Bendigo on the bus they did remove their rabbit skin leggings which I think they usually wore 24/7. They had their own method of tanning the rabbit skins, which they wore fir-side inwards for warmth.

Both Dave and George were gentlemen who clearly had been well brought up and educated. Plain, unpretentious, intelligent, articulate and well-mannered. They asked for little and were grateful for all they had. They had no goals for themselves and thought no ill of others. They were honourable and honest—as straight as a gun barrel, as my father would say. I never saw any sign of religion in them. They both played the violin and attempted painting in oils and clay modelling. The violins were dreadful old blackened devices with cracks that had been bogged up with some sort of substance for glue, but both brothers could play them with basic skill and, I noticed, could read music. I thought their oil paintings were dreadfully dark and dreary and their clay modelling very primitive. They had quite a first-class deposit of white clay on the property that they were at one stage negotiating to sell to the Bendigo Pottery. I can't recall if anything came of it.

When we visited, they always met us at the door cheerily and with a respectable and pleasant familiarity. They were frank and pleasant, albeit slow, conversationalist, philosophical about their circumstances and used to dealing with the irritations of life including attending to minor injuries and flesh wounds incurred in the business of farming or the bunions, blemishes, boils, carbuncles and insect bites suffered in daily existence. They had their own remedy for all these things whether it be stitching up with a needle and thread, administering kerosene, eucalyptus oil, Condy's crystals, raw linseed oil, turpentine, castor oil or even creosote or a raw onion.

One day George turned up at The Crown and said to my father, "Reg, I am worried about Dave. He is refusing to talk to me. All he does is sit in his chair and ignore me. I am worried about him and wonder if he is sick. Would you please come out with me and have a look at him?"

Naturally my father obliged and when he entered the house and saw Dave sitting in the chair it was clear that he was dead and had been so for quite some time. Poor old George probably knew that in his heart of hearts but refused to admit to himself that he had lost his lifelong companion. Dave's death was recorded as 18 July 1958 at an age of 88 years. He had been born in 1870 and lived his entire life at Axedale. In the year that he died, the Americans succeeded in putting their first satellite into orbit and yet another animal was shot into space when Gordo, a squirrel monkey, was fired up 600 miles. Gordo was okay until splashdown when he drowned due to failure of his flotation device. One year and 17 days after Dave's death, George died on 5 August 1959 aged 85 years.

The main asset in George's estate was of course the land, which was valuable. Before he died, George told my father that there were several stashes of money in the property, one of which was in the roof and that he should be careful when accessing that because there was a booby-trap set up to stop anyone stealing it. While this cautionary information was conveyed to the lawyer attending the property to take an inventory, he discounted it almost to his detriment when, as he accessed the manhole from the top of a ladder, a large log of red gum slid down and just missed his ear. In the roof we discovered a number of old treacle tins jammed full of coins and notes in the old currency of King George VI who died on the 5 February 1952. More tins were found jammed full of the same currency in the wall cavity between the kitchen and Dave's bedroom.

Of particular interest to me at the time were a number of muzzle loading double-barrelled shot guns on the premises. They were found under the beds and in the other rooms fully loaded with powder and shot, capped and ready to go. Some were very old with Damascus twist barrels that were prone to blow up if overcharged. My father tied them all to a tree and pulled the trigger with a long cord attached to fire them separately off from a safe distance. Also found were powder flasks, ram rods, nipple caps, shot pouches and bullet moulds plus a very early model muzzle loading Colt 45 revolver which my father wanted to throw in the dam. I counselled him against doing this and it was eventually sold for a tidy sum that went to The Benevolent Home.

I still remember Dave and George as tall, broad-shouldered, square jawed-imposing persons who in their younger days would have been handsome examples of manhood. Although overlaid with years of extreme frugality, dirt and grime, they somehow radiated a presence of goodwill. I have often wondered what brought them to their peculiar existence as gentlemen hermits. It was, in retrospect, a privilege to know them.

29. The Harris grave at the Old Axedale Cemetery.

Chapter 27

THE BEAT GENERATION

The 1950s in Bendigo were pretty calm but some exciting new developments in music, fashion and entertainment primed us for the radical changes to our coming youthful years when the term 'teenager' would be used for the first time. Up until now we were just called boys, girls or young people. The term 'teenager' defined the gap between adults and kids. We were becoming a new cohort with our own identity and I was one of the pioneer teenagers.

At the end of the 1940s and into the early 1950s American artists like Nat King Cole, Tony Bennett and Perry Como continued to maintain their popularity, and together with American swing, still formed a significant part of commercial radio. But then a quasi-cult developed among some rhythm hungry teenagers, the males of which were called bodgies and the females widgies. They seemed to have been born out of the jitterbuggers and jivers of the big band swing era in the 1930s and 1940s. Bodgies had their own dress style with big shouldered jackets tapered down to hug the hips, and trousers with narrow tapered cuffs. Navy was a popular colour, often worn with canary yellow socks and ox blood brogues or suede shoes. Hairstyles copied the cut of film star Tony Curtis or combined a crew cut top with long lengths of hair in a ducktail at the back of the neck. Widgies' haircuts were often a slightly longer version of the 'Tony Curtis' or, later in the 1950s, a beehive style hairdo or ponytail. They wore short skirts, round-necked sleeveless blouses and flat shoes with bobby socks.

Newspapers occasionally provided lurid reports of depraved bodgie and widgie parties. They generally came from tough working-class areas and were often regarded as louts and illiterate hoons. An allegation that at times contained more than just a little substance. One well-known Bendigo identity had a reputation for carrying a bike chain in his pocket for use as a weapon. Victoria Police formed a special 'Bodgies and Widgies' squad to bust up gangs. The Melbourne *Sun-Herald newspaper* reported in November 1952 that about 200 bodgies and widgies had clashed with police in a Swanston Street milk bar. Luckily, being then only aged eight and in Grade 2 at Gravel Hill, I was more interested in Hopalong Cassidy than joining Bendigo's teenage gang, the existence of which was confirmed by a report in the *Sun-Herald* on 17 June 1956. For the next two years, Australia's newspaper editors generated an atmosphere of fear through their articles on the violent behaviour of bodgies causing many people to believe that the country's teenagers were uncontrollable. They had seen nothing yet. The 'Rock 'n' Roll' generation was still to come.

Few people had good record players in the 1950s, the best were 'radiograms' which were a piece of furniture that combined the radio and record player, fitted with larger quality loudspeakers than an ordinary radio. The first time I heard one of the wonderful old 50s hits on a radiogram I was overawed. It was at the back of Lou Robinson's butcher shop in Lyttleton Terrace in the residential part where the family lived. A leap in technology from old-fashioned records played at 78 rpm came in 1956 with the appearance of the first 45 rpm records. The sound was better and the new records didn't break when you dropped them. Stereo sound did not arrive until 1958 when the first two channel stereo records were published but it was a sound not heard much until the 1960s when stereo record players became more common as rock 'n' roll and pop gained more followers.

Back at The Crown, Zel and I were left with an old 'His Masters Voice' windup console gramophone in the dining room that we could only access at evenings after all the guests had finished their meal. We had just a handful of old 78 rpm bakelite records in our sound library. Chad Morgan got a good run with his 'I'm The Sheik of Scrubby Creek' and another favourite was 'The Green Door' by Jim Lowe. Meanwhile, by the late 50s the bodgies and widgies faded away leaving only their haircuts, adapted by the early rockers dressed in jeans with turned up cuffs, as they took over their predecessors popular meeting places at local milk bars with jukeboxes, where they could listen to the current genre of rhythm and blues and hit parade music.

Rechter's Café in Mitchell Street called 'The American' was a popular haunt for teenagers with a slightly rebellious attitude. Set up in US style, with booths containing slide-in bench seats for three on each side of a table in the middle, plus additional seating provided on high stools in front of a long counter. Fully equipped with ice cream dispensers, hotdog machines and milkshake makers, you could order pretty much any kind of ice cream sundae or shake known to mankind, or a soft drink from the multiplicity of choices in the fridge. Hamburgers were assembled to your specifications and, from the extensive display behind the counter, you could buy cigars and American cigarettes such as Chesterfield, Pall Mall, Salem, Kent, Lucky Strike, Camel, Lark, Newport, More and Temple Bar.

The jukebox was the beating heart of this café culture and a central part of its attraction. A spectacle of sight and sound with lights and chrome held together in a colourful bakelite plastic chest with a domed window in the front that allowed you to see the selected records retrieved and played under a mechanical arm. They received the newest recordings first, played music on demand without commercials and were most popular during the 1950s and early 1960s. Choosing your own songs from the jukebox was more than a fun thing—it was an expression of teenage power and control. The only way to get music of your choice without hiring a live band. With a shilling in the slot, I had the musical world of pop at my fingertips. Jukeboxes kept customers around and that meant more money spent in the premises on other items. Girls in blue denims, twinsets and ponytails, and boys in black jeans, crêpe sole desert boots and "slickem back" Brylcreem hairdos congregated to play the latest rock 'n' roll hits of the day from Buddy Holly, The Big Bopper, Elvis Presley, Johnny O'Keefe and others.

When I walked through the doors into Rechters Café as a teenager, I immediately felt a few inches taller because my universe had got smaller. That's what happened when I slid into a booth with a malted milk and a packet of American cigarettes while in the background Elvis was vocalising Jailhouse Rock and the pinball machines were pinging away. It was reality, even better than the set of *Happy Days*. I went there often as I could in the 1950s with my mate Jon Rechter who was a nephew of the proprietor. Some parents took a dim view of such premises which they considered to be breeding grounds for delinquent teenagers. While it was the age of the 'Beat Generation' it was also the era of the diehard, middle-of-the-road, stick in the mud, Man in The Grey Flannel Suit.

At the other side of the fountain at the top of View Street opposite the Queen Elizabeth Oval (QEO) another milk bar popular with young rebels without a cause was run by Bert Butters. Bert's specialty was thick shakes. He had the thickest malted milks in Bendigo. Nobody knew what his secret thickness ingredient was that made them difficult to suck up a straw. His malted milks were made into an art with specialty mixes such as 'The Purple People Eater', 'Dracula's Blood', 'Choc Muck', 'Blue Heaven', 'The Witchdoctor', and such like which drew young people from far and wide to his shop. Making milkshakes was quite an art, requiring a variety of ingredients apart from milk and flavoured essences. Yeast, malt, caramel, honey, chocolate, butter, ice cream and cream (and sometimes fruit) were added, depending on the texture and strength of taste required. It took a certain skill to get all these components right. Then the density of the final shake could be varied between thick and thin by adjusting the rotational speed of the electric mixer and the time the ingredients were mixed. Bert Butters was a master of the art.

'Rock Around The Clock' heard during the opening and closing credits of the movie *Blackboard Jungle*, screened here in 1956, was the first rock and roll number to top the charts. Around the world, kids danced "wildly and defiantly" in the aisles of picture theatres wherever the movie played (I saw it happen in Bendigo) with some audiences tearing up theatre seats. In Australia, the chief censor had banned the film outright. His decision was reversed on appeal but it was similarly banned in some 15 different countries. The film was described as a vivid and hair-raising melodrama of juvenile violence , and an unsettling piece of work that was tense and disturbing. A group that danced in protest outside police headquarters in Melbourne on 22 September were charged with offensive and indecent behaviour.

The visit of Bill Haley and his Comets to Australia in 1957 with live renditions of 'Rock Around The Clock' absolutely launched the teenage youth movement of the 20th century embodied in rock and roll. The song eventually sold 25 million copies to be dubbed "The National Anthem of Rock and Roll." There was no doubt now that teenagers were a distinct social category with their own music, clothing fashions and heroes. And guess what? I was now 13 and qualified.

Elvis Presley had recorded his first hit in 1956 with 'Heartbreak Hotel' followed by 'Let Me Be Your Teddy Bear', 'All Shook Up', 'Don't Be Cruel' and others. My favourite was 'Blue Suede Shoes', recorded in 1956 with its legendary introduction—

Well it's one for the money, two for the show, three to get ready and go cat go! But don't you step on my blue suede shoes!

My father was horrified by Elvis's energised interpretations of songs and provocative performance style and did what he could to counsel me not to be influenced by him. My father's attitude was a reflection of opinion in the USA. A judge in Jacksonville, Florida, ordered Presley to tame his act. Crowds in Nashville and St Louis burned him in effigy! In Australia, Perth's *Daily News* on 14 November 1957 under the headline "Filth and Eroticism" argued that Presley's records should be banned. In Sydney, *The Sunday Truth* on 9 February 1958 claimed that Elvis's movie *Jailhouse Rock* was "sex crazed and disgusting". Teenagers still flocked to his movies and bought his records and as rock 'n' roll erupted across Australia, the public alarm over perceived teenage delinquency escalated.

But Elvis was a role model to us, particularly in his movies. Always polite and courteous addressing ladies with "Yes M'am/ No M'am," never using swear words, always fighting for and doing what was right. Throughout most of his life Elvis was a teetotaller, fiercely opposed to drugs, although he became hopelessly addicted to opioids in the end. More than anyone else he gave us teenagers belief in our own identity and somehow unified and empowered us with self-esteem arising from belief in our own culture. His music and songs appealed to kids from all socio-economic groups creating a commonality of interest and amalgamating influence. Many of us imitated the hairstyle, lumber jackets or narrow ties made popular by Elvis and although denim jeans had been around for some time, they now became really popular. My father hated them. In his mind they related to denim work wear worn by manual labourers. He was even less impressed when he first saw me with a pair of suede ripple-soled shoes we called "brothel creepers" and bright "Presley purple" socks. A "slickem back" Brylcreem hairdo and duffel coat completed my sartorial splendour when I went to Saturday afternoon movie matinees.

Just as the post-war period spawned the golden age of western movies and the golden age of radio dramas it also produced a golden age of pop music writers and singers. I didn't appreciate at the time that I was living through what I think was the richest period in the history of pop music. Elvis changed everything, music, language, clothes, and he unleashed the raw, sexual appeal of rock and roll. Being a teenager through this amazing transformation was a wonderful and exciting experience. [A selected list of hits from the Golden Age of Pop Music is in Appendix 6.] In 1959, Aussie great Col Joye's number one hit 'Oh Yeah Uh Uh' was a title which the older generation thought was proof positive that the social mores of the younger generation were in decay and several radio stations refused to play Johnny O'Keefe's 'Shout' because they thought it was too loud for listeners.

The day the music died warrants special mention. It was on 3 February 1959 when a private plane carrying Buddy Holly, Richie Valens and The Big Bopper (J.P. Richardson) crashed, killing all three. Teenagers were devastated, particularly the girls, with the loss of heart-throb Buddy Holly. His first big hit was 'That'll Be the Day' in 1957, reaching number one in the USA. His next hit, 'Peggy Sue' followed shortly after. The last hit single he had, released just before he died, was 'It Doesn't Matter Any More'. I was a fan and loved his work. I was an even greater fan of The Big Bopper. His bestseller in 1958 had been 'Chantilly Lace' sung with his animated baritone scaling pop voice. I was then 14 and in Form 2E at Bendigo High School, bursting with testosterone and whipped into a frenzy by the Bopper's words:

> *You know what I like—Chantilly lace with a pretty face and a ponytail hangin' down, a wiggle in a walk and a giggle in a talk make the world go round. There ain't nothing in the world like a big-eyed girl make me act so funny, make me spend my money, make me feel real loose like a long-necked goose, like a girl!—Oh, baby that's what I like!*

Now a declared member of the group adults disparagingly called 'teenagers' I was on my way to knowing absolutely everything that was worth knowing—so I thought.

Chapter 28

CALGULLY
AND LOSS

By the end of Grade 6 at Gravel Hill State School I had every expectation of being rejected as unsuitable for high school due to my appalling performance with maths subjects. Our Grade 6 teacher Mr DeeDee continually reminded us that if we failed to reach an adequate standard in all subjects, we ran the risk of being kept at Gravel Hill's Year 7 and 8 Forms. I was genuinely resigned to that prospect and astonished to discover I had been accepted at Bendigo High School.

When school started on 5 February 1957, it was soon apparent that the 780 students enrolled for the year would not fit into the school buildings. Not all first form (Year 7) students in particular could be accommodated. For the first few weeks several large groups of us took classes in the school hall while the problem was sorted. Mixing such a large number of on-the-cusp teenage boys with growing gonads together in cheek-by-jowl proximity inevitably led to friction between those unknown to each other until the pecking order was established and friends made.

Having made it to high school from such a tough school as Gravel Hill, I thought I was pretty good and at the first hint of a confrontation found myself in an after-school fight. That was my first mistake. My encounter was with Valentine Ignatenko and I figured I'd be okay because he was smaller than me. Unfortunately, he knew nothing about the Marquis of Queensbury Rules and belted the living daylights out of me. My father used to say, "Experience is a good school my son, but its fees are high." Val and I later became good friends.

The announcement was eventually made that Forms 1A and 1C would be based at California Gully (Calgully) State School located more than half-way to Eaglehawk. For me, allocated to 1A, the difference was a five-minute walk through the park to the main high school compared with an almost 30-minute bike ride. Most kids caught the 8:30 tram at the fountain, which I used as my limit starting point to get to school on time riding my Malvern Star semi-racer bike. Arriving before the tram wasn't hard as it had to stop for passengers on the way.

30. Calgully tram.
Photograph by Alan Eldridge Smith, State Library of Victoria.

I felt quite at home in Calgully State School built around the same time and in the same architectural style as Gravel Hill State School, only considerably smaller but with similar classrooms, two of which were to house around 40 students each, allocated to Bendigo High School. It was more relaxed than Gravel Hill with less corporal punishment, a more rural environment and had better teachers. The call to classrooms was made with an old hand-held cow bell. I felt lucky to be assigned to Calgully as it was a kind of a halfway house or transition between state school and high school. With only around 80 students, it was a much smaller and more cohesive environment than the main high school. Except for a few tussocks, our 'sports ground' was pretty much devoid of grass and made up largely of gravel clay and stones but the surrounding environment provided wonderful scope for adventure. The peaks of mullock and sand heaps were great to slide down on old sheets of tin and a concrete water race made a fabulous bike track in the dry season enabling you to ride on the wall going around a sharp bend due to the centrifugal effect. Alas, sometimes misjudged by the cyclist causing him to fly off the edge into the bush resulting in considerable loss of skin. At the back of the Calgully swimming pool there was a huge sand heap where we used to ride our bikes down a soft angled slope. I saw Ian Scarfe ride down it one day when the front wheel of his bike dug into the sand causing him, while still seated, to cartwheel several times and then continue on sedately.

Old mining areas near the school sprinkled with peppercorn trees were an ideal place to sneak into after-school to have a clandestine smoke and also a popular venue for after-school fights. The fights became a regular thing that happened almost every day after school. It was a practice, common among testosterone-charged youths, to challenge someone during the day to a fight.

It was a spectator sport with a regular number of supporters attending to cheer on the opposing pugilists. No one was seriously hurt although there was many a blood nose and black eye and I suspect an occasional missing tooth. It was an open slather no holds barred show with just a few rules such as no hitting below the belt or someone on the ground. Fights ended quickly if someone submitted and never seemed to result in any lasting animosity between contestants. The novelty wore off after a while and the fights stopped. It was really a no-win caper and contestants eventually decided they'd had enough.

One of the highlights of Calgully was its woodworking class based at the school and run by Mr Hamilton. It provided instruction for students from a number of district schools who wished to undergo training in the subject. Being students in situ, it was logical to provide a weekly class for us. It was a boy's own affair with the girls being directed and instructed to pursue what were thought to be more artistic and domestic goals. Although never becoming highly skilled I enjoyed the subject and learned some techniques that stayed with me for life. Mr Hamilton was a fairly humourless and stern fellow who happily applied the strap to any student who fooled around, earning him the nickname 'Strappo Hamilton'.

The rest of my academic year at Calgully was largely uneventful. I thought that our two teachers Mr O'Shannessy and Miss Woodman were better than fair average quality but both respectively failed to inspire me in mathematics and French. The endorsement in my report book "maths rather weak" was a considerable percentage understated from what I deserved.

* * *

Five days before Christmas, our grandmother Sarah Walker, who we called 'Nana', died at the age of 89. I had known her for 13 years and most of that time I had seen her every day. Her loss was the first time I experienced the death of someone close. I still remember little things about her, the incredible softness of her skin, the little doilies she crocheted to put over milk jugs, the smelling salts she sniffed as a cure for headaches and colds, the mint sauce she insisted on making for herself and especially her dark brown eyes. Born in 1869 she was a very straight, mild-mannered, right-wing Protestant Victorian era lady. It was as though she had popped out of one of Charles Dickens' novels.

As I started to grow and swear, Nana constantly berated me for my conduct, counselled me not to take the Lord's name in vain and made repeated references to the Bible which she told me that I should, like her, read every night. When she got really cross with me, she would break into Dutch Afrikaans quasi-English with exclamations like, "My mucktith Mackie! My mucktith! You will brack de piano." I didn't think I was pounding hard enough on it to break it.

I got the impression that Nana strongly disapproved of the hotel environment and alcohol consumption. She was not happy with my mother's drinking habits. She never took part in the management of the hotel or interfered with it in any way and always accorded my father great respect, which he returned to her in spades. She was a constant and it was comforting for me and my sister to know that she was always there even though, as a veritable reference library on morality, she continually told us what was right and where we were wrong.

Each day she would leave her bedroom to come downstairs and sit in the family's little room where she ate and read and knitted and crocheted and adopted a low profile. At day's end she would then retire upstairs to her bedroom equipped with her own commode and next day go through the same life experience again. She did not seem happy. Occasionally I would engage her to talk about Africa and its monkeys and lions and elephants and she enjoyed that interaction. She suffered great discomfort from a tropical ulcer on her leg which deteriorated over time as did her comprehension and general mental capacity. Before her death she was rapidly enveloped by Alzheimer's and became completely unable to cope in the hotel environment. She was then admitted to the Bendigo Benevolent Home where she spent the rest of her time in an ever-thickening mental fog. I visited her with my mother regularly at first but less as time went on. She didn't recognise me and I hated going there anyway. All these old people were there just waiting to die. As you walked down the passage old ladies and men in their chairs would sit and stare and shake and dribble in shrunken and wrinkled bodies. It was horrible and frightening. I was glad when she died. She had not spoken to me for ages. I wish I had learnt more from her about her time as a military nurse in the Boer War and as a prisoner in one of the British concentration camps where over 26,000 women and children died. Indeed, about her life experiences in general. Much had changed in her lifetime. Born in South Africa in 1869 when it was mind-boggling to think you could put a man-made object into space, she had lived 78 days past the first successful launch of a satellite in 1957. Who would have then thought that 11 years and nine months later USA would land a man on the moon!

My mother was aged 51 when my grandmother died and Nana's death after all those years with her, seemed to emotionally drain my mother and create in her a maudlin melancholy and depression. Nana had been proud of her daughter when she followed in her footsteps and became a nurse but, although she tried, could not hide her disappointment at her daughter marrying a publican. Her particular right-wing Protestant ethic encompassed total abstinence. She was absolutely convinced on the evils of drink, thought that drunkenness was the worst kind of slavery and became distressed when she observed the demon drink taking hold of my mother. Her mother's torment and disapproval contributed to my mother's depreciating self-esteem and sadness.

Chapter 29

DEPRESSION AND ESCAPE

I was delighted when school started in 1958 to be able to attend the main Bendigo High School campus right in the heart of the city on the edge of beautiful Rosalind Park and less than ten minutes walk from The Crown. I often rode my bike because in the days before school backpacks I was equipped with a leather Gladstone bag to carry school books and found that the best way to move it was on the handlebars. Enrolments continued to exceed the 600 students the school had been originally designed for, requiring the use of temporary classrooms constructed on the playground. Further plans were afoot to relocate the occupants of the adjacent Girls Secondary School to Flora Hill so that the campus could be acquired for the high school. In the meantime, some additional classes took place in the adjacent Camp Hill State School, the old sandstone police barracks and an old timber hall behind the Trades Hall in View Street.

It was when my mother arrived inebriated at parent teacher interviews in my early high school years, causing me extreme embarrassment, that I began to grasp the gravity of her situation. I often caught her, late in the day after the hotel had settled down, the staff had gone home and she had consumed too many brandies or whiskies, staring into the large mirror over the small faux fire place in the hotel office. She usually had a drink in one hand and a cigarette in the other. At times when I saw her doing this she was crying and I would ask her what was wrong. She would always say, "Nothing." But I knew that it must be something.

She clearly was not at peace with the face that stared back at her. At the least, I think now, in her fifties, she was depressed by the vision of the ageing woman she had become in the mirror in comparison with her earlier younger self, and it was not just a matter of looks but a question of the person she knew she had become. A stranger to her youth, she saw herself as addicted, overweight, very tired and hopelessly locked into a self-punishing environment from which she could not escape. While she was never paranoid, neurotic or unstable, the black dog of depression continued to envelop her and her drinking got worse. Often times she was so drunk that she could not manage to walk up the stairs to her bedroom by herself requiring my sister, Zelda, and I on either side to help her accomplish the task. It was a case of three steps up and two steps back but we always made it in the end.

Next morning the first thing my mother did, in order to face the hotel staff and public, was to swallow one of two popular headache powders. A dose which she would often repeat during the day. Both Vincent's APC Powder and Bex Powder were compound analgesics, containing a mix of aspirin, phenacetin and caffeine often, leading to addiction. Phenacetin was later found to be carcinogenic to humans and responsible for an increased risk of death due to kidney failure, cardiovascular diseases and various cancers. Advertising blurbs for these two 'cure-alls' were "Take Vincent's with confidence, for quick three-way relief," and "Have a cup of tea, a Bex and a good lie down". Both were banned in Australia in 1977 and all pharmaceutical use of phenacetin banned in the early 1980s. Another strange, albeit benign, habit of my mother's was to suck peppermint Lifesaver lollies all day.

I began to notice that she seemed to be losing interest in the hotel business. In the past she had been obsessive about floral arrangements and displays in the hotel but now it was noticeable how her formerly precious flowers and plants drooped and wilted through lack of care. I remember well the sickening smell of rancid dead flower water poured out of the vases when they eventually received attention and the vision of my mother snipping the stems of smelly Christmas lilies with cigarette in hand, and a glass of scotch and soda in close proximity. Most concerning were the arguments between my mother and father. I don't recall the detail, just the frequency. Because I knew she was unhappy I tried not to upset her by keeping my feelings to myself. If I did something 'wrong' or talked back I was afraid It might make her drink more.

The overall hotel environment was chaotic. I felt not in control of my situation and insecure. There were also my circumstances at school, my prospects in the future and the worldly context of everything to take on board. There was a lot of stuff to sort out and reconcile. In my early high school teens, I spent a lot of time worrying about what was to come. I could not imagine any occupation that I would be good enough to study for and be. I worried about major issues such as death, religion and survival and how I might be able to get a job to support myself, or using my father's words "pull my own weight". I was in a perpetual state of emotional crisis, confused and seriously muddled up. The only place that

I could confidently get control was in the privacy of my own bedroom where I could place my belongings where I wanted and think my thoughts without being interrupted. In there I became an obsessive-compulsive.

As time went on my anger increased. I resented my parents, each night after the evening meal had finished, retiring to a locked bar room for a drinking session with other staff, leaving my sister and I in charge of the hotel office. On repeated occasions we would knock on the bar room door pleading to be allowed to come in and join them only to be refused. It was a straightforward rejection and it was often not till after 9 o'clock that they surfaced to have their evening meal. We would then be sent to bed. Until then, I sometimes got rid of some of my frustration by tossing a tennis ball at the end kitchen wall and catching it on the rebound in the hope that it might improve my 'ball sense'. The result was a wall pockmarked with ball shapes that my father had to repaint. At the end of the evening meal each night my mother prepared specially carved butterballs for breakfast by using a curved serrated metal instrument dipped in hot water. The balls left in covered dishes on a bench for the morning breakfast proved to be ideal ammunition to fire at the ceiling at the end of a flexible knife. There they stuck and stayed until the arrival of a very hot day. I began to become more argumentative and rebellious, particularly when it came to dealings with my mother. But on the other hand, my underlying desire was always a need to please my parents.

I found that a sense of control comes with achievement. I enjoyed escaping from my parents, the customers and staff of the hotel on my pushbike. Riding long distances, solo, in the surrounding countryside became a common modus operandi on weekends. In the solitude and silence of my riding adventures I did not feel alone. I found that being by myself with just my surroundings to observe, only my thoughts to contemplate and the physical challenges before me to confront, was restorative and gave me a sense of accomplishment. I rode to Lockwood, Goornong, Bridgewater, Castlemaine, Heathcote and back with shorter rides to Marong, Axedale, Huntly and Strathfieldsaye. In doing this I was imitating my hero Russell Mockridge who was described at the time as Australia's greatest all round cyclist. I knew him personally because he stayed at The Crown when he came to Bendigo to compete in cycling races at The Bendigo Showgrounds, that had an excellent bicycle circuit attracting top riders during the Easter Fair each year. I was devastated when, early in this year, 1958, he was killed by a bus during a road race. During my absence on bike rides my parents had no idea where I was. I simply told them I was going for a ride.

For several years my mate Robert Iser and I had ridden our bikes regularly in the evening to the smallbore rifle range at Junourton where, for a small fee, we could hire a .22 rifle to shoot at targets. We were the youngest members of the club and well looked after by responsible senior men who trained and instilled in us correct firearms safety and protocol. I became reasonably proficient at the exercise which helped my self-esteem. When the club moved into Bendigo I decided to purchase a proper target rifle from money I had saved through hotel chores and a contribution by my father for my birthday. I placed an order with Rupe Hartley, a licensed gun dealer, who had a shop in Allen's Walk known as Hartley's Shoe Repairs opposite the delicatessen. Most of the shop was devoted to guns. Shoe repairing activities took place on the floor above where cobblers were summoned from below by radio and a hand-operated dumbwaiter lift that cranked boots and shoes up and down. Rupe was notorious for taking forever to repair your shoes. It was not uncommon for him to have them for a month or more before you got them back. He was, however, a wonderful character that would happily talk to anyone, regardless of age, on the subject of guns. He always had a laugh and was entertaining and polite.

When I collected the gun Rupe took me upstairs to the cobblers' room where he had constructed a rifle range with a long concrete pipe that led to a target at the end. He explained that as the gun was new, he had to "shoot it in" to make sure that the sights were accurate. We pinged away with .22 cartridges on the first floor of Allen's Walk for half an hour before he was satisfied with the setting on the sights.

Downstairs in the shop there was a loose floorboard which Rupe often removed to "let a few go" to make sure that the gun in question was operating satisfactorily before delivering it to a customer. Some future urban archaeologist will one day be scratching his head over the discovery of the cache of lead under the floorboards of Allen's Walk.

My new gun, a single shot Sportco designed for target shoot-ing, improved my performance so much that I was invited to be part of the Victorian Pennant Team shooting championships in Melbourne. Regrettably my father refused to allow me to participate. I couldn't reconcile why he was happy to allow me, at the age of 14, to ride my pushbike to the gun club each week, with rifle slung on my back and a box-full of ammunition, through the main streets of Bendigo, but wouldn't allow me to travel to Melbourne under the constant supervision of responsible senior men in order to participate in the Pennant Team shoot. The police stopped me a couple of times on the way to the gun club but after being satisfied that I had disabled the gun by removing the firing pin bolt and was on a bona fide trip to shoot at the club, allowed me to proceed. It's impossible to imagine that happening today.

In April this year (1958) the Commonwealth Government issued a list of 178 banned books which would be confiscated by Federal Customs because they were "indecent", "obscene", "disgusting", or "offensive", and should not be read by Australians. The list included several books on the exploits of Casanova, *The Decameron, Lady Chatterley's Lover, Naughty Hilda* and *The Sexual Life of Robinson Crusoe.* They became hot property the moment they were banned and several well-thumbed editions were soon circulating around Bendigo High School. Meanwhile, Duane Eddy took to the air with his twangy guitar and Peggy Lee recorded 'Fever', perhaps the greatest hit of her career. Back in Bendigo the new Olympic Pool was declared open and in the final year test in Form 2E at Bendigo High School I was awarded 40 per cent for arithmetic and 25 per cent for French with an endorsement on my report book which read: "Attitude must change for the better! More co-operation is required! Capable of much better work."

31. Madge, Zel and Mickey, circa 1958.

Chapter 30

SHOPS

Cruising around the streets and shops after school, Saturday morning or any time in the day during school holidays was a kind of solace or relief to me from the chaos of The Crown. Sometimes I would just wander or I might go to one of my favourite shops such as Army Disposals in Hargreaves Street to browse. It was not long since World War II and the Korean War which came to a 'close' in 1954, meaning there was still plenty of surplus army, navy and air force stuff to dispose of. I loved going there just to look. There was everything from tank aerials, backpacks, gas masks, World War II leather fighter pilots' helmets and goggles, leather gauntlets, army, air force and navy jackets and jumpers, heavy overcoats, leggings, shirts and all sorts of tools from shovels to spanners, wrenches, sledgehammers, rope, twine, buckets and billies. It was, to me, a reality show of much of the stuff I had seen in war movies.

In the late 1950s, Bendigo was still struggling to emerge from parts of its pre-war and post-war persona. Some shops had hardly changed at all. Dowell's hardware store, two doors up on the left from The Crown, was a tiny little shop and a time-warp from an earlier era. At the front there was a hand operated 'Plume' brand petrol pump from which Mr Dowell manually pumped petrol out of an underground tank into a large glass bowl marked with graduated quantity measures at the top of the bowser. When the bowl was full to the required amount, another tap was then turned on to gravity feed the fuel into the vehicle that was being supplied. He specialised in providing dairy fittings and parts for dairy farmers but also had a never-ending range of hardware bits and pieces and always seemed to stock what I wanted. If you asked for a doover wacky in imperial size he would scratch around through the drawers behind his counter until he found one. I was a regular customer of his from a very early age and would often go in with the smallest of orders such as a single washer or bolt I needed for my billy cart and he would willingly supply me. He was one of many retailers in Bendigo's CBD who was caring, attentive and kind to me as a kid.

Bennett's Arcade was a wonderful Victorian era time tunnel that joined Hargreaves Street with Pall Mall. In the same genre as London's famous Burlington Arcade and Melbourne's prestigious Block Arcade in that, like them, almost its entire length was roofed in glass panels forming an apex to allow in natural light. A system of light canvas blinds allowed the glass panels to be covered on hot days and if the weather got too gloomy, large pendulous lights hanging down from the apex could brighten up the precinct. Big station clocks with Roman numerals were mounted at each end of the walkway with the one at Bennett's Hardware store painted with the face of a policeman wearing an English style 'Bobby' helmet, perhaps intended to deter shoplifters. The arcade was unfortunately destroyed by fire in the 1960s.

As a child it was the hardware store on the Hargreaves Street entrance to Bennett's Arcade that attracted me. Goods were displayed on wide sloping shelves tilted to the walkway so that when you went past you couldn't fail to notice them. In addition to hardware there were children's tricycles, scooters, rocking horses, pushers, cane baskets, bags and suitcases, cooking utensils and crockery, tennis rackets, cricket bats and all sorts of sporting goods, tins of paint and, it seemed to me, absolutely everything in the world that you could ever possibly want. I loved going there just to look, or, if I had money, to spend.

The arcade was paved in tessellated tiles with many wonderful little shops on each side of the walk. There were bookshops, tailors, dressmakers, ladies lingerie shops and hairdressers, shoe stores and men's barbers, jewellers, a fabric shop and a flower shop that had an external gully trap that I recall peeing in at the direction of my mother as a very young child. I remember one shop had a clock in the window with a little girl on a spring that danced up and down. At the Pall Mall end, Dr Beischer had his dental surgery upstairs and fronting the street was George's café run by Angelo, a Greek gentleman.

Angelo's specialty was the extraordinary variety of chocolates he always had for sale and displayed in his shopfront window and his expertise in the art of dispensing ice cream sundaes according to individual specifications of taste or his own special ingredients. Banana sundaes were done in a flash, starting with two dollops of ice cream, crushed raspberries or cherries plopped over the dollops, a dob of whipped cream in the centre, a split of banana on each side and a sprinkle over the whole lot with chopped nuts, grated chocolate or cinnamon if you wanted. Then you could add, if you liked, maple syrup, honey or your chosen syrup flavour. Finally, it was served with wafer biscuits stuck into each ice cream dollop. There were all sorts of ingredient variations that could be made with different flavoured ice cream, fruit such as peaches, pineapple or pears, and a choice of different nut sprinkles with the final topping always in the power of the purchaser.

My father ran an account at several of the major stores including Myers, The Beehive, Morley Johnsons and Matthews Brothers which enabled me, as long as I had my father's permission, to book up purchases on his account at any of these shops. I did my own shopping for clothes at a very early age and got to know some shop attendants personally. Some already knew me as they were customers of The Crown.

Matthews Brothers was one of my favourite places to shop. It was an old-fashioned, manchester, haberdashery and general clothing store fronting Hargreaves Street, where the mall currently is, painted predominantly a post office red on the outside. It looked like it hadn't changed since the 19th century. Inside seemed as though it was from the same era with long rows of wooden counters behind which stood shop assistants in front of a system of high wooden shelves and pull-out drawers jammed with items for sale. In response to a customer's enquiry, helpful staff retrieved items from the shelves for inspection. When payment was made the assistant jammed your money together with a hand-written invoice into a little brass cylinder and, after hooking it onto a network of wires that ran across the ceiling of the store, shot it with the aid of a rubber catapult device across the shop to the cashier's office on the other side. The cashier then put any change and the receipt back into the cylinder and fired it back to the sender. When the shop was busy it was mesmerising watching dozens of these little brass cylinders whizzing all over the shop like tiny cable cars on the network of wires. The system was clearly a hangover from

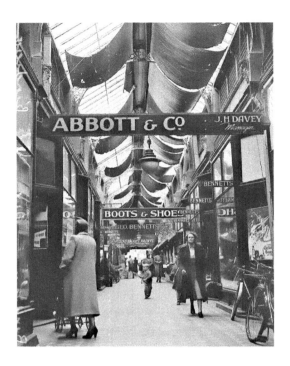

32. Bennetts Arcade.
Photos by Travis McScratchey, 'Lost Bendigo and District',
lostbendigodistrict.weebly.com.

the times when ordinary staff were not trusted to handle money. Matthews Brothers was a real blast from the past.

When I charged a sale to my father's account the cashier had to confirm the account was good for the sale to proceed. On a busy day this sometimes took a while requiring the sales staff to entertain me with pleasant chat until the cashier's confirmation was returned. Only then were the purchased goods wrapped in brown paper drawn from a silvered cast-iron dispenser and tied with string dangling from a ball which skilled shop assistants could snap in their fingers.

Two doors down from The Crown towards Bull Street was Basil Tonkin's tobacconist shop. Basil's specialty was his own pipe tobacco mixes prepared according to his personal recipes. They were stored in large glass jars along the counter and displayed labels alleging some of their secret ingredients such as honey, maple syrup, cinnamon, rose petals, sugar and spice and everything nice. The entire shop had an amazingly heady smell about it with scents and aromas causing an intoxicating effect as soon as you walked in. He stocked a huge array of different sorts of pipes, specialised in an extensive choice of cigars, roll your own tobacco and supplies and every brand of Australian and overseas cigarettes you could imagine plus all related smoking paraphernalia such as lighters, matches, pipe cleaners and tampers, ashtrays and cigar cutters.

One door closer to The Crown, next to Basil's shop, was Bill Holland's electrical fix it shop where you could take your old radio, radiator, jug, vacuum cleaner or blender and he'd repair it to last you for another few years. As time passed it eventually became cheaper to buy a new one than pay to repair the old item.

On the other side of Basil's towards bull Street was Allan Mallalieu's tiny little chemist shop. My father ran an account there and it was a go-to place for me to get a quick fix for a sneeze or sniffle, have film from my Brownie box camera developed, seek Allan's advice on current rashes or minor injuries or collect pre-ordered items on behalf of my parents. A calm, considerate and attentive man, he was always willing to spend time listening to my complaints, whether real or imagined, and was a constant source of assurance and comfort over a period of 20 years of my life. During that time, he served four generations of the Beck family and when he retired, we presented him with a silver plate with words engraved expressing our gratitude for his service. In the 1950s he often compounded medicines in the shop and made prescribed tablets on the premises. He typed directions with a manual typewriter on pre-printed gum labels with the heading "The Tablets", "The Ointment", "The Mixture" or "The Cream". Most of the time we had no idea what we were taking as the ingredients were not disclosed. Chemists also sold chemicals such as sulphur, sulphuric acid, permanganate of potash (Condy's crystals) and even arsenic.

I bought my shoes from Crawford's Shoe Store at the corner of Bull and Hargreaves Streets where I could charge them to my father's account. In the shop they had an x-ray machine where you could stand and shove your foot in the bottom while you looked through the top to see if the x-ray vision of your foot revealed whether it was a good fit in the shoe. Every time you bought a pair of shoes you got a free dose of radiation.

Chapter 31

RESPONSIBILITIES

I n 1959 the non-aboriginal population of Australia reached 10 million and the population of Bendigo High School was twice what it was 10 years previously. With many classes exceeding 40 students, the pressure of numbers brought problems. One of my problems was French. I figured that I was on a hiding to nothing in that subject and decided to drop it. Meanwhile I continued to struggle with arithmetic. My track record to date had been so appalling in that subject that I had lost all heart for it. I just couldn't 'get it'. My maths teacher, Mr Mick Morrisey, did nothing to help my confidence. In one test he gave me three out of 10 and then four off for neatness, equalling minus one, which he gleefully disclosed publicly to the rest of the class causing much merriment at my expense. I had always had problems with numbers. I think I suffered from 'arithmetical dyslexia' arising from my fear of getting things wrong and being exposed as a numerical idiot. Mick Morrisey's public outing of my problem just made things worse and added to my simmering anger. Later in life the calculator saved me from a fate worse than monetary death.

My mother's drinking got worse. My father counselled her to cut back but it had no effect. Her habit of seeking the company of women drinkers in the ladies lounge to join them for a drinking session particularly annoyed my father. If he thought my mother had enough to drink, he would instruct the barmen not to serve her. She would then get her drinking mates to obtain drinks for her. Several times when my father discovered that my mother had been supplied drinks by other women, he had blazing rows with them and threw them off the premises. After a short break most of them came back again. This conflict distressed my mother resulting in screaming arguments between my parents when he would say to her that if she kept it up, she would "drink herself to death." My mother also recruited staff members to obtain drinks for her. She hid them to keep them from my father's eyes in such places as the letterbox under the office counter where customers' mail was posted.

My father then recruited my sister and I as spies to report to him the location of drink hiding spots, which caused arguments with our mother when she found out we had informed on her. My exchanges with her at times became highly emotional and, I regret, sometimes abusive on my part. After one such altercation I 'left home' riding off into the dark of night on my bicycle to the Whipstick Forest with just a packet of cigarettes and a box of matches for sustenance. I lit a camp fire in the bush and sat around it all night smoking cigarettes until dawn and then rode back to The Crown.

Towards the middle of the school year, I was called to the headmaster's office and told that my father had phoned and that he wanted me home straight away as my mother was not well.

When I arrived at The Crown, I was told that she had been taken to Melbourne in an ambulance after collapsing with a headache, and vomiting. My father explained that she had difficulty in speaking and that her condition was serious. She had been taken to Epworth Hospital, and he was going to drive to Melbourne immediately to be with her and was leaving me in charge of the hotel. The staff had been informed and if there were any problems, they should come to me and I could then talk to him when he phoned me regularly during his absence. He handed me the keys to the hotel including the bar and the safe and instructed that each night after bar staff had gone home, I had to count the cash from the three tills and, after leaving the sum specified by him as the 'float' in the tills for the next day's trading, bag the coins in ANZ bank denomination packets, sort and wrap the notes with a rubber band, complete the banking deposit slip, add the total and deposit the money at the bank. I am sure that if my father had been aware of my arithmetic grades at school, he would not have given me this responsibility. I found the task an onerous one and due to my lack of confidence had to count all monies several times before I was sure of the total.

Zelda and I had to book people into accommodation and receive their payments on checkout making sure that we wrote them an official Crown Hotel receipt. Zel had to type the menus for the dining room, which was a task that my mother normally attended to and help as required in the kitchen. Each night with the large bunch of hotel keys that my father left me I had to make sure that the hotel was properly locked. Except for the upstairs fire escape door which was always left open, there were a total of nine doors to check, three external, three bar doors, two dining room doors and one office door. And, finally, my bedroom door. To this day, checking that doors are locked at night has remained an obsession of mine. As a 14-year-old with a poor record with numbers I felt an onerous responsibility in being left to handle the hotel's daily monetary concerns but somehow managed to do it.

My father remained in Melbourne for days. I can't remember how long. It seemed like forever. Several times a day he would phone me and report on my mother's progress and I would report on The Crown. In the meantime, the staff at the hotel were very caring and kind to me and Zelda. I decided that our family circumstances were a good reason for me to completely avoid school for the time being and applied myself to doing what I could to help run The Crown. I spent my days physically helping where I could and asking all staff individually if there were any problems or things, they wished me to do or ask my father when he phoned, or that they wanted to talk to him about personally. On his return the staff very kindly praised my efforts which helped boost my self-esteem.

After receiving medication and close monitoring in an intensive care unit at Epworth for several days my mother seemed to improve. She was then transferred to a general hospital bed where her treatment continued. She had suffered a cerebral haemorrhage or stroke and was lucky to recover from it without any major physical impediments such as difficulty in speaking, weakness in an arm or leg, tingling or numbness. She was, however, still generally not a well person.

On her release from hospital, it was decided that instead of returning to the hotel environment immediately she would stay with a friend at Heathcote. She remained there convalescing for several weeks and continued to improve. While she was there, I decided on one hot day I would ride there on my semi racer bike to visit her. The return distance from Bendigo was more than 90 kilometres and while I had a strong tailwind to Heathcote which helped me considerably, the journey back took me nearly twice as long butting into a hot headwind. Her doctors advised her that she was at risk of having another cerebral haemorrhage and that risk factors included high blood pressure, excessive alcohol consumption and cigarette smoking. She was told that she should cut down on drinking, cigarettes and lose weight.

Chapter 32

A CHALLENGE

In the year 1959, teenagers were pushing the boundaries to test the strength of their revolution. Popular music such as 'Rock Around The Clock' that had featured in the movie *Blackboard Jungle* reflected the emotion of the times and, while Bendigo High School was never a blackboard jungle, it did have some students who fancied they could follow in the footsteps of some of the characters from the movie. Even to the point of copying some of the dialogue. The film featured a rebellious bully and gang leader by the name of Artie West who showed no respect for his teacher, was involved in his assault, and in the end pulled a knife on him. The teacher refused to back down and ultimately was supported by the majority of the class and one student in particular to subdue West. In my class of 3E we had a student who I will call Jack (not his real name) who clearly did not want to be there and did his conscious best to disrupt classes with a repertoire of disturbances. He would interrupt the teacher, ask stupid questions, talk out loud to other students and make belittling, offensive, rude and intimidating remarks to them and the teacher. He particularly intimidated less assertive teachers where he knew he would get away with it.

We had a kind and gentle art teacher of Dutch background who equipped us in each class with the usual watercolour paints and small jam tins to wash brushes in. After filling our tins with water from a sink tap, we would take a seat at our desks. In a typical performance, Jack punched a hole in the bottom of his tin with a compass point so that, when he slowly walked back to his seat at the rear of the class, water trickled along the full distance of the floor. The teacher then said, "Jack! Jack! Your tin it is leaking on the floor." Jack then replied, "Oh yeah Teach! Where?" as he turned the tin upside down to look at the bottom resulting in the entire contents being dumped on the floor, creating a mess that disrupted the whole class.

Sitting in my usual position in the back row of a science class one day I heard a thumping noise to my left and upon looking saw Jack holding his erect penis and thumping it on the desk to the embarrassing amusement of girls further along the row who had a clear view of the performance. I am sure our teacher who had not long arrived in the country from England had a good idea what was going on. Looking at Jack with eyes that could have burned a hole in the back wall he said, in a wonderfully eloquent and meaningful English dialect, "Jack! If you don't put away what you are playing with, I will come up and take it off you!"

We had an American geography teacher, who was out here on exchange from the US. He was tall, well-built and strong with a short-cropped crewcut hairstyle. There was an altercation between him and Jack one day, resulting in the teacher calling Jack to come out to the front of the class. Jack refused and in a scenario that was almost a replay of the scene from *Blackboard Jungle* said, "Come on Teach! Come up here and make me."

After again asking and again being refused, the teacher walked up the aisle to Jack who, in general terms, repeated the challenge to the teacher. In the altercation that followed Jack lost and was marched off to the headmaster's office.

Jack's conduct was having a seriously adverse effect on all the other students in Form 3E and in the schoolyard his reputation as a bully was flourishing. He was a stand over merchant who would pick on individuals constantly to frighten them. There was one student, the son of a church minister, whose nickname amongst all the kids was 'Jelly'. Jack made a point of terrorising him. After a particularly disruptive performance by Jack in our class one day, the teacher, Mrs Griffiths, made an emotional speech to the class accusing us of all being stupid and cowards for putting up with Jack who was causing lasting damage to our education and our future. She said she knew that some of us wanted to learn and that we were being stopped from doing so by Jack who, it seemed, none of us had the guts to stop. It was time she said, "For you to put him in his place." She then stormed out of the class.

Some of the kids cheered but most of us yelled at Jack and told him that we had enough of his nonsense which should stop. In typical stance he threw challenges out saying, "Yeah! Will you?" As he went around poking kids in the chest. When he came to me, I said I would like to. "Yeah?" he said, "Then meet me in the park after school at 4 o'clock and you can have a go!" This was a direct challenge to me in front of the whole class. To refuse I would be deemed a coward.

I found it hard to concentrate in the remaining classes that day. I kept going over in my mind what Danny Morrison had taught me about boxing. Not to close my eyes if I saw a punch heading for my face, to hold my head up and never to duck it, which would simply be an invitation to my opponent to lay me out with an uppercut. I should swerve, or bob left, right or back to avoid punches with head up, fists up, elbows in and eyes open at all times and if I landed a good punch make sure I always followed up quickly. I had also learned from experience that if you are going to get into a street fight you can't rely on the Marquis of Queensbury rules.

Word got around and by 4 o'clock there were 30 or 40 kids in the park waiting for the fight. It was short. After a momentary stand-off Jack charged me with his head down and seeing him coming, I let go with a roundhouse uppercut that hit him square in the face and laid him out. Then, jumping on his back, I grabbed his ears and rubbed and rubbed his face into the lawn. In answer to my question, he very soon replied that he'd had enough. When I released him and told him to clear off (in terms more explicit than that) he ran out of the park followed by a mob of spectators chasing and yelling at him.

The air of rebellion around at the time rubbed off on me and compelled me at times to join in disruptive practices in class. We had an excellent teacher, Shirley Clarke, whose main task was to instil into our psyche the concept of 'Musical Appreciation'. With the tsunami of pop music and rock and roll exuding from the radio waves on a daily basis, Ms Clarke had serious competition when it came to introducing classical music to the minds of an unreceptive student body. While I don't remember the details, I admit that I must have been a disruptive element in class because I clearly remember Ms Clarke sentencing me to the punishment of writing out by hand, 1000 times, "Manners maketh man". By the end of the year, I was forever indebted to her for opening my ears to classical music. She seduced the entire class with loudly played renditions of popular classics on the school's stereo radio gram.

I couldn't believe my ears when I first heard Tchaikovsky's '1812 Overture'. She followed up with popular orchestral presentations such as 'Four Seasons' by Vivaldi, Handel's 'The Arrival of The Queen of Sheba', Eine Kleine Nachtmusik by Mozart, Beethoven symphonies and 'The William Tell Overture' by Rossini (known to us then as the theme from the TV series *The Lone Ranger*) and others.

Back at The Crown I started pushing the boundaries of my own teenage revolution by sneaking out of the hotel at night. After announcing that I was going to bed and locking the door from inside the room, I would then exit via the second storey bedroom window and shimmy down a cast-iron sewerage pipe to the ground. Equipped with a packet of cigarettes purloined from the trail of half-smoked boxes left by my mother I would then venture forth into the night in search of my identity, which I invariably found at Rechter's American Café in Mitchell Street. where I could buy a milkshake and play the latest hits on the jukebox.

As 1959 came to an end, American evangelistic preacher Billy Graham wrapped up his Southern Cross Crusade in Australia which was claimed to be not only the most important religious event in Australian history but the most successful evangelistic endeavour in the history of the world! It was estimated that at least 50 per cent of Australians heard his gospel message either at a live event or on the radio. Some of his rallies attracted greater crowds than attended the grand finals of the Victorian Football League. At the MCG he set an attendance record of more than 130,000 people. I clearly remember him ranting on the radio, but I wonder how many of his religious precepts actually stuck after he left.

As a sign of the different times back then, TV stations still played 'God Save the Queen' before they shut down for the night around 11 p.m.

Chapter 33

A HOUSE AND FUNERALS

When my mother returned to The Crown from her rehabilitation in Heathcote, she was a lesser version of her old self. Still smoking a bit, drinking a bit, not quite as sharp as she had been mentally, and physically not as strong. As time went on, she resumed the level of her old habits and in the end my father knew that he had to get her away from the hotel environment. My sister and I had been pleading for years to live in a house and had begged him to buy one. The problem my father had was, that under the liquor licensing laws, it was compulsory for a publican to live on the licensed premises. In the end he decided to buy a house only two streets and a little more than five minutes walk away in Myers Street. This, he reasoned, would enable him to maintain his domicile at the hotel and come and go to the house as he pleased. The plan was to install us two kids and our mum in the house on a permanent basis while he attended there part-time.

Zel and I were delighted with the beautiful two-storey house with a large kitchen, separate dining and lounge rooms, four bedrooms and a small study in lovely garden surrounds. When we moved in at the beginning of 1960, I took with me my little miniature fox terrier dog 'Patch', who until now had been living in the territory of the hotel backyard where he developed a number of special skills including using the wood heap to climb up on the roof and then run along the top of the brick wall that bounded the Bull Street side of the yard. He soon settled into Myers Street where he enjoyed digging in the garden and chasing sparrows and the neighbours' cats. The rest of the family had more difficulty adjusting to the new environment.

When my sister and I went to school in the morning and my father was at the hotel, this left my mother at the house by herself. Having spent most of her married life up till now in a busy hotel atmosphere she just could not stand the loneliness and each day made her way back to the hotel and the company of others. If my sister and I went home from school for lunch it was to the hotel we would go. At day's end our mother would often stay overnight at the hotel. A convenient practice, facilitated by her drinking during the day. This left my sister and I by ourselves in the four-bedroom double-storey house.

It became clear to us that our mother did not like living there. She did sometimes make an effort on weekends to cook a meal at the house and slept there occasionally. Rarely did our father sleep there. Each day Zel and I had breakfast, lunch and dinner at the hotel and then went home to the house to sleep. It was a strange existence for two teenagers. The realisation of our fervent wish of an idealistic happy family existence in our own house had come to much less than that. Our joint worries about our mother brought us closer together as did living together alone largely unsupervised.

While there was an unspoken understanding between us that we had to support each other, our circumstances weighed heavily on us causing Zel, then aged 16, to become depressed and me to keep struggling with my anger. At the time, although aware of it, I did not realise how bad her depression was and only fully appreciated its depths when much later in life I discovered through reading her diary that she was seriously contemplating suicide. I think my sister's poor self-image and lack of personal confidence was in part a reflection of our mother's situation and my anger, in part, an echo of my father's plight. I regret, in retrospect, that at times my anger was unjustly directed at Zel and my mother.

The present state of my mother's health handicapped her from performing her former hotel duties. She had always been the one to type the hotel menu after conferring with the cook and agreeing on the dishes. But, due to her ill-health, this task now fell to my father who was advised on one occasion by the cook that the evening main course would be 'Roast Beef and Horseradish Sauce'. By the time he got around to typing the menu he was a little worse for drink and instead typed with his two fingers 'Roast Horse and Beef Radish Sauce'. The waitresses picked up the error straight away but rather than bringing it to my father's attention decided to present it as typed to the diners causing great astonishment and laughter in the dining room.

During Easter and other busy periods Zel was called upon to fill her mother's shoes in kitchen and dining room duties as well as servicing upstairs accommodation. At the house, I willingly and enthusiastically applied myself to doing what I could to maintain the garden and regularly mowing the extensive lawns. It was an activity that I then enjoyed due to its novelty.

My grandfather, Alec Beck, known to the family as 'Daddy Beck', had been having frequent trips to hospital and, on his last visit, died on 30 May, aged 86 years. I was aged 15, and for all those years he was the one constant that I could rely on as being always there, always available, always accessible. I would miss him more than I thought and, as time went by, appreciated more and more having known him. Then, on 4 August, my mother died after another cerebral haemorrhage, aged 53 years. My father had travelled with her in the ambulance to Epworth Hospital, Melbourne, where they planned to operate but she died a few minutes after arriving. Only 15 days later my favourite Uncle Alf and fishing mate died on 19 August, also from a cerebral haemorrhage, aged 64. The impact of these three deaths in the space of 82 days on my sister and I was enormous. In the middle of this, her pet dog also died on 3 July, adding to the weight of death she must have felt all around her.

My father too was crushed having lost his father, his wife and only brother-in-law in that 82-day period. In addition to the weight of personal loss there was also the burden of attending three funerals (two of which my father had to arrange), including the lead up to them and the aftermath. It was particularly difficult for my father having to deal, on a daily basis, with the constant expressions of sorrow and condolences, relating to the three deaths, from hotel patrons.

Zel missed her mother terribly. She was only 17 years old when mum died and I think she suffered more from the loss than me. There are some things that a girl just needs to talk to her mother about. My father's maudlin state made it difficult for her to talk to him about anything of significance, let alone important womanly matters. She must have felt so lonely with only her younger brother as a shoulder to cry on, a listening ear, or just someone to hang out with. For a long time, she retreated into her shell and avoided social contact, particularly around The Crown.

Most of my grieving for my mother had been done long before she died, so when she did, most of my grief was over. I knew her condition was serious and, at the age of 15, had thought of the possibility that she might have a fatal stroke. It was an anticipatory grief for the loss before it fully unfolded. But my mind had difficulty in accepting the reality of her death, and I kept thinking that I would have to ask her for something, maybe money, but then realised she was not there and I now had only one parent. My mother had always been the go-to source for gratuitous remuneration. While my father was not mean in remunerating me for work done around the hotel, he had always been less generous when it came to gratuitous payments.

After her funeral, I just wanted to hide from everything and all the people in The Crown who kept saying how sorry they were that my mother had died. It seemed dozens of people told me that every day. I never quite knew how to react to what they said. To say "thank you" somehow seemed wrong to me. I just wanted to cower, draw-back and cringe from people. I knew they were trying to be kind to me but I just wanted to hide from them and be alone. At the same time, I felt lonely and still angry. I was tired of people leaving me and angry with my mother for dying. I knew I had to support my father and sister and help them and was afraid of the additional responsibilities that I would now face and anxious about the future. I recall reading an article somewhere that gave me great solace in dealing with the grief. It said that I had to accept, adjust and achieve. This simple little formula of the three A's helped me then and has continued to do so throughout life. Eventually I reached the stage of acceptance and relief that my mother's passing was over. I was not embittered by her death. In many ways it was to me a welcome release from her depression, the concerns I had for her and the embarrassment I felt in relation to her situation. I long pondered her sorrowful life and eventually resolved that there is no way I can know her whole story, not now or ever.

My mother had been held in high regard by many people who knew her as an accomplished hostess and professional hotel manageress who paid meticulous attention to detail, always extending a warm and sincere welcome to all. The large gathering at her funeral was eloquent testimony to her wide popularity. A letter received from His Honour Mr Justice R. Sholl extending condolences to my father and Zel and I typically expressed the esteem and respect many people had for her. He wrote:

> *I have the warmest and most grateful recollection of Mrs Beck's kindness and friendly care for myself and my associate during many circuits at Bendigo in past years, as I have of course, of your hospitable attention also. I had heard that your wife was not well and that was why you could no longer take us at The Crown, but I had not realised that her illness was so serious. Circuit in Bendigo has not seemed the same since Colonel Latchford and I ceased coming to your hotel, and the Colonel, like myself, will feel the loss of a charming lady whom we regarded as a personal friend.* [The letter of Mr Justice Sholl appears in Appendix 7.]

My father's memory of my mother's easy access to alcohol in hotel premises during almost 21 years of their married life, with a direct causal link between that and her death, created an intensely painful connection that led to his overwhelming guilt and a severe depressive grief reaction that lasted beyond six months. Dealing with the public on a daily basis, it was hard for him to get her loss out of his mind for more than a few minutes at a time as he was constantly told how sorry people were for his loss and asked how he was going and how were the children, and so on. I felt truly sorry for him. He was stuck in a state of bereavement and drowning in remorse.

As a young girl, Zel was passionate about horses and dreamt of one day owning one herself. She pleaded with our father many times to buy her one. He had an anti-horse mentality arising from adverse experiences he'd had with them as the son of a blacksmith and refused outright to contemplate Zel owning a horse, adding that accommodating one at the hotel was untenable.

Not long after our mother's death, he told Zel that he would buy her a horse and make arrangements for it to be stabled at the house in Myers Street. In her diary Zel wrote: "Mum once said the only way I would get a horse would be for dad to die—but it has happened the other way around. I have wanted a horse for as long as I can remember but I didn't think I would be getting it this way." A stable was built on the side of the garage and a small exercise yard fenced off where a well-trained former stock horse by the name of Jimmy was installed.

Apart from a tendency to threaten strangers with a nip, Jimmy proved to be amiable and eager to please. He was comfortable around motor vehicle traffic and Zel rode him successfully around Bendigo's central business district. She also allowed me to ride him a little, once we got to know each other and gained Zel's approval. One Sunday morning Jimmy and I had a memorable ride when, thinking I would show off my horsemanship skills to the congregational gathering at the front of the Sacred Heart Cathedral, I turned Jimmy's head off High Street to head up Wattle Street past the church. Unbeknown to me at the time, one of Jimmy's traits was that he had only one speed going uphill and that was flat out. He laid back his ears, dropped his head, gave a snort and galloped hell for leather past the astonished Christian assembly. There was no way I could stop him. In any event, I was far too busy hanging on to think of anything else. Somehow, I managed to stay in the saddle until the top of the hill when Jimmy just stopped dead in his tracks and gave a big blow.

Unlike Zel, I never did develop an abiding interest in horses. I was far more interested in Ford's new Australian car, the Falcon, launched in September in answer to the Holden. The standard Falcon, which had a more modern look than the Holden, could be bought new for £1,137 ($2,274).

Towards the end of the year John F. Kennedy was elected president in USA. The 'Pill' was finally cleared for public distribution. Chubby Checker released his hit dance craze single 'The Twist' and portable record players started to emerge.

Chapter 34

PARTIES, PONTIACS, PACKARDS AND PEERS

An exhaustive study by Dr H. S. Wyndham of the education system in New South Wales in 1958 found that only 16 per cent of all school students survived to do Year 11 'Leaving Certificate'. Most students left school as soon as possible. Shortly after our mother died, my sister Zel withdrew from her eleventh school year after successfully applying for a job at the 'Fashion House' ladies wear shop that specialised in upmarket dresses for women of maturity. Having unsurprisingly failed mathematics in the previous year, I had somehow passed seven other subjects and at the start of 1961 was pushed into Year 11 with the unlikely prospect of obtaining a 'Leaving Certificate'. The title at least gave me some hope that I might finally get away from school and meanwhile I was able at last to abandon mathematics from my subject study list.

Zel and I continued to live by ourselves in the large two-storey house in Myers Street and kept having our meals at the hotel. I was now 16 and she was 17, due to turn 18 in June. Our father never stayed at the house although he visited at times during the day to do some gardening. I think the place reminded him of our mother and what might have been if things had worked out well. As time went on, he increasingly enjoyed gardening and his visits more. Staff from the hotel were sent to the house on an irregular basis to clean and service it and most of our laundry was carried out at the hotel by staff. We did have an early model concrete mixer style Lightburn washing machine that gave little intermittent electric shocks every time you used it, which fortunately was not very often.

We were now almost entirely free of any kind of parental supervision and, as a matter of necessity, forced to live in an 'odd couple' relationship together. That worked well most of the time but not always. If push came to shove, there was no doubt that we would fight to the death to save each other's backs but there were times that we did clash. Although television had been available for five years, our father would have none of it and refused to have a set anywhere near the hotel or the house. He finally relented later in the year as he started to surface from his mourning and recover somewhat from his overwhelming guilt and negativity. Until then Zel and I managed to entertain ourselves with radios and a portable record player that he provided as a concession.

On Mother's Day in May 1961, we all went to the cemetery with flowers. When Zel returned to The Crown she threw herself on the couch and howled her eyes out. I think this was the first time that she truly acknowledged her pain and despair. Only after this did she find a way to pick up the pieces and move on with life.

As a teenager, Bendigo's Saturday night dances were the place to be and I soon started to go. By the mid 1960s, Peter Rechter's band, 'The Tol Puddle Martyrs' (formerly called 'Peter and The Silhouettes') were hosting their own dance night at the Golden Square fire station hall. They played their own brand of keyboard driven music with social commentary and lyrics that drew crowds and made them one of the hottest and most popular bands in the region. Their successful song, 'Claudette Jones', was my favourite. It was Peter's brother, Jon who was my schoolmate and his uncle Bob Rechter, that ran Rechter's American Café in Mitchell Strteet Bendigo.

The most popular dance was at the YMCA in Mundy Street just one block and only several minutes walk from our house. I became a regular attender. The live music there was shared by The Reg Bridgeland Band, with a wide repertoire of traditional jazz, big band swing and pop, and The Esquires who were more into straight pop and rock and roll. When Reg's band played 'The Golden Wedding', featuring a clarinet solo introduction backed by drums, the gathered throng was silenced by one note after the other until a sensational top note pierced the air prompting loud applause and the rest of the band to join in. Frenetic dancing followed under the large rotating mirror ball hanging from the ceiling as it reflected colourful lights on the walls.

The dance started at 8 p.m. by which time there was often a queue lined up outside to get in. Bouncers on the entrance doors were there to exclude intoxicated persons and other troublemakers. The pubs closing at 6 p.m. didn't stop young people from drinking in their parked cars with purchases made before closing time. In typical country dance hall fashion, the protocol dictated that girls should line up on one side of the hall while boys lined up on the other. When the music started for a new dance, it was a long lonely walk to the other side of the hall to ask a girl for a dance. Requests refused were the greatest source of embarrassment imaginable. Police often attended to do a 'walk-through' in the hall during the evening and always manned the exit at midnight when the dance finished.

Zel developed a practice of using most of her weekends to go horse riding with friends where she and Jimmy would stay. This left me in sole possession of the house which I soon realised had great potential as a venue for parties after the Saturday night YMCA dance. It was easy for me to invite friends back to my place where we could kick up our heels for another couple of hours with music generated by the portable record player. It was tea and coffee provided but BYO drinks—and they did. It became a regular party house with friends often asking, "Is it on again at your place tonight, Mick?" There were never any drugs but plenty of cigarettes and alcohol, never any fights but surely a few hangovers next day. I am not proud to say that I hosted these parties at the age of 17–18 but relieved to put on record that there were no lasting adverse consequences arising therefrom.

My mate Andrew Long was the son of Dr Long who had a new V8 Pontiac Parisien conveniently parked in a detached garage some distance from his house. Andrew was in the habit of 'borrowing' it and calling at our house in the middle of the night where he would rattle small stones on my bedroom window to wake me up so I could join him in going for a 'burn' in the Pontiac. At times we would pick up another mate, Ted Ryan, to join us. After dropping us off in the early hours of the morning, Andrew would refuel the Pontiac at the Provincial Motors coin-operated pump and return the vehicle to his dad's garage before dawn.

I envied Andrew's daring and expertise, and decided to employ a similar 'modus operandi' with my father's 1949 straight-8

Packard which he had bought, second-hand, from George Pethard, the principal proprietor of Tarax soft drinks, who lived in Bendigo. It was in mint condition when my father took possession of the vehicle, save for a very strong smell of cigar smoke which seemed to just add to its classy ambience. It had a 'three-on-the-tree' column shift and a kick down switch on each gear operated by the accelerator which disengaged the overdrive to provide an instantly higher revving and faster accelerating ratio, effectively providing six forward gears in all. I eventually proved that it could do 75 miles per hour (120 kilometres per hour) in second gear overdrive—so long as it was in a straight line. There were no seat belts or airbags then. I managed to complete quite a few expeditions, returning favours to my mates, in this impressive machine before I was discovered.

Along with my new-found freedom came an unwarranted sense of confidence and a dose of bad attitude on top of my angry young man syndrome. Although I was unaware of it, my teachers at high school clearly were not. If I continued on in this vein there was a danger that I might become a hopeless under-achiever and nothing more than a boil on the bum of society. I was pulled up by a blistering, paint-peeling, riveting lecture I received at the hands of a teacher by the name of Laurie Cross. And I mean "at the hands" because he pushed and poked and shoved and prodded me constantly while he tongue lashed me to the bone. He knew all about my circumstances and stated that I had an absolute duty not to let my father down. That he was in need of my help and to do that I had to change my ways and be a better person and student. Furthermore, that I had potential and needed to realise it. I am forever indebted to Laurie Cross for taking the time to stop and graphically explain all that, and more, to me. His lecture changed my life. If he had not taken the time out to speak to me in the manner in which he did, I believe I would not be here today in my present form. I have never forgotten it. Looking back I cringe to recall how confused I was. Seriously muddled up with no sense of direction.

The other thing that helped straighten me out was that, before the year was finished Bendigo High School injected an enormous dose of self-esteem into my psyche. It came largely through my involvement in the school's production of Gilbert and Sullivan's *Iolanthe* where I had a low-level role as a Peer in the Peers Chorus. It was an amazing production with a cast of 61 students and teachers plus another 83 people acting as stagehands, make-up artists, costume designers, ushers and organisers. We played to over 3300 people in five performances in the old Capital Theatre which then sat only 700. The production made a profit of £280 ($560) for the school.

Major benefits from the show came from intangibles such as the increased prestige of the school in the community, improved student–teacher relationships through the involvement of both in the pursuit of a common goal leading to a better understanding of each other and, above all else, the spades of self- esteem that everyone involved received.

My low-key involvement in the performance meant a great deal to me. There was also the simple happiness that it provided. Two teachers who played important characters actually fell in love in real life and got married. While the success of the production was the result of combined efforts of many it was especially due to the exceptional work of Producer Mr Keith Pyers and Musical Director Shirley Clark, both teachers at the school. Performances took place at the end of Term Two in the winter months when it was cold backstage at the Capital Theatre. To keep us warm and give us courage each night I smuggled out of The Crown and into backstage at The Capital a flask of black coffee laced with rum. By the final curtain call each night my mate Tony Conolan and I were near three sheets to the wind!

My admission to hospital, not long after *Iolanthe,* for an appendicitis operation gave me a pause for thought. I liked the idea of achievement and the sense of direction it gave. If direction could be attained through achievement, then, logically I could make my own decisions where to go. With achieving I might get a sense of control, gain approval from my father and fulfil my responsibilities to him. I did desperately want to please him. On the other hand, I was still enjoying my clandestine excursions in the 1949 Packard and the freedom of hosting parties at the house on Saturday night. My father had no coaching advice when it came to school studies or what potential occupation I might aim to pursue save that, after intense discussions with him on a subject, he might say that he thought I should be a lawyer. He had received a very rudimentary education himself and had no appreciation of what really serious study was like except for his training as a professional violinist. But he was keen for me to succeed and kept saying repeatedly "Study self-sacrifice my boy—self-sacrifice is the secret!"

This was my father's way of explaining that it was possible to attain something better later in life if I gave up or sacrificed some present social activity or pleasure to apply my efforts to acquiring knowledge and skill that would bring future rewards. Gradually it dawned on me that denying myself immediate gratification to spend time on studying could lead to real benefits down the track. I had the option of taking that direction. When it came to anything to do with educational school expenses, my father was always extremely supportive and, for example, readily agreed to my request to be fitted out with a tailor-made school blazer from Ashman's Menswear, "The Home of Better Suits". He always counselled me to "study hard" and to continue on with my education as far as I could and constantly warned me to be careful how I spent my time because that was part of my capital and once it was spent that was it, it was gone.

Only a few weeks after the anniversary of my mother's death, my father received another blow when the founder and chairman of the Richmond Brewery, Peter Grant Hay, died. His brewery had been a remarkable success and, since his argument with Carlton and United Breweries, my father had formed a close personal working relationship with Grant Hay who regarded The Crown as one of the best and most successful outlets for his products. The relationship between him and Reg Beck had been one of mutual admiration. The loss of a friend and business ally just added to my father's grief.

Chapter 35

THE END OF THE BEGINNING

After being given a pass in five subjects and granted my 'Leaving Certificate' I realised that I didn't want to leave after all. The year 1962 began with 960 students in the school. Year 12 had around 60 students with about 40 boys and 20 girls. Starting elections and appointments made it clear that no one thought I was qualified to be a prefect. That was the truth. Surprisingly, although endowed with only very average sporting skills, I was elected Captain of Freeman House. Also, I think because of my tailor-made school blazer, I was shanghaied into being President of the Social Service League, an organisation with 46 student representatives from all years devoted to raising funds for charity.

The school year was substantially different to the previous ones I had experienced. Students did not do all the same subjects which meant that in any given class there was a different group of students. Most days there were non-class periods in your timetable where you were able to do private study. If your first class period was not till 10 a.m. then you could get away with turning up at that time. Likewise, if your last one finished at 3 p.m. you could sneak away and go home early. Such practices, while never formally encouraged by teachers, were known by them and ignored. The reasoning was that students in Year 12 attended school because they wanted to and not because they had to. It followed that if you didn't want to learn it was better if you did not attend. I made the most of the time table system, often sneaking down to Rosalind Park for a cigarette with my mate Tony during a non-class period or recess. Cigarettes were cheap to buy. Most Year 12 teachers wore black academic gowns, giving them a more authoritative and learned appearance as they walked briskly through the quadrangle with gown flowing behind. It provided a visible role model for students and gave the school a more scholastic appearance. It was also easier to pick out teachers in a crowd which could be handy at times. Many of the teachers were given nicknames by the kids. One senior teacher seemed to constantly clear his throat or cough and was given the name 'Crump'. I eventually found out that he had endured mustard gas poisoning during the First World War which increased the respect I already had for him.

My best mate Tony Conolan who had been in school with me since preps at Gravel Hill was by now an accomplished musician and violinist. Together, we formed a pop vocal trio with fellow student Ted Ryan. We performed at the High School Senior Social singing 'Do You Wanna' Dance', 'Wolverton Mountain', 'Speedy Gonzalez's' and songs of a similar genre, but our signature number was 'The Bendigo High School Rock' [see Appendix 8], a plagiarised and bastardised version of the school song which

Tony and I put together in collaboration, and also sung, to the astonishment of the teachers, at the Senior Social. Branding ourselves the TMTs we performed on behalf of the school Social Service League at pensioners' afternoons in the Trades Hall and at the Bendigo Benevolent Home where we added some softer numbers like 'Swing Low Sweet Chariot' to our repertoire.

33. The 'TMTs' performing at the High School Senior Social 1962.
Left to right: Max Beck, Ted Ryan and Tony Conolan.

Tony had been appointed secretary for Freeman House and with me as House Captain we conspired together by the end of the second term to organise sports rosters so that all students except us were gainfully employed playing sport. We would then casually sneak down to The Crown to either play pool in the bar parlour or practice our singing in the dining room where there was a small stage and a piano that Tony could play. He went on to do a Bachelor of Music at Melbourne University and became lead violinist in the Melbourne Symphony Orchestra and later Artistic Advisor to the State Orchestra of Victoria (now Orchestra Victoria).

Meanwhile the weekend parties continued at the house in Myers Street as did the occasional night time jaunts in Dr Long's Pontiac and my father's Packard. Looking for some new challenge in the Packard, I decided one night to do a solo trip to the Eppalock Dam near Axedale on the Campaspe River. Construction was under full swing at the time with 24-hour shifts that operated under lights at night. I knew there was a viewing platform and figured I would go and take a look. Somehow, in the dark, I took the wrong track and found myself heading to the main gate on the construction road. Having decided to do a U-turn, I managed to solidly bog the Packard. Leaving the vehicle, I walked to the gatekeeper's house where I pleaded with him to pull me out of the bog. Luckily for me, I thought at the time, the gatekeeper was a customer of The Crown, knew who I was, happily pulled me out of the bog with a 4×4 and sent me on my way.

I drove straight back to the hotel where I hosed all the mud off the car in the dark and returned it to the shed, thanking my good fortune that I seemed to have survived the experience. Several days later I was summoned by my father who clearly had a very serious demeanour. He advised that the customer in question had recently dropped in for a drink and explained, "I pulled young

Mickey out of a bog in the Packard the other night!" Fortunately, I was not there at the time to see my father's reaction. I was in serious trouble for a long, long time after that. Shortly after, this felony was compounded when my father turned up at the house early one Sunday morning to discover the place in a considerable mess. Glasses in the sink, empty grog bottles, ashtrays spilling over and general detritus about the place were clear evidence of further serious offending. Having discovered me asleep in bed he grabbed me by the ear and led me downstairs on a tour of inspection, cross-examining as he went. All I could do was to plead guilty and promise full restitution, reparations, reform and remorse—the latter of which was already obvious.

My father's worst fears were realised when the news broke that, after negotiations with the heirs to the estate of Grant Hay, Carlton and United Breweries would purchase the Richmond Brewery. Shortly after, CUB closed it down which meant my father was now left dealing with his old enemy, CUB, from which he had to buy all his beer. The news was devastating to him. He had created a new identity for The Crown around the Richmond Beer product. No other hotel in Bendigo had stocked it, giving him a marketing edge and now he was levelled off with all the other hotels. As a consequence, there was a noticeable drop in his trade. More importantly there was a significant drop in his level of satisfaction with the hotel business. The demise of Richmond Brewery was yet another loss he had to deal with. For a considerable time, there had also been gradually decreasing income from the hotel's guest accommodation due to the growing popularity of new motels with ensuite facilities, television, breakfast service to the bedroom and car parking outside the door, none of which The Crown could provide. The hotel was becoming a lesser version of its former significant self.

After reading a comment in my school report book "A very sincere effort is necessary in the final term" I resolved, as the final term approached, to get serious and study properly. With my father's support I bought a number of books on 'How to Study', 'How to Pass Exams' and 'How to Improve Your Memory'. The considerable time I spent reading these books might have been better spent on studying itself but I did learn and understand some very valuable skills and principles from my reading. The most important thing I learned was that there is no education without motivation. I guess I already knew that but to read it in a book with explanations and illustrations gave it new meaning. I found, when it came down to it, I had plenty of motivation. First, I felt that I had let my father down on several fronts and I wanted to make it up to him by doing something that would please him. He wanted me to be a lawyer and as I was hopeless at maths I couldn't think of a better idea. This meant I had to get high marks to get into University Law School. Deciding I really did want to do that made all the difference. That was the second part of my motivation. While I was going to study seriously to please my father I was also doing it for myself because I wanted to. Because I could see, in the distance, a hazy view of where it might take me.

Shortly after the start of the third term I cleaned out my school locker and took all my books home to the Myers Street house. There I set myself up in a small study with a reel-to-reel tape recorder I had requested my father to buy and on which I dictated all my subject notes. Once recorded I played back the notes during the day and at night as I went to sleep. The tape would play on while I was asleep and eventually turn itself off at the end. The theory being that my brain would absorb the facts and details subliminally while I was asleep. I also spent hours reading and studying in conventional ways during the day and night before bed. This routine was broken during the day by my bike rides to The Crown and back for breakfast, lunch and dinner. It was a long, lonely, cloistered existence by myself in the house in the months leading up to exams. I saw Zel, briefly in the mornings when she took on the responsibility of getting me out of bed, for which I am forever indebted, and again at evening. At times, I became very depressed but managed to find inspiration to keep me going from such unlikely sources such as President Kennedy's speech on 12 September when he said: "We choose to go to the moon in this decade and do the other things, not because they are easy, but because they are hard …." I thought going to the moon was just like me trying to get into Law School at Melbourne University but resolved again to maintain my efforts. I kept reminding myself of the school motto '*Qui Patitur Vincit*' which translated loosely meant 'The one who endures conquers'.

In the middle of my study marathon, I was awoken one night by the rattle of pebbles on my bedroom window to find Andrew Long extending an invitation to join him on a jaunt in his dad's V8 Pontiac Parisien. Having resolved that for me there would be no parties, no car rides and nothing else but study, at least until the final exams were over, I declined his persistent pleas to join him. After collecting another mate, the two enjoyed a pleasant joy ride half way to Geelong and back. On returning the car to his father's garage in the early hours of the morning Andrew found, when opening the doors, that his dad, Dr Long, was sitting at the end in a large armchair waiting for him. I was so glad that I had said "no".

Not many years later Andrew married and was the proud father of a lovely baby daughter when, driving alone, he ran off the road and hit a tree between Melbourne and Bendigo. I went to his funeral and cried. It seemed wrong and unjust that this had happened now when we had got away with our joyride escapades without accident, without police intervention, without any serious incident and almost entirely scot-free.

As the year came to a close so did the golden era of rock and roll after the Beatles released their first single 'Love Me Do' in October 1962, which began the popularity of the music genre known as Merseybeat. Like rock, it too would have its own particular and different impact on popular music and youth culture. The following year, the Beatles single 'Please Please Me' became number one. A string of successes followed including 'She Loves You', 'I Want to Hold Your Hand', 'Can't Buy Me Love' and 'Hard Day's Night'.

When the exam results were in I discovered to my astonishment that I had scored a first-class honour in so-called British History which was in fact really Australian History, a second-class honour in Economics and passes in Modern History and English Expression. I then found that not only had I been admitted to Melbourne University Law Faculty as a first-year student but also to Queens College as a resident. This all meant that I was out of here. I would no longer be around Bendigo. No longer around the bend would I go. It was a case of be careful what you wish for.

34. Bendigo High School Emblem: *"The one who endures conquers"*.

Chapter 36

EPILOGUE

Bendigo High School had been a wonderful place for me. It had just the right balance of discipline, education and freedom. I left with a new self-esteem and a lifelong debt to those teachers who steered me through a difficult time and changed my life permanently. My debt to them is not just for the teaching but for the total experience of those years. I was lucky also to be brought up in the environment of The Crown where I had to weigh up risks and make my own decisions as to where the limits were. I think I had more freedom than any other kid in Bendigo. I had a few close shaves and lost some skin on the way but, with the support of my father, managed to survive. Members of staff were often like extended family and interaction with them was generally very beneficial to my sister and I as children, and our parents as well, who profited from their nurturing of us while they attended to other matters.

My father, who had continued to lose enthusiasm for the hotel business after Carlton United Breweries closed down Richmond

Brewery, was now in his 60s and had been running hotels for nearly 40 years. He decided that he'd had enough and that he would surrender the liquor licence, which he did on 23 May 1963. He then converted the bar and its parlours into commercial shops to lease to tenants. Bendigo's remaining publicans continued with 6 o'clock closing time until 1 February 1966 when 10 o'clock closing came into force in Victoria.

35. Chevron Hotel, Melbourne on 17 July 1965.
Left to Right: Reg Beck, Wally Shaw, Jack Jeffrey and Tom Norris.
(*Melbourne versus Richmond AFL game, Richmond won by one goal.*)

Reg thought he could continue to run the accommodation side of the business as a bed and breakfast private hotel but found that, without the liquor licence, the accommodation trade depleted so much that it was not worth his while to keep the dining room open for breakfast and consequently closed it with all the tables remaining fully set. It remained closed for years with the blinds pulled down and the dust gathering until it became like Dickens' description of Miss Havisham's dining room in *Great Expectations*, "everything which ought to be white had been white long ago and had lost its lustre and was faded yellow." When cutlery settings remaining on the table were lifted, they left an outline in the dust and fading linen tablecloths. The clock also, as in Miss Havisham's dining room, had stopped. When my father surrendered The Crown's licence in 1963 there were around 52 hotels in Bendigo. When he purchased the hotel in 1949 there had been 72. The residential accommodation side of the hotel business continued to struggle on, providing bed and bathroom facilities only which attracted a considerably more downmarket, customer base, that over time, became numerically less and less.

Two remaining long-term tenants in the dying stages of The Crown during this period were Arthur Smith and Stan Aldridge. They were men passed their middle age who always presented as quiet, self-contained and lonely. Arthur lived in the downstairs tiny flat and Stan in a single room upstairs. They became good friends and drinking mates over the years and could often be seen on a warm summer's evening sitting on the rear external staircase having a beer and a yarn. Years of hard manual work and many beers downed over that time had detrimentally affected them both. Neither looked well with their flushed faces, bloodshot eyes and undernourished appearance. Still, they were always gentlemen, always polite and always amiable.

One day, Arthur turned up at the hotel office with a worried look on his face to ask my father whether he had seen Stan, who he hadn't seen for several days, explaining that he had knocked on his door, which was locked, but there was no answer. Arthur was wondering whether Stan had told my father that he was going away for a few days. Reg replied in the negative and took a house key to check Stan's room. He found the door locked but couldn't insert the house key to open it because of a key left in the lock on the other side. At this point my father became quite concerned and worried as to whether Stan might be unwell, or perhaps worse, locked in his room.

Summoning the assistance of Arthur, the two of them managed to manhandle a high extension ladder up the side of the building to the second story window of Stan's room. As my father was then approaching his seventies and not in good enough trim to climb a high extension ladder, he managed to coerce Arthur into tackling the task. This he did with initial hesitancy and then a great deal of trepidation. After a slow-motion ascent there followed an arduous struggle between Arthur and the fly wire screen on the window before he eventually managed to remove it. Having discovered the window unlocked, Arthur disappeared into Stan's bedroom. There followed a lengthy pause after which Arthur stuck his head out the window and said, "He's dead Reg." My father then replied, "All right, unlock the door then, and get out." Arthur obediently turned the key in the door and having satisfied himself that it was open, instead of walking through the door and into the passage, to the amazement of my father, slowly climbed out the window and descended the ladder.

Arthur continued to stay at the old Crown and was one of its last residential tenants.

Stan, like all persons who died on the premises, was removed, under police supervision, quietly from the hotel precincts. It was not a common occurrence but it did happen. An even rarer occurrence was the arrival of a dead person. It happened once when a well-dressed, suited gentleman from a small Mallee town checked in very late one evening and parked his vehicle in the backyard. On rising early next morning my father discovered a hearse, complete with coffin, lined up with the other vehicles. A cross-examination of the driver revealed that he was a funeral director en-route to

Melbourne to deliver the corpse in the coffin. My father took umbrage against a cadaver being stored on the premises without his consent and after threatening to charge double for the insult, advised the funereal miscreant to immediately leave or run the risk of himself been laid to rest.

* * *

At Melbourne University and Queens College, I was out of my depth and completely overwhelmed by the loftiness and status of it all. I felt intellectually and socially outgunned by my fellow students at Queens who had nearly all come from a metropolitan private school background. I found it difficult to manage the changed environment from my living circumstances in Bendigo to the collegiate atmosphere of a large number of students living together. After spending too much time socialising and not enough time studying, I achieved a pass in only two out of four subjects in the final exam and was advised that my place in the Law Faculty was terminated.

Fortunately, Monash University was due to start the first year of its Law Faculty the following year and, again with the continuing support of my long-suffering father, I applied and was accepted. It was a five-year course requiring the completion of a prerequisite Bachelor of Jurisprudence degree before completing the Bachelor of Laws degree which was needed to apply for admission to practice. Having already wasted one year at Melbourne University it meant that it was going to take a total of six years to complete my law qualifications.

After the five years study at Monash, I graduated in both degrees with two more subjects than needed, achieving 13 clear passes, seven creditable passes, one distinction pass and not failing any of the 21 subjects completed. Halfway through the course I obtained a Commonwealth Scholarship and each year during the annual vacation I worked in various jobs including truck driving and farm work in the Mallee, as a labourer at the Snowy Mountains scheme in two consecutive years, and delivery driver of a Marchant's soft drink truck in Melbourne. I used the money saved from these sources for my daily living expenses during the academic year while all other expenses, including private board, books, university fees and so forth, were met by my father. During my final year, I married my first wife who worked as a teacher. The first of our three children arrived three years and six months later.

After completing my year of articles and then a year as an employee solicitor with the firm of Byrne, Jones and Torney in Ballarat, I returned to Bendigo in 1971 to set up my own law practice in a tiny shopfront office in The Crown that my father provided rent-free for the first 12 months. Over the years the practice grew until it occupied a large proportion of the hotel. Its success was substantially due to the support of my father and the excellent, highly motivated loyal and industrious people who worked with me. At its peak, personnel exceeded 25 and the annual trust account turnover was more than $30 million. The descendant of the firm still thrives today and trades under the name of 'Becks'. In April 1989 my first wife and I separated after a marriage of 21 years. Six months later I left the law practice I had been devoted to for 18 years. The loss of my marriage, contact with my children and my professional life was devastating. The story about that is not for telling here. Maybe another time.

My father died on the 3 May 1980. My understanding had developed to see him for what he was, as a respected man in the community, a capable businessman and manager, an excellent host and an all-round good bloke who was, to use one of his favourite phrases, "as straight as a gun barrel" and could be relied on always.

He didn't teach me how to play football or cricket, or shoot, or, regardless of my constant pleading, to drive, but he did teach me how to fish and how to handle a boat. What he did teach me were the really important things like the importance of keeping your word, to accept responsibility for what you do, to tell the truth, to do what he called "the right thing", to work industriously and to choose words carefully and curb really bad language. To aim always to be civil and polite unless the situation clearly warranted differently. He was a great raconteur and loved by his customers. He was proud of me and supported my legitimate endeavours.

My sister always stood behind me and supported me, even when some of my endeavours were not legitimate. She covered my back many times when we were living together as the odd couple at 44 Myers Street and even pitched in to help clean up the mess after some of the parties I held, which, for the record, she never took part in. While she never encouraged such goings-on she always covered my back, never complained and never reported my activities to my father. I forever remain indebted to her for her caring and loyalty, particularly after my marriage broke down and I left my law practice. She, and my brother-in-law Garry, looked after and nurtured me while I lived in a caravan at the back of their house until I could sort myself out. Zelda died on the 7 December 2014 after a long illness with cancer, aged 71 years.

In February 1990 I accepted a salaried position as a solicitor with the firm of Herring and Bathurst in Maryborough where I remained for two and a half years performing mainly Magistrates Court appearance work with the occasional County Court appearance on pleas. The work took me back to my grassroots and I found it, and the congenial firm that I worked in, thoroughly restoring. After 22 years career as a lawyer, I was then appointed a Magistrate and Coroner for country Victoria and believe I was the first country solicitor to be given that honour. Upon completion of a training period in Melbourne I spent two years as Co-ordinating Magistrate at Shepparton Headquarters court and then was transferred to Geelong Magistrates Court. During the fifteen years I was on the bench, I sat at 28 different courts throughout Victoria, mainly in the country. [See Appendix 9.] That's also a story for another time.

Five years after the failure of my first marriage I married again. We have enjoyed a happy and successful 28 years and look forward to many more together.

The advancements in science, technology, welfare, health, medicine, industry, aviation, poverty education and a long list of other areas where boundaries were smashed in every direction in my lifetime were greater than ever before I was born. I am now 78, have lived long enough to see the future become history and the world's population triple in my time. Today young people are better informed, better organised, there is more of them and they are probably smarter than they were in the 1960s. But I doubt they are happier. I doubt that they realise that those of us who have lived as part of western civilisation since 1945 and avoided military service have been among the luckiest people since the beginning of man.

I enjoyed being a Magistrate. For the first time in my legal career, I was able to practise total intellectual honesty. Free at last from having to present jaundiced one-sided arguments espousing a particular position and able instead to weigh up both sides to come to an honest conclusion about the truth. It was as much of a joy as a burden. When you think about it, practising lawyers, like I was for 22 years, are often not much more than intellectual prostitutes hiring out their brains for the satisfaction of their clients. I found also that everything I had ever done in the past, every experience

I had, all my education and anything else that had gone into the databank of my brain from every source was material that as a Magistrate I, subconsciously, drew on. I felt as though my entire past had prepared me for sitting on the bench. My upbringing in The Crown, my education at Gravel Hill and Bendigo High School and everything else was somehow, in some way, now relevant to everything before me. I owed a lot to many people. It has been said that good judgement comes from experience and that you only get experience from making bad judgements. Well, on that ground at least, I had some qualifications to be a Magistrate.

There were many instances when my past life experiences helped me deal with hearings fairly, as was the case of 'Mrs Brown' (not her real name), a defendant in proceedings brought against her by her husband for a restraining order, sometimes called "an apprehended violence order". The case was unusual as normally it was men who were the defendants in such proceedings facing allegations that they had assaulted their wives.

The hearing was booked in for a contest estimated to last one day and allocated to me as presiding Magistrate. Mr Brown appeared with his lawyer and four witnesses. Mrs Brown turned up by herself, in a distressed state, with no witnesses, and demanded an adjournment on the grounds that she was unrepresented and did not have any witnesses in court. A check of the court listings revealed that the case had been listed and adjourned no less than four times previously over the last three months, this being the fifth hearing.

I said to her, "Mrs brown, you have had ample opportunity over the last three months and four adjourned hearings of this case to arrange legal representation and the attendance of any witnesses. To grant your application today would cause substantial inconvenience and expense to six people including the applicant, your husband, his lawyer and four witnesses. Furthermore, this case has been booked in for a contested hearing and the court has budgeted and allocated one day of its time for me to hear it which will be lost at substantial cost to the public purse if the case is adjourned. Your application for an adjournment is therefore refused."

"Well," she said, "If that's the case! If … If that's the case—you can shove it up your arse!"

When the laughter died down, I said to her, "Mrs Brown, I will need some time to consider that difficult submission (more laughter), so I'll stand this case down to enable you to have a talk with the duty solicitor and I will call it on again in half an hour."

When I called the case back on after she had spoken to the duty solicitor, Mrs Brown meekly came back into court and consented to the orders sought by her husband against her. Sometimes instead of confronting people it's better to give them breathing space. The broad and extensive education that I had received in Bendigo schools and at The Crown equipped me better for retaining my sense of humour at all times while dealing with people like Mrs Brown.

If that's the case, and I can tell you that it is, it's time I rested my case.

APPENDICES LIST

Appendix 1
HOTELS WITHIN 250–300M
OF THE CROWN IN 1949
(Chapter 4)

1. The Royal Mail, cnr. Hargreaves and Williamson Streets.
2. The Shamrock, cnr. Pall Mall and Williamson Streets.
3. The Metropolitan, cnr. Hargreaves and Bull Streets.
4. The Arcade, Hargreaves Street (Hargreaves Mall).
5. The Belfast Arms, Hargreaves Street (Hargreaves Mall).
6. The Harp and Shamrock, cnr. Hargreaves and Mundy Streets.
7. The Criterion, cnr. Mundy and Hopetoun Streets.
8. The Cumberland, cnr. Williamson Street and Lyttleton Terrace.
9. The Limerick Castle, Williamson Street.
10. The Sandhurst, cnr. Lyttleton Terrace and St Andrews Avenue.
11. The Law Courts, cnr. Bull Street and Pall Mall.
12. The Court House, cnr. Mundy Street and Pall Mall.

Appendix 2
DISTINGUISHED GUESTS
AT THE CROWN
(Chapter 4)

His Honour Judge Moore

His Honour Judge Mitchell

His Honour Judge Stretton

His Honour Judge Mulvaney

His Honour Judge Gamble

His Honour Judge Reid

His Honour Judge Norris

His Honour Judge Barber

His Honour Judge Sholl

His Honour Judge Stafford

The Honourable Sir James MacFarlane

The Honourable Sir Charles John Lowe KCMG

The Honourable Sir Charles Gavin Duffy

The Honourable Sir Norman O'Brien

The Honourable Sir Alexander Duncan Grant Adam

The Honourable Sir John McEwen—Deputy Prime Minister

The Honourable Sir Albert Dunstan—Victorian State Premier

The Honourable Sir John McDonald—Victorian State Premier

The Honourable Sir Robert Vincent Monahan

Police Superintendent Charles Wright

Police Superintendent Alf Weightman

Police Superintendent Jack Webb

Police Inspector Herbert Parker

Police Inspector Armstrong

Appendix 3
LETTER TO REG
(Chapter 4)

From Mr Justice John V. Barry's associate, 3 May 1949.

Appendix 4

PAT McGINTY'S GOAT
Song lyrics (Chapter 5)

Mr Patrick McGinty, an Irishman of note,
Came into a fortune and bought himself a goat.
Said Patrick, "Of goats' milk I mean to have my fill!"
But when he got his Nanny home, he found it was a Bill.

Now little Nora Murphy, the knot was going to tie,
She washed out her trousseau and hung it out to dry,
Along came the goat and saw the bits of white.
He swallowed all her falderals—t'was on her wedding night!

And now all the ladies who live in Killaroo
Are all wearing bustles like their mothers used to do
They each wear a bolster beneath their petticoat
And leave the rest to providence and Pat McGinty's goat!

Off the West coast of Ireland one morning there was seen
As plain as a pikestaff a German submarine
The Coast Guard Maloney fell over in a fit
Said Pat McGinty's goat, "It's up to me to do my bit!"

He dived into the water, as frisky as a whale
He swam around the U-boat and wagged his little tail
He upped with his horn and stuck it in the boat
And sent those Huns to Helligoland—did Pat McGinty's goat!

The brave Irish guards, though you may think it is romance
Adopted Paddy's goat and took him off to France
The day that he landed he heard the bugle blow
And ducked his little head as he ran to meet the foe.

Now the Germans retreated and hurriedly they fled
The Krauts held their noses as they tumbled over dead
"Yuck!" said the Kaiser, "There's poisonous gas aboot."
But t'was only the effluvia From Pat McGinty's goat!

McRiley went to the races on a fine summer's day
He won $20 and shouted "Hip Hooray!"
Holding up the notes he shouted "Look what I have got!"
Then along came Paddy's goat and he gobbled the bloody lot!

"He's gobbled up my bank-notes!" said McRiley with a humph.
They ran for the doctor who fetched the stomach pump.
He pumped and pumped and pumped for that $20 note
But only got a gallon of beer from Paddy McGinty's goat.

Now that Paddy McGinty's goat had a mighty appetite,
One night he swallowed up two plugs of dynamite
Then ate a box of fuses and quaffed a quart of gasoline
Even with his constitution he felt a little green.

He sat by the fireside and didn't give a damn
He gobbled up a spark and exploded with a bang!
And when you get to heaven I'll bet you a dollar note
That the angel with the whiskers on is Paddy McGinty's goat!

Appendix 5

GRAVEL HILL STATE SCHOOL
STUDENTS, GRADE 6, 1956
(Chapter 12)

Robert Iser, David Wilson, Trevor Pearce, Roland Kurtske, John Race, Ian Roberts, Peter Allan, Eddie Marriot, John Harris, Harry Watts, Gordon Lowry, Jon Rechter, Robert Lee, David Lee, John Stanistreet, Des Byrnes, Lionel Henry, Ken Prior, Lesley Gouge, Ken Gouge, Leon Scott, Billy Letts, Michael King, John Gibson, John Connolly, Tony Conolan, Barry Ripper, Keith Threlfall, Jeff Holland, Francis Daly, Geoff Whatmore, Frank Tout, Dennis Kolle, Max (Mick) Beck. (34)

Madge Richards, Vivian Chamberlain, Raelene Jones, Bronwyn Townsend, Heather Hansford, Beverly Knight, Beverley Dowsey, Heather Kilby, Sue Percival, Heather Beer, Lorraine West, Carol Cook, Denise Schade, Joan Unmack, Sandra Goddard, Judith Allan, Brenda Griffiths, Helen Clarkson, Beverly McGreehan, Margaret Underwood, Christine Tzaros, Jill McClay. (22)

[Apologies in advance for any errors or omissions.]

Appendix 6
SELECTED HITS FROM THE GOLDEN AGE OF POP MUSIC
(Chapter 27)

Elvis Presley: All Shook Up, Blue Suede Shoes, Don't Be Cruel, Heartbreak Hotel, Hound Dog, Jailhouse Rock, Shake Rattle and Roll, Return to Sender, Let me be Your Teddy Bear, Love me Tender, Hard Headed Woman, It's Now or Never.

Little Richard: Good Golly Miss Molly, Tutti-Frutti, Long Tall Sally, Lucille, Ready Teddy, Rip it Up, Keep a Knockin'.

Jerry Lee Lewis: Great Balls of Fire, Whole Lotta Shakin' Going On, Wild One.

Johnny Cash: I Walk the Line, Folsom Prison Blues, A Boy Named Sue, Ghost Riders in the Sky, Ring of Fire.

The Temptations: My Girl, Hey Girl.

Buddy Holly: That'll Be The Day, It Doesn't Matter Any More, Rave On, Peggy Sue, It's So Easy to Fall in Love, Raining in My Heart.

Chuck Berry: Johnny B Goode, Roll Over Beethoven, Sweet Little Sixteen.

Bill Haley and The Comets: Rock Around The Clock, See You Later Alligator.

The Big Bopper: Chantilly Lace, White Lightning, It's the Truth Ruth.

The Everly Brothers: All I Have to do is Dream, Wake Up Little Susie, Till I Kissed You, Bye Bye Love, Cathy's Clown.

Richie Valens: La Bamba, Donna.

Fats Domino: Aint That a Shame, I'm Walking, I Hear You Knockin, My Blue Heaven, Blueberry Hill, Walking to New Orleans.

Paul Anka: Diana, Lonely Boy, Put Your Head on My Shoulder.

Connie Francis: Whose Sorry Now, Stupid Cupid, Lipstick on Your Collar, Everybody's Somebody's Fool, Among my Souvenirs.

Johnny Horton: North to Alaska, The Battle of New Orleans, Sink the Bismarck.

Doris Day: Secret Love, Whatever Will Be Will Be, A Guy is a Guy, Teachers Pet.

Johnny O'Keefe: So Tough, Shout, I'm Counting on You, Move Baby Move, Sing.

Col Joye: Oh Yeah Uh Uh, Yes Sir That's My Baby, Bye Bye Baby, I Need Your Love Tonight, Be-Bop-A-Lula.

Frankie Avalon: Venus, Young Love, I'll Wait for You.

Gene Pitney: 24 Hours to Tulsa, The Man Who Shot Liberty Valance, Town Without Pity.

The Beatles: I Want to Hold Your Hand, She Loves You, Love Me Do, Let it Be, Hey Jude, All You Need is Love, Penny Lane.

Appendix 7
CONDOLENCE LETTER
(Chapter 33)

POSTAL ADDRESS:
Box 61, P.O.
BALLARAT
TELEPHONE:
BALLARAT 102

*as from: Judges' Chambers,
Supreme Court,
Melbourne.*

LAW COURTS,
BALLARAT.

June 23rd, 1961.

Dear Mrs. Beck,

I have been sitting here on circuit this week, and in the course of meeting local solicitors was told by Mr. R. A. Must that you had lost your wife. Apparently he learned of it when in Bendigo before Xmas last. I am deeply sorry to hear the news, the announcement of which I am afraid I must have missed at the time, though it is a wonder it did not reach Judges' Chambers through one or other of the Associates who have been to Bendigo since.

Please accept my very sincere condolences on your bereavement, and if your son and daughter remember me, please give them a message also.

I have the warmest and most grateful recollections of Mrs. Beck's kindness and friendly care for myself and my associate during many circuits at Bendigo in past years, — as I have, of course, of your hospitable attention also. I had heard that your wife was not well, and that that was why

From His Honour Mr Justice Reginald Sholl, 23 June 1961.
Page 1 of 2.

(2

You could no longer take us at the Crown, but I had not realised that her illness was so serious. Circuit in Bendigo has not seemed the same since Col. Latchford & I ceased coming to your hotel, and the Colonel, like myself, will feel the loss of a charming lady whom we regarded as a personal friend.

The Colonel has retired some time since, but he comes into Judges' Chambers from time to time, and will, I know, be shocked to hear of your loss.

Please do not trouble to answer this; I expect in a way it is likely to freshen again wounds which time slowly makes less painful.

With very kind regards to yourself and the children,

Yours sincerely,

A.P. Crol

Page 2 of 2.

Appendix 8
BENDIGO HIGH SCHOOL ROCK
(Chapter 35)

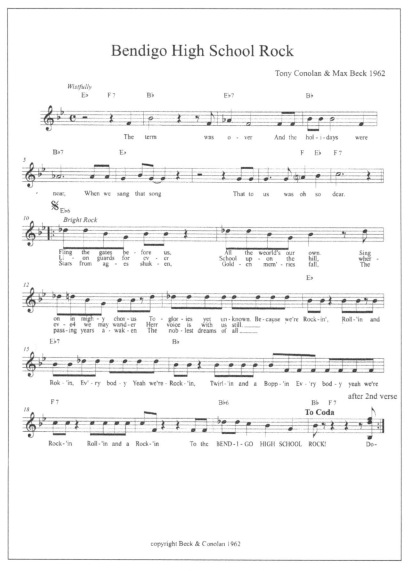

Music and lyrics, page 1 of 2.

Music and lyrics, page 2 of 2.

Appendix 9
LIST OF MAGISTRATES COURTS
(Chapter 36)

Old Melbourne Magistrate's Court

Old Children's Court

City Coroner's Court

Prahran Court

Coburg Court

Shepparton Court

Cobden Court

Seymour Court

Benalla Court

Wangaratta Court

Myrtleford Court

Mansfield Court

Wodonga Court

Corryong Court

Geelong Court

Colac Court

Ballarat Court

Bendigo Court

Kyneton Court

Castlemaine Court

Maryborough Court

Warrnambool Court

Portland Court

Hamilton Court

Mildura Court

Ouyen Court

Swan Hill Court

Robinvale Court

BIBLIOGRAPHY

PRIMARY SOURCES

Crowley Frank, *Modern Australia 1939–1970: A Documentary History of Australia*, Vol. 5, Wren Publishing Pty Ltd, Melbourne, 1973.

Bendigo High School, *Old Gold Magazine 1957–1962*.

Bendigo High School, *Class Report Book*, (Max C S Beck) 1957–1962.

Grossman Vasily, *A Writer At War: With The Red Army 1941–1945*, The Folio Society Ltd, 2015.

SECONDARY SOURCES

Arnold Ken, *Historical Hotels Within the City of Bendigo*, Crown Castleton Publishers, Bendigo, 2020.

Beevor Antony, *Berlin: The Downfall 1945*, The Folio Society Ltd, 2007.

Blainey Geoffrey, *Before I Forget: An Early Memoir*, Penguin Random House Australia, 2019.

Blainey Geoffrey, *Black Kettle and Full Moon: Daily Life in a Vanished Australia*, Penguin Books Australia Ltd, 2003.

Bolton Geoffrey *The Oxford History of Australia Vol. 5* (The Middle Way) 2nd edition. Oxford University Press Australia, 1996.

Borel Brooke, *Infested*, The University of Chicago Press, 2015.

Butcher Mike and Collins Yolande M J, *Bendigo at Work: An Industrial History*, Holland House Publishers for the National Trust of Australia (Victoria) Bendigo and District Branch, 2011.

Byrne Bob, *Australia Remember When*, University of New South Wales Press Ltd, 2015.

Connors Jane, *Royal Visits to Australia*, NLA Publishing, 2014.

Crouch Wallace J, *Commonwealth of Australia Jubilee Celebrations 1901–1951: An Official Record*, Government of the Commonwealth of Australia, 1952.

Deutsher Keith M, *The Breweries of Australia: A History*, Thomas C Lothian Pty Ltd, Melbourne, 1999.

Dunbar-Hall P and Hodge G, *A Guide to Rock and Pop*, Science Press Marrickville NSW, 1988.

Erlewine M, Bogdanov V, Woodstra C, et al, *All Music Guide to Rock*, Miller Freeman Books San Francisco, 1995.

Fraser Bryce, *The Macquarie Book of Events*, Macquarie Library Pty Ltd NSW, 1983.

Gilbert Martin, *The Second World War 1943–1945*, The Folio Society Ltd, 2014.

Glover Richard, *The Land Before Avocado: Journeys in a Lost Australia*, Harper Collins Publishers Australia Pty Ltd, 2018.

Golub Adam, *A Transnational Tale of Teenage Terror:* The Blackboard Jungle *in Global Perspective*, Red Feather, no date.

Gould Tony, *A Summer Plague: Polio and its survivors*, Self-published, USA, 1997.

Griffen-Foley Bridget, *Changing Stations: The Story of Australian Commercial Radio*, University of New South Wales Press Ltd, 2009.

Hardy Phil, *The Encyclopaedia of Western Movies*, Octopus Books, London, 1985.

Haynes Jim, *On All Fronts: Australia's World War II*, Harper Collins Publishers Australia Pty Ltd, 2010.

Heywood Victoria, *Possum Pie Beetroot Beer and Lamingtons*, The Slattery Media Group, Melbourne, 2011.

Hocking Geoff, *Bendigo on My Mind*, New Chum Press, Castlemaine, 2016.

Houston Pamela, *A Pub on Every Corner: Bendigo and Surrounds*, 6 Volume Compilation, Self-published, 2009–2010.

Jenkins Alan, *The Forties*, Book Club Associates, London, 1977.

Jones Colin, *Something in the Air: A History of Radio in Australia*, Kangaroo Press Ltd, NSW, 1995.

Kirkby D, Luckins T and McConville C, *The Australian Pub*, University of New South Wales Press Ltd, 2010.

Lane Richard, *The Golden Age of Australian Radio Drama (1923–1960)*, Melbourne University Press, 1994.

Larkins John and Howard Bruce, *Australian Pubs*, Rigby Ltd, 1976.

Lerk James A, *Bendigo's once Flourishing Tomato Industry*, Published by JA and ERS Lerk, 2020.

Low Liz, *Eaglehawk Girl*, Brolga Publishing Pty Ltd, Melbourne, 2018.

Maraini Fosco and the Editors of Time Life Books, *Tokyo*, Time Life International, 1977.

McLennan Wayne, *Tent Boxing*, Granta Publications, London, 2007.

Messenger Charles, *World War II Chronological Atlas*, Bloomsbury Publishing Ltd, London, 1989.

Miller David Ed, *World War II*, Salamander Books Ltd, London, 2003.

Moore Dr Keith, *Bodgies, Widgies and Moral Panic in Australia 1955–1959*, School of Humanities and Human Services, Queensland University of Technology, 2004.

Morrow B with Maloof R, *Rock and Roll*, Imagine Publishing Inc. NJ. USA, 2009.

Murphy John and Smart Judith (eds), *The Forgotten Fifties: Aspects of Australian Society and Culture in the Nineteen Fifties*, Melbourne University Press, 1997.

Niall Brenda and Britain Ian (eds), *The Oxford Book of Australian Schooldays*, Oxford University Press, Melbourne, 1998.

O'Connell Jan, *A Timeline of Australian Food*, New South Publishing, University of New South Wales Press Ltd, 2017.

O'Neal Bill, *Reel Cowboys*, Eakin Press, Austin Texas, 2000.

Perry George and Aldridge Alan, *The Penguin Book of Comics*, Penguin Books Ltd UK, 1989.

Perry Roland, *The Fight for Australia*, Hatchette Australia Pty Ltd, 2017.

Philp Peter, *A History of Radio Drama in Australia: From 1920s to 1970s*, Eureka Media Communications, 2016.

Robson L L, *Australia in the Nineteen Twenties*, Thomas Nelson, Melbourne, 1984.

Sharpe Alan, *Nostalgia Australia*, Dominion Publishing NSW, 1975.

Simons Gerald, and The Editors of Time Life Books, *Victory in Europe*, Caxton Publishing Group, London, 2004.

Spenceley G, *The Depression Decade*, Thomas Nelson, Melbourne, 1984.

Wright Clare, *Beyond the Ladies Lounge: Australia's Female Publicans*, Text Publishing Melbourne, 2014.

ELECTRONIC SITES

Australian Bureau of Statistics: www.abs.gov.au

Wikipedia, the free Encyclopaedia: www.wikipedia.org

London Prize Ring Rules

William Abednego Thompson (boxer)

TROVE Digitised Newspapers, NLA: www.trove.nla.gov.au

Classic Australian Radio Serials: www.screensound.gov.au

The Great Detectives of Old Time Radio: www.greatdetectives.net

YouTube

Bendigo—Harp and a Monkey (The Victorians)

Milton Keynes UK
Ingram Content Group UK Ltd.
UKHW021302120923
428528UK00016B/447